WEiRD
TEXAS

STERLING
New York / London
www.sterlingpublishing.com

Weird TEXAS

Your Travel Guide to Texas's Local Legends and Best Kept Secrets

By Wesley Treat, Heather Shade, and Rob Riggs

Mark Sceurman and Mark Moran, Creative Directors

WEIRD TEXAS

STERLING and the distinctive Sterling logo
are registered trademarks of Sterling Publishing Co., Inc.

Library of Congress Cataloging-in-Publication Data Available

12 14 16 18 20 19 17 15 13

Published by Sterling Publishing Co., Inc.
387 Park Avenue South, New York, NY 10016
© 2005 by Sterling Publishing Co., Inc.
Distributed in Canada by Sterling Publishing
c/o Canadian Manda Group, 165 Dufferin Street,
Toronto, Ontario, Canada M6K 3H6
Distributed in the United Kingdom by GMC Distribution Services,
Castle Place, 166 High Street, Lewes, East Sussex, England BN7 1XU
Distributed in Australia by Capricorn Link (Australia) Pty. Ltd.
P.O. Box 704, Windsor, NSW 2756, Australia

Printed in China
All rights reserved

Sterling ISBN 978-1-4027-3280-5 (hardcover)

Sterling ISBN 978-1-4027-6687-9 (paperback)

For information about custom editions, special sales, premium and
corporate purchases, please contact Sterling Special Sales
Department at 800-805-5489 or specialsales@sterlingpublishing.com.

Design: Richard J. Berenson
    Berenson Design & Books, LLC, New York, NY

CONTENTS

A Note from the Marks

Our weird journey began a long, long time ago in a far-off land called New Jersey. Once a year or so, we'd compile a homespun newsletter called *Weird N.J.*, then pass it on to our friends. The pamphlet was a collection of odd news clippings, bizarre facts, little-known historical anecdotes, and anomalous encounters from our home state. The newsletter also included the kinds of localized legends that were often whispered around a particular town but seldom heard outside the boundaries of the community where they originated.

We had started *Weird N.J.* on the simple theory that every town in the state had at least one good tale to tell. The publication soon become a full-fledged magazine, and we made the decision to actually do our own investigating to see if we could track down where all of these seemingly unbelievable stories were coming from. Was there, we wondered, any factual basis for the fantastical local legends people were telling us about? Armed with not much more than a camera and a notepad, we set off on a mystical journey of discovery. Much to our surprise and amazement, a lot of what we had initially presumed to be nothing more than urban legends turned out to be real—or at least to contain a grain of truth, which had sparked the lore to begin with.

After a dozen years of documenting the bizarre, we were asked to write a book about our adventures, and so *Weird N.J.: Your Travel Guide to New Jersey's Local Legends and Best Kept Secrets* was published in 2003. Soon, people from all over the country began writing to us, telling us strange tales from their home state. As it turned out, what we had perceived to be something of very local interest was actually just a small part of a larger and more universal phenomenon.

When Barnes & Noble, the publisher of the book, asked us what we wanted to do next, the answer was simple: "We'd like to do a book called *Weird U.S.*, in which we could document the local legends and strangest stories from all over the country." So for the next twelve months, we set out in search of weirdness wherever it might be found in the fifty states. And indeed, we found plenty of it!

After *Weird U.S.* was published, we came to the conclusion that this country had more great tales than could be contained in just one book. Everywhere we looked, we found unwritten folklore, creepy cemeteries, cursed locations, and outlandish roadside oddities. With this in mind, we told our publisher that we wanted to document it ALL and to do it in a series of books, each focusing on the peculiarities of a particular state.

But where would we begin this state-by-state excursion into the weirdest territory ever explored? At the top of the list was Texas. Perhaps it's due to the enormous size of the place, but truth be told, the Lone Star State has more than its fair share of the bizarre.

For a state this big, we needed not one writer, but a team. And we assembled a fine one. The first person we asked was Heather Shade (known to just about everyone as Shady). Shady is an El Paso gal, but she spent a couple of years here in New Jersey, where we got to know her through her Web site, Lost Destinations. On the site, Shady chronicled weird abandoned places, haunted locations, and creepy cemeteries. Her writing and photography brought these places to life. As luck would have it, Shady moved back to Texas just as this book was in the planning stages—coincidence or fate?

The next person we contacted was Wesley Treat, an Arlington resident. For years, Wesley has been traveling the highways, byways, and back roads of Texas in search of offbeat places and stories for his Web site, Texas Twisted. His photos of roadside oddities, crazy characters, and outrageous properties are nothing short of stunning. Add to that his keen wit and nose for strange stories, and you have one heck of a roving reporter.

The final addition to the team was reporter and author Rob Riggs of Manchaca. Rob has been tracking down stories of bizarre Texas beasts, unexplained phenomena, and ancient mysteries for decades. His scientific investigations of ghost lights and other mysterious occurrences will leave you asking yourself if such things are natural or supernatural.

All three of these authors possess what we like to call the "weird eye," and that is what is needed to search out the sorts of stories we were looking for. It requires one to see the world in a different way, with a renewed sense of wonder. All of a sudden, you begin to reexamine your own environs, noticing your everyday surroundings as if for the first time. And you begin to ask yourself questions like, What the heck is that thing all about, anyway? and, Doesn't anybody else think that's kind of weird?

So come with us now, and let Shady, Wesley, and Rob show you their home state as they see it, with all of its cultural quirks, strange sites, and oddball characters. It is a place we like to call *Weird Texas*.

Mark Sceurman, Sam Houston, and Mark Moran

iNTRODUCTiON

Howdy, Podnuhs, and welcome to *Weird Texas*! All three of us have spent the better part of our so-called adult lives chasing the weird, so we were pleased indeed when Mark Moran and Mark Sceurman, the grand masters of all things weird, called us and asked if we'd like to team-write a book about all the weirdness in Texas. No hesitation on our part—we all signed on for what has been one wild and weird ride.

Weird: What does that word mean, anyway? It makes you think of something mysterious, possibly forbidden, and better off left alone. It's a subjective term, and like beauty, it is in the eye of the beholder. To us, it means anything that is so out of the ordinary that it piques your interest, intrigues, and perhaps even confuses you. And in our huge state, there's a whole lot of weird to be found.

The sites you'll find in this book are a culmination of years of research, interviews, and road trips. Many of the legends have never before been heard outside the towns in which they originated, and sometimes only a handful of people can remember the tales. While we've sought to find truth behind the legends, we've often found that truth isn't always an essential ingredient for a good story.

Legends live and grow as the years pass. Details can change with each retelling, to the point where even a well-documented historic event can become mythologized. Often, a great tale will grow out of a single seed of fact, and sometimes it takes even less than that. Some of these stories will be passed down and embellished upon by subsequent generations.

Where the line between history and mystery begins to blur is the tightrope we like to tread. For that reason, *Weird Texas* is as much about asking questions as it is about answering them. We present mysteries of the Lone Star State to you for examination, and often, we ourselves wonder just what they mean. Perhaps together we can make some sense of it.

But, hey, we're not concerned with telling only fact-based stories here, folks. We're also interested in the rumor and conjecture that has arisen around the actual events, people, and places we seek to document in this book. Be it in search of fact or fantasy, traveling Texas in search of the state's oddities is a fun ride, whether you find them or not.

Readers frequently ask why there are often no directions given to the sites we write about. While *Weird Texas* is a travel guide, we wouldn't want to lead others to trespass on private property or into a situation that might be dangerous. Some sites are better left to the imagination. But most are accessible to travelers, and we encourage everyone to get out there and see them before they disappear.

One can only imagine the countless tales yet to be told. Even after years of traveling, we know that we've only scratched the surface. In this respect, *Weird Texas* is a lot like life: It's the journey itself, not the destination, that's really important.

So thank you, Mark and Mark. We've had a blast putting together weird tales, Texas-style. And we think all of you fellow travelers are going to enjoy the ride too.

—Wesley, Shady, and Rob

Local Legends

People need mythology in their lives. Whether or not we admit it, most of us want to believe that, even in our technologically advanced society, there exist mysterious places that defy rational explanation. These places are like springboards for our collective unconscious and serve to fuel the dark side of our imagination—the really interesting side. Knowing that a frightening fable took place somewhere you can actually go and visit just adds to the thrill.

There are certain sites throughout Texas that have attained legendary status. Sometimes the location may be nothing more than an apparently ordinary bridge. The stories that have grown out of these humble landmarks, though, are the stuff of nightmares.

How do these dark and disturbing legends start, and why do they continue to be told from one generation to the next? The answer might lie in the need for people to prove themselves to their peer group and to themselves. Sometimes it takes a little more than the polite ceremonies we've adopted in Western culture to mark one's passage into adulthood. Sometimes it takes a late-night ride to confront some hideously deformed creature in the woods to separate the men from the boys.

The Legend of La Llorona

El Paso, a dusty desert city along the Mexican border, is a town rich with folklore—possibly because of its very bloody history, which lends itself to all kinds of interesting tales. The story of La Llorona is one of our favorites.

Part sorrowful banshee, part angry spirit, part cursed creature, La Llorona is known to almost every Latin culture. The first story dates all the way back to 1550! The name (pronounced la yo-ro-na) literally translates to "the Crier," which is exactly what this spook is said to do eternally. There are different versions of the story depending on the region where it's told, but all of them center around a woman who murdered her two small children hundreds of years ago. This is the version they tell in El Paso.

Long ago, there was a widow with two small children who lived in the poorest section of Juarez, Mexico, the town across the border from El Paso. Somehow, she met a man who was rather wealthy and began a relationship with him. The problem was that the man did not want to marry her, because of the two children. So the woman turned on her kids. She took them down to the Rio Grande, the huge river that runs right through El Paso and Juarez and that divides them and forms the American-Mexican border. There, in the dead of night, she heartlessly stabbed her children, then threw them into the river, where they drowned.

Still wearing her bloody nightgown, the woman slipped through the night to her lover's house to show him the lengths she'd gone to in order to be with him. When her wealthy lover saw her at his doorstep in the blood-streaked white gown, far from being impressed, he was horrified. He immediately rejected her. Suddenly realizing what she had done, and all for nothing, she went mad. She ran back to the river, screaming and tearing at her hair, trying in vain to save her poor children, but it was too late.

The story varies here, as some people say she stabbed and drowned herself in the same river. Others insist that she was caught by an angry mob of people, killed for her crimes, and thrown into the river. Either way, the result was the same. The woman died.

There, in the dead of night, she heartlessly stabbed her children, then threw them into the river, where they drowned.

That's when the creepiness began. Not long after her death, people who lived near this spot along the Rio Grande started to report hearing a horrible wailing in the dead of night. Then the sightings began. People described a grotesque apparition wandering the river-banks at night, something with the body of a woman but the head of a HORSE! The creature was said to be wearing a long, white bloody nightgown as it glided up and down the river, searching the water and wailing. It was undoubtedly the spirit of the woman, cursed to wander the banks of the Rio Grande for all eternity in her blood-stained gown, looking for her dead children. As punishment for her unspeakable sins, she was given the head of a horse.

Locals are warned against going near the river alone at night and are told that if La Llorona finds you there, she will take possession of you and force you to keep her company in her awful vigil by the water. To this day, whenever someone is found drowned in the Rio Grande, which happens constantly, people whisper that La Llorona is still lonely and looking for company.

The Bloody Box on the Bridge

When I was a teenager, we used to pile into a car and drive down to the river at night, daring each other to get out and look for La Llorona. There actually were quite a few times when we heard hair-raising, blood-curdling sobbing and what almost sounded like, I don't know—some weird, garbled babbling coming from the banks. It could have been animals or even pranksters, but of course, when we heard that, we'd get into the car and peel outta there in under five seconds!

But I did have one extremely freaky experience there. We had driven across a bridge that took us to the other, darker side of the river. Then we all got out and looked around a little bit, walking down the banks. One friend went alone back up toward the bridge. All of a sudden, we heard him yell out. When we looked to where he was, we saw him hurl something at the bridge, then come running back toward the car. He was

The box was filled with blood, bloody organs, pieces of bone, hair, and other unidentifiable stuff.

yelling at us to get in and go! We jumped in, and he told us that he'd seen a terrible monster woman standing in the middle of the bridge, looking at him. He was so scared that he had thrown his pocketknife at it.

We were all totally thinking he was trying to scare us, so we didn't take him seriously. As we headed back over the bridge to the other side (which was the only exit out of there), we suddenly stopped laughing as we found our way blocked by a box that was sitting in the very center of the narrow bridge. There was no way it was there before or we wouldn't have been able to cross the bridge in the first place. Needless to say, we were all scared witless, and there was a big debate about who would get out and move the thing. We finally decided that half of us would leave the car and move it together. When we went over to it, we could see some dark liquid stuff dripping down the sides, and when we lifted the lid, we freaked! The box was filled with blood, bloody organs, pieces of bone, hair, and other unidentifiable stuff. I even recall clearly seeing an eyeball!

My friend shoved the box to the edge of the bridge so we could get by while the rest of us ran back to the car. We sped out of there as fast as we could and pulled over at the first place we found, an old bar, where we ran in and called the cops. They met us at the bar and asked us to lead the way to the bloody box. We did, and to our surprise, it was still there. We had half expected it to have disappeared.

As soon as the cops opened the box and shined their flashlights in, they both unholstered their guns. One of them called for backup, while the other shined his light on the bushes around the riverbank while holding his gun in the other hand.

Meanwhile, we were all sitting in the car, totally tripping out on all this. More cops came and took statements from us. The only explanation they gave us was, "Well, maybe it was bait from a fisherman who left it there by the river after fishing."

I would almost think that I imagined all this if it weren't for the fact that seven other people (including my mom and my aunt) were there that night, and there are police statements to prove it. My friend still insists that he saw La Llorona, and he's convinced that she left the box there for us. My other friends think we almost stumbled across a murderer who was dumping what was left of his victim. I don't know what I believe, but that was an experience I'll never, ever forget! —*Shady*

La Llorona's Choice

There is an old Mexican folktale around where I live about La Llorona. In the story, no specific towns are named, but it was supposed to have happened in the Castroville and Hondo area. Well, as the story goes, a young woman married a man she does not love. He loves her and is rich, so she decides that she will marry him to make her family happy. As the years went on, she gave birth to two sons that this man loved dearly. As it so happened, the woman met another man in a nearby town. She fell in love with him and began an affair. Well, her husband found out and threatened to leave her with the two boys. In a fit of anger, she slipped out one night with the children and went to her lover.

The husband leaves, never to return, because of the pain he went through in the town. His wife is confused to find her world so changed without her wealthy husband to support her. She had no sisters or brothers to leave her children with. One day, she stopped to have a picnic with her children near a river, what would later become the Regional Park and the Medina River. Well, as she went over in her mind what she could do, something snapped. She smiled and calmly plucked up one boy, the youngest. This boy was said to be three or four. She walked to the edge of a cliff and gently tossed him into the river. This boy didn't know how to swim and drowned quickly. As her other son rushed over to try to save his brother, she promptly grabbed him under his arms and plopped him into the river as well.

It was said that she was truly insane at that moment. She rushed to her lover and told him that the children were with their grandparents. A week after the drowning, the lover was bored with her and disappeared. It was at this point that she realized what she did to her children. Frantic, she ran out into the night howling. It was said that people who saw her after that viewed her as a woman wearing all white, crying as she wandered along the river. If approached, she would run away screaming, "I did it for him! They were my children!" The bodies of the children were never found.

Two years passed, and she somehow made an amazing journey around the Texas rivers and streams, looking for her lost children. She found herself at the same spot where they had their little picnic. She could see the children playing about in the sun. She remembered them having so much fun that day. In all her grief, she leapt off the same cliff she had tossed her children from, two years to the day after she killed them. It was said that a week later to the day her lover abandoned her, her body was recovered.

There are various endings to this tale. One is that she came back as a woman dressed in black, a symbol of her guilt for her crime. One version cloaks her in red to symbolize her adulterous ways and the blood of her children soaked into her dress. It was also said that she was very pretty and as punishment for her sins, she was given the face of a white horse with sunken-in features.

My grandfather is one of the people who have seen her. He was walking home one night with his brother. They were tired from a hard day of work in the fields and were headed to the house that my grandfather and grandmother still live in today. This house is but a few blocks from the river. As they walked across a field in front of the house, they realized a

woman was walking just ahead of them. She was wearing all white. She began to cry. They both ran up behind her, asking her what was wrong, but she answered them back only with her cries. As they got closer to her, my great-uncle began to realize something. He yelled to my grandfather to look at her feet. As he did so, he saw that she was floating two feet off the ground. Both ran to the house, locking it tight. When they told my grandmother what they saw, she whispered to them, "La Llorona?"–*Jaime Burvato*

La Llorona Wants Your Bones

Right before my great-grandma died, she told me this weird story. One night, while she was walking home in Corpus Christi, she saw a lady in black ahead of her carrying a lamp. (Remember, it was a long time ago and there weren't streetlights.) So she walked up to the lady and asked what she was doing out so late. There was no reply, so she asked again. This time, the lady stopped and looked up at my grandma. She screamed. The lady did not have a human head but that of a horse. At this point, my grandma got the heck out of there, tripping and falling all the way home.

In another variation, La Llorona did not have enough cash to feed her children, and not wanting them to suffer, she tossed them off a cliff. Too guilty to live with her sin, she also jumped. When she got to heaven, the Lord wouldn't allow her to enter till she found her children's bones (which had been scattered by the river). To this day, she still searches, willing to take anyone's bones, anyone who crosses her path.–*James*

Cruisin' with La Llorona

My soon-to-be brother-in-law, Wero, my brother, and I were cruising around in Wero's car just listening to music one hot summer night. We decided to head to Lasara, a little town west of Raymondville. For some reason, we stopped by an old ranch house that had been there for ages. As we were standing beside the car, we heard some noise inside the old house. We yelled out some things and continued what we were doing. All of a sudden, the wind started blowing pretty weird, and from the side of the old house, I saw her: the Lady in White, or La Llorona.

I told Wero, "Look! It's La Llorona!" We just stood there, unable to move, seeing with our own eyes what before had been only a tale our grandmas used to tell us. She moved in front of the car about ten feet in front of us, floating about two feet off the ground with her dress swirling all around her. She moved toward a gate that started to open all by itself with a loud groan. She passed, and the gate closed hard behind her.

As the shock wore off, we jumped into the car. My brother was almost under the backseat, he was so scared. We tried to start the car, but it wouldn't start. Finally, the engine turned, and we took off meaning to go home, but in our scared state we turned back toward Lasara instead. Just as we were getting to the bridge, the car died. I mean, everything turned off. Then, as I looked out toward the field, I saw her coming straight for the car. Man, my heart started beating like crazy, and I'm yelling, "Start the car, start the car!" She was about five feet from the car when it started.

Wero did a one-eighty right there in the middle of the road, and we took off, never looking back. My brother was so scared, he never went cruising with us again. Wero, well, he's my brother-in-law now, and from time to time, we talk about that night, the night that made us believe in La Llorona. –*Eddie Rodriguez*

Woman Without a Face

Once, my friend saw La Llorona. He said that he and his parents were just passing by, and that all of a sudden they saw a lady dressed in white. But once they saw the front of her, they said she didn't have a face, and she was carrying a baby all covered in white, but they didn't get to see the baby's face. They said it was like three o'clock in the morning. They punched the gas and went faster because they were scared.–*Anonymous*

Woman Hollering Creek

Located off of Interstate 10 in Seguin, between San Antonio and Houston, there is a creek that is said to be haunted by the spirit of a woman who drowned her two children there. Now it is said that she walks along the bank trying to find them. Many have claimed to hear her wails, and some have even seen her. People are warned not to get too close to the creek or her hand will reach up from the water and pull you in. *–Tim Stevens*

Woman Hollering Creek

The Legend of the Donkey Lady

Anyone who has gone to school in San Antonio has heard of the Donkey Lady.

Now, the way I heard it, back in the fifties, a young woman had been in a fire. (My wife says she heard the Donkey Lady had lost two children in that fire and that her husband had started it.) She was left horribly disfigured. It is said that when her face healed, the skin had something of a drooped, baggy appearance. Her fingers had all fused together, leaving dark stumps, or hooves. Disfigured and totally insane, she stayed mostly in the rural areas of Bexar County and terrorized anyone who approached her. As children, when we could stay out late on summer nights, we were absolutely positive that she waited in the darkness for us to separate so that she could pounce on a lone victim, ripping and chewing . . . well, you get the idea.

Most of the Donkey Lady stories have faded into memory, but one was a little harder to shake. One of my best friends told of a cousin who was with his father and brother on a weekend outing. They were going to do a little fishing. The group pulled up to a weed-infested area off a dirt road and began to make camp. The two boys had the task of unloading the pickup truck while the father found a suitable spot for the tent. While unloading the truck, one of the boys heard a rustling in the weeds and called out to their father to come to the truck. The three of them watched the tall weeds beneath the oaks along the road bend under the weight of what was apparently a large animal. Then they heard an odd snorting sound and a high-pitched snarl. The father, not recognizing the sounds coming from the "animal," decided they probably ought to find another spot to set up camp.

The three of them quickly threw the tent, sleeping

bags, and gear into the back of their truck. The father was just pulling out into the road when something fast and large burst out of the weeds. Seconds later, a horrible apparition bounded up onto their hood and began shrieking at them through the glass. It was the ugliest thing any of them ever saw. They swore it looked like a donkey, but it was mostly human. It screamed at them more as the truck continued to move away from the weeds and into the road. It used its deformed hands to punch at the windshield and broke it in many places.

The father hit the brakes. The thing slid off the hood and onto the dirt road. Throwing the truck into reverse, the father floored the gas pedal and put some distance between them and the thing, backing into the weeds off the road. He then put the truck into first and stepped on it again. They said it almost looked like a wild animal with an incredible look of rage and hatred in its eyes. Dirt sprayed up from the road at the beast as they pulled out, slowing it down just enough for them to get away.

The Donkey Lady supposedly finally dropped back and headed into the weeds. After the story was told, my friend let it be known that he thought it was a nice story, but, well, it was a nice story. Then he was taken outside and shown the truck. The windshield was almost knocked out. The hood was dented, and its paint was scuffed and scraped. *–Tim Stevens*

Occurrence at Donkey Lady Bridge

The Donkey Lady Bridge crosses Elm creek via Applewhite Road, approximately four miles North of Loop 1604 on the south side of San Antonio. One night in late 1987, while I was at my best friend's house, four fellow companions showed up, looking for something to do. We suggested they visit the Donkey Lady Bridge, a favorite for late-night stories. They agreed and were soon driving out of sight. My friend and I stayed home.

About six hours later, their vehicle returned to our driveway with only one occupant. Assuming he had taken the girls home, we went out to greet him. What we found at the car was something I'll never forget: The windshield was busted, the front dented, and there was what appeared to be blood all over the hood. We immediately ran to the driver's door to see if John (not his actual name) was all right. He was just sitting there, staring out the windshield with a blank expression on his face. After several minutes of badgering, we finally got him to talk.

He told us that he and his friends Lisa, Terri, and Jill had arrived at the bridge. They began to honk their horn and call for the Donkey Lady (according to legend, this is how you are supposed to get her attention). After about fifteen minutes of not seeing anything, they decided to go into the woods and look for her themselves. What happened next was truly unbelievable, and if I hadn't known John all my life and seen the car, I would not have believed it myself.

While walking in the woods, John said he got the feeling they were being watched. Looking around and evaluating the situation, he discovered in the distance what appeared to be two eyes staring at them. These eyes seemed to be reflecting from the moonlight and were of a color that he said was indescribable. The girls panicked and began to run back to the car. John was quick to follow, and soon after he turned away, there was a horrible scream from the direction of the eyes. Too afraid to turn around, he picked up his pace as he ran to the car. When he got there, the girls were already inside screaming at him to get in and leave.

As he was trying to find his keys, he heard the sounds of what seemed to be a horse running in their direction. Starting the car, he put the gas pedal to the floor. Suddenly, a figure appeared in the road in front of them. Too afraid to stop, John collided with the figure. It hit the hood of the car and rolled over the roof. Looking in his rearview mirror, he said he thought the figure got up and continued to pursue them.

After hearing this and seeing the condition of the car, my friend and I felt this deserved a second look. John told us that he would never return to that bridge again, but if we wanted to risk our lives, to go right ahead. Grabbing two flashlights, we jumped in my pickup and made for the bridge. As we drew closer, we slowed down and turned on the many off-road lights my truck had. These lit the road and the woods to the side of us as if it were daytime, giving us an outstanding view of the bridge as we approached. The first thing we noticed as the bridge drew close was the large amount of blood on the road. However, this was the only evidence we could find of the incident described by John.

Upon our investigation of the woods on foot, we discovered what seemed to be several tracks of a small horse (unshod) leading to the road. After several hours of looking and not finding anything else, we returned to the house. By this time, John had already found his way home, and we went to bed, too excited to sleep.

To this day, none of the people involved in this story have returned to the bridge. Did John actually see and strike the Donkey Lady that night, or was it merely a stray pony startled by their presence? All I know is that something was there that night, and it did scare our friends half to death.—*Airborne*

Hello, Donkey Lady...Is That You?

My friend had a phone number where you could call the Donkey Lady, and she called it and had me listen. The sound coming from that telephone made me hang up immediately. It was the horrible sound of a donkey being tortured, or worse. I called the number myself a few times after that. One time I even tried to scare my mom with it, but she seemed unfazed. —*Anonymous*

Donkey Lady Is Busy, Please Hang Up and Try Again

The number for the Donkey Lady was "KEEP-IT-1." A classmate told me about it when I was in about the sixth grade. Supposedly, when you called it, you could hear a donkey. I tried it a couple of times, but it was always busy.—*Anonymous*

Attacked at Donkey Lady Bridge

One weekend in 1989, some friends and I were driving around in the 1973 Impala one of them owned. We were showing the younger cousins of the driver, Todd, around; they had turned thirteen that year and were being "inducted." We decided to drive to Donkey Lady Bridge, partly since we had never been there, partly to give them a good scare. Any child who has grown up in San Antonio knows about the Donkey Lady.

We drove out to the bridge, turning off the headlights before we were actually on it. It is very eerie out there at night. Todd started to slowly advance across the bridge, when a figure appeared seemingly from nowhere in the middle of it. He stopped the car, and we whispered speculations as to who or what it was.

We were NOT expecting to see anything, much less this. Todd placed the car in gear again and, honking his horn, slowly inched his way toward the figure, which promptly vanished. Then the car was stopped again, and this made us shut up. Todd sat listening to our suggestions to back up or gun the car to the other side when something landed on the hood. Everyone screamed, and Todd slammed the car into reverse and floored it. The dark figure rolled from the hood,

and Todd didn't stop until we reached the main road. Getting out, we all stared at the hood, which now sported two very deep dents in it. No one had an explanation for where the figure had dropped from to make those. Todd took his car to a body shop the next day and had to replace the entire hood—the dents were too deep to pound out. Incidentally, I was seventeen when this happened and am thirty today, and I have never been back out there.—*Backlash*

Munching Muffins with the Real Donkey Lady

I met the lady people refer to as the Donkey Lady. She was a recluse, and she may have been a nut (though she was very lucid when I spoke to her), but she told me she was the Donkey Lady, so make up your own mind if she really was.

I was riding my horse and came across a beautiful Appaloosa colt tied up. A woman came out of the bushes when I was petting the colt and said she had seen me riding around. She was very old (this must have been around 1980ish) and took me to her "house," which was made up of garbage bags and plywood. She told me that her real house had burned down and her husband had died and she had nowhere to go. She had donkeys, horses, skunks, and several other animals.

We sat and talked, and she brought out an old photo album of herself and her husband. They had ridden horses for years and ran a dude ranch many years before. We spent several hours together and she was very kind.

I went back and brought her some muffins, as she liked sweets, and we talked again. I went back once more, and she was gone. I'd like to get the story on the woman who called herself the Donkey Lady. She seemed to have lived a great life but with a sad end.—*D*

Saw the Donkey Lady in the Pale Moonlight

I have lived in San Antonio my entire life, and like all the other kids who have gone to school here, I was familiar with the Donkey Lady. I never really went out hunting her. I didn't have the guts to be hanging around any dark bridges in the middle of the night, so my first and hopefully last encounter with her was a fluke.

One night in late January, when the weather was still frozen, a girlfriend of mine and a boy were going to meet some other friends to see a show. The girl and I picked up our other friend, who lived out in the boondocks, past the tracks and the bridge where the Donkey Lady is supposed to hang out. The midnight road was lined with transients, sleeping in alcoves and packs along the road, which was very creepy in and of itself. As we drove, watching out in the dark, a large animal the size of a deer came bounding out of the scenery, moving parallel to our vehicle. Everyone in the car freaked out screaming, and the animal outside the window did the same. We sped up as fast as we could, trying not to hit Donkey Lady so she couldn't rip through the windshield and kill us off. —*Hailey*

Donkey Lady Bridge: January 2004

One night in January, around 12:30 a.m., a few of us decided to go to the Donkey Lady Bridge and check it out. There were two girls (including me) and two guys. We girls decided to stay in the car. The two guys proceeded to head into the woods, leaving us wondering if anything would happen. All of a sudden, there was the sound of hooves next to the car. They stayed pretty loud for about ten seconds, then faded slowly toward where the guys had entered the woods. We waited until we couldn't hear them any longer, then we called the guys' cell phones. There was no answer, and one of the phones indicated that they were unavailable. We were about to drive in there to find them when they came running out. We sped off toward the main road. We didn't actually see her, but I think it's better off that way! Please be careful if you ever go out there!—*PinkcheekedQT*

Escaped in the Nick of Time

During the first week of fiesta, my husband and I invited his sixteen-year-old brother from Arizona to come down. So me, my husband, Juan, his brother Johnny, and my best friend, Lizzette, went to the carnival and had a good time. After leaving there, my friend Lizzette asked us if we had ever heard of the Donkey Lady's Bridge. We said no.

So she took us all the way down Applewhite Road to a one-way bridge. We were all skeptical when she told us to turn off the lights and just sit there and wait. The whole car was silent, and Lizzette goes, "Do you hear that?" It sounded like a horse running in our direction, and it kept getting louder and louder, and we were all screaming. Finally, it sounded really close so we took off burning rubber and all. I just wanted to let you know that I think it is true about the Donkey Lady. I'm just glad I didn't meet her!—*Suzy Galindo*

The Dancing Devil

San Antonio is a very interesting place year-round. There are citywide parties at the drop of a hat. During the Christmas season, the River Walk is lit by eighty thousand colorful lights and roamed by tourists from all over the world. Each of the many ethnic groups (Hispanic, German, Czech, Polish, Greek, and so forth) that contribute to the history and heritage of Texas have festivals throughout the year.

But in October, Hispanic traditions dominate, giving Halloween in San Antonio a unique twist on the day's theme. On Halloween, it is said, el Diablo (the Devil) appears for a night on the town. He dresses in the finest attire, with one notable exception, but we'll get to that in a moment. He visits many nightspots across town, having a preference for the low-lit, smaller establishments. He wines and dines the prettiest young woman he can find. She is enchanted with him, not knowing his true nature. Then he asks her to dance.

Intoxicated by his charm and uncommon good looks, she accepts the invitation. The dance begins. The young woman is held spellbound by his eyes as they dance in the close confines of the club. Invariably, however, she looks down at the floor, after a misstep, perhaps. What she sees then makes her scream in horror. The impeccably dressed man with whom she has been infatuated all night has the feet of a chicken!

The Devil then laughs, and during the confusion that ensues, he retreats to a dark corner and vanishes in a foul, sulfurous cloud of smoke.—*Tim Stevens*

Crimes in the Dark of Spring Lake Park

Texarkana is a town you might classify as interesting. To start with, it is in both Texas and Arkansas. That in itself is worth a look. And it's huge on sports. You have race fans and hockey lovers, and it's an outdoorsman's dream for hunting and fishing. It also has some very popular parks.

One of spookier interest is known as Spring Lake Park, where locals tell a legend that begins with a real-life tale of murder. The story goes that a young couple had stolen off for a romantic interlude on a secluded lover's lane in the park. Unfortunately, they were murdered in the middle of their tryst—shot to death. Before being killed herself, the young lady was tied to a tree and made to watch her boyfriend's gruesome demise.

Legend has it that if you lean against just the right tree, you will feel constriction, as if a rope is tying you to the very spot. Perhaps this is the girl's spirit struggling for rescue. Or maybe she's looking for someone to take her place so she can be free from the sight of her lover's murder.

Perhaps the scariest part of this legend is that it is based on something terrifyingly real, one of Texas's most famous unsolved serial killings. They were called the Texarkana Moonlight Murders because the killer usually struck at night. The killer himself was dubbed the Phantom, a hooded, menacing figure who went on a rampage in 1946, targeting young couples in secluded areas and attacking them with a gun and a knife. Without mercy, the Phantom left a string of bloodied young bodies in his wake. Despite a massive manhunt by Texas Rangers and the investigation of over three hundred suspects, the killer was never caught. There are those who fear he still roams Texarkana's darker, shadowy regions.

In 1976, a film called *The Town That Dreaded Sundown* was made about the crimes of the Phantom. It's actually a pretty cool '70s-type movie and worth a look.

Hell's Gate

Somewhere deep inside the tangled green depths of River Legacy Park, in Arlington, there is rumored to be a very old trail surrounded on either side by murky swamps and overhanging trees. This long dirt trail is said to end at a dirt mound, a spot where captured spies of the Union Army were executed. They call this place Hell's Gate.

If you can find the spot, you might see the remains of the posts where a gate once hung. This passage was supposedly one of the last things the Union prisoners saw as they were led through it at the end of the trail to the tree where they would be hanged. Some believe that because of all the deaths that took place here, there are many tormented spirits still residing at Hell's Gate. If you walk the trail, they say, you can still hear the disembodied whispers, sobs, and prayers of the men and women who once

took their final steps in this awful place.

Unfortunately, River Legacy Park covers acres and acres of area, and the *Weird Texas* team was never able to turn up the trail, gateposts, or any tormented spirits other than our own as we plowed through the woods. A park ranger, however, said there were some very old artifacts from the Civil War era, including pieces of cannons, in different parts of the park. She didn't know about the remains of any gateposts, though. Curses! Foiled again.

Ancient Mysteries

it's *difficult* to associate Texas with anything ancient. Even though much of its cowboy-western heritage is still intact, that ranching tradition dates back scarcely more than a hundred and fifty years. Texas, as we know it, has a short and recent history in the grand scheme of things. Not only that, but its population is growing ever more urbanized, and its cities are ever more modern. The image and identity of the state is increasingly defined by Houston's sleek skyscrapers, Austin's high-tech industry, and the concrete freeway sprawl of the Dallas–Fort Worth Metroplex.

But there are vestiges of ancient cultures and places that have yet to be swallowed up by the suburbs. These remnants of the distant past reflect a view of the world that had a healthy respect for the mysteries of nature. In fact, the Lone Star State owes its name to one such ancient culture—the Caddo. When the Spanish began to colonize Texas in the early nineteenth century, they came in contact with the Kadohadacho group of the Caddo Indians near the Red River and with the Hasinai group in the valleys of the Neches and Angelina rivers.

The state's name is derived from the word *tejas*, which is the Spanish spelling of the Hasinai word *tayshas*. The Hasinai used the word to mean "friends" or "allies," and it was a form of greeting, as in "Hello, friend." It may also have referred to various peaceful groups allied against the war-loving Comanche.

The Caddo in Texas are said to have been warm and friendly people, traits for which modern Texans are also frequently known. It seems appropriate, then, that the official Texas state motto, Friendship, conveys the original meaning of the word used by the Hasinai and that the name Texas itself comes from that same ancient word.

Ancient Mound Builders

Near the town of Alto in Cherokee County on State Highway 21 are the remains of an important city of the ancient Caddo—the Caddoan Mounds State Historic Site. This is one of the best-known and most thoroughly investigated Indian archaeological sites in Texas. Some people believe that subtle but powerful energies known only to its ancient residents are still present there.

The Caddo had a thriving and sophisticated agrarian society on the western edge of the great forests of eastern North America from about 1000 years B.C. until about A.D. 1500. Inhabiting lands extending from East Texas into Louisiana, Arkansas, and Oklahoma, the Caddo traded with tribes as far away as the Gulf Coast and the Appalachian Mountains.

The mounds, generally referred to as the George C. Davis Site by archaeologists, are thought to have been built as a permanent settlement around A.D. 900. There are a total of three mounds. Two were probably connected with religious activities and served as platforms for temples

or for the chiefs' houses. The third mound was for the burial of elite members of the Caddo.

The building of mounds to serve as platforms for temples and other important buildings was a widespread practice among ancient peoples in what are now the southeastern United States and the Mississippi Valley. The Caddo shared this practice, and the religious beliefs associated with it, with many other tribes, including the Creek, the Chickasaw, and the Muskogean. Collectively, these tribes make up what is known as the Mississippian Culture, or the Mound Builders.

The Mississippians were successful farmers, who raised livestock and stored grain crops. Because of their

Many Native Americans and spiritual groups believe that places like Cahokia and the ancient Caddo site near Alto are still sources of powerful, potentially spiritually transforming energy even today.

agrarian base, they evolved into a settled culture and eventually built cities and great civilizations in North America that rivaled those of Egypt and Mexico. They also built large, flat-topped temple mounds similar to the pyramids of the Mexican Indians, a custom they may have adopted through their trading contacts. Some of the mounds were topped by elaborate temples, where ceremonies led by priests were held.

The largest Mississippian city was Cahokia, located in present-day southern Illinois. Its population was estimated at fifteen thousand to twenty thousand at its peak, and it was one of the largest urban centers in the world at that time. Cahokia is believed to have existed from A.D. 700 until 1300. It had more than one hundred mounds—base platforms for burials, temples, and the houses of the city's elite. The largest, a temple mound now known as Monk's Mound, is bigger at the base than the Great Pyramid of Egypt. It covers about sixteen acres and is about one hundred feet tall.

Many Mississippian peoples, the Hasinai among them, practiced a set of religious beliefs that anthropologists call the Southern Cult, which included a form of sun worship. The so-called Woodhenge at the Cahokia site, for example, was a "sun circle." Forty-eight wooden poles made a 410-foot-diameter circle that was used for astronomical observations, such as the determination of the exact date of the spring and autumn equinoxes.

Fire was an important part of the cult's traditions, since it was believed to be part of the sun, which represented the highest god. Each household kept a fire burning at all times, and a sacred perpetual fire was maintained at the principal temple, or fire temple.

Some scholars believe that the Mound Builders may not have been mere sun worshippers but, rather, possessed a knowledge of the subtle, sacred energies in the earth similar to the knowledge attributed to the ancient Celts and Chinese. This energy, which formed an important link to the spirit world or the land of ancestors, is thought to sometimes manifest in the

form of the mysterious lights that you can read about in the "Unexplained Phenomena" chapter of *Weird Texas*.

For reasons not known, the Davis Site was more or less abandoned by about A.D. 1300, and it never regained its former status. This was about the same time as the decline of Cahokia. By the time the European settlers arrived in the eighteenth century, the remaining Hasinai Caddo lived in scattered villages with less political and social organization, and they no longer built mounds.

It is not entirely known why the Mound Builders' civilization fell apart. Incursions by the Europeans, with their unfamiliar and—for the Indians—deadly germs, no doubt hastened the decline of the Mound Builders, but that decline had started long before the Europeans were on the scene. Whatever the reasons, many still consider the sites of the mounds and temples to be sacred places.

In August 1987, more than a thousand people met at the Monk's Mound in Cahokia to take part in a worldwide event that came to be known as the Harmonic Convergence, designed to bring peace to the planet through a heightened awareness of the subtle energies the ancient cultures had possessed. Many Native Americans and spiritual groups believe that places like Cahokia and the ancient Caddo site near Alto are still sources of powerful, potentially spiritually transforming energy even today.

Enchanted Rock

This is a truly ancient site. It is a pink granite dome that is more than a billion years old, which makes it one of the oldest exposed rocks in the world. The rock covers six hundred and forty acres in southwestern Llano County, about twenty miles north of Fredericksburg, and towers more than four hundred feet above the surrounding area. It is the second largest batholith, or underground igneous rock formation uncovered by erosion, in the United States. (The first is Stone Mountain in Georgia.)

But such mundane descriptions do not do justice to the wonder that this legendary rock mountain has inspired. Its name, Enchanted Rock, is attributed to the Indians' supposed belief that it is haunted. The Tonkawa, the story goes, saw ghostly campfires flickering near its summit and heard the mountain groan. Both the Tonkawa and the Comanche regarded the rock with fear and reverence and were even rumored to have offered sacrifices at its base. The Apache said it was inhabited by mountain spirits. Because of these beliefs, many Indians would not set foot on the "talking rock," which they believed housed the restless souls of the dead. This was handy for nineteenth-century European settlers and frontiersmen, who took refuge at the rock when raiding war parties roamed nearby.

According to one legend, the rock became haunted when a band of brave warriors, the last of their tribe, defended themselves on its high ground against the attacks of another tribe. The warriors were finally overpowered, but ever since then, their wandering, wailing spirits roam the magnificent granite undulations of the giant rock.

Today, learned scientists theorize that the Indian legends probably arose from the way the rock glitters on clear nights after heavy rainfall or from the creaking noises that are reportedly heard when cool nights follow warm days, causing the rock's outer surface to contract as it suddenly cools. Such theories do not credit the Indians with having much sense, and assume that they were a superstitious bunch, ignorant in the ways of nature. Much of this attitude may result from our own ignorance of the forces of nature, of which the Indians were very much aware.

Not far from Enchanted Rock, still in Llano County, is a place where a ghostly light is said to appear. Called the Six-Mile Light, it is most likely another manifestation of the weird energies that converge near Marfa in West Texas and on Bragg Road in East Texas. The Marfa Lights and the Bragg Light occur at the same latitude—within less than one percent variation from latitude 30 degrees N. Similar unexplained mystery lights occur in scattered locations around the world at that latitude, at which

Enchanted Rock also lies. It is very likely that at least some of the lights witnessed there come from an energy source similar to the one that produces the ghostly lights at Marfa and on Bragg Road.

Nights on a Moaning Mountain

The region surrounding Enchanted Rock is called the Llano Uplift, or the Central Texas Mineral Region. There are a number of other large outcroppings of the same pink granite in the area, including Bee Rock Mountain, Cedar Mountain, and Sharp Mountain. Over the years, some members of the *Weird Texas* team have spent time camping on these mountains, particularly during the solstices. On several occasions at night, they heard a strange sound, one that could not possibly be explained by cooling rocks. It was more like an electronic hum, as if one were standing next to a high-voltage power line. But in each case, there were no such power lines within miles. Is it possible that the lights and sounds produced by the mysterious energy within the granite is the basis of the native legend of the moaning sacred mountain, not contracting rocks and reflected moonlight?

Harmonic Convergence at Enchanted Rock

Places where mysterious energy periodically intensifies to high levels and manifests as light and sound were known to many ancient cultures. Such places were considered sacred, and the energy was thought to provide a conscious link to the spirit world. Although such beliefs and practices are age-old and virtually universal among shamanistic cultures, they have been mostly forgotten in modern times. A vestige of this belief, however, and a growing desire to return to a direct experience of the subtle mysteries of nature might account for the huge role that Enchanted Rock played in the Harmonic Convergence event of 1987.

Based on writer Jose Arguelles's interpretation of ancient Mayan texts, this loosely coordinated event sought to promote world peace through a heightened awareness of subtle energies in the earth believed to have been the basis of much of ancient Native American spirituality. Participants were encouraged to gather at ancient sacred sites around the world, such as Mount Shasta, Cahokia, Stonehenge, and the Great Pyramid. Park officials at Enchanted Rock lost count of the attendance there when the number of ticket stubs reached seven thousand. But taking into account the number of people who might have slipped in under the fences, the final estimate was that more than ten thousand people gathered at Enchanted Rock for the event. That made it the biggest gathering for Harmonic Convergence of all the ancient sites.

Enchanted Rock was designated a National Natural Landmark in 1970. Since the Harmonic Convergence, the average weekly attendance has more than doubled, and on any given weekend, would-be visitors are turned away when the park has reached capacity. Clearly, the pink granite mountain that rises majestically in the geographical heart of Texas and that once was sacred to many ancient Texans occupies a place in the hearts of the state's modern inhabitants as well.

Pimple Mounds of Southeast Texas

The first time the *Weird Texas* team really noticed these curious mounds was during a two-and-a-half-mile hike through flooded woods in the Big Thicket National Preserve. We were on our way to a campsite on a slight rise near the border of the Lance Rosier Unit, not far from Black Creek. From the time we left the trailhead, we were splashing through water that ranged from ankle-high to just below the tops of our knee-high boots. Though the trail was completely submerged, we began to notice that there were a few small circular patches of higher land jutting as much as two feet out of the water.

At first, we assumed they were eroded root-balls of giant trees that had dominated the virgin woods hundreds, perhaps even thousands, of years ago. But the farther we went along the trail, the more it became obvious that there was more to them than that.

The high water made the rises more obvious, and there were lots of them. We had hiked in woods all over Hardin County and hadn't noticed them elsewhere. If these were the remains of ancient root-balls, shouldn't they also be common in other parts of the woods? Why were they found only here? Some were almost forty feet across and over three feet high. It was hard to imagine that even an ancient tree could have had a root-ball that large.

We also noticed that some of the rises had what looked like pits nearby that might have been holes remaining from whatever process had created the mounds. Was it a coincidence that they occurred in a frequently flooded part of the woods?

Given the regularity of their shape, the rises could have been made by humans. If so, the obvious reason would have been to create patches of high and dry ground for the wet season. If the rainy seasons in ancient times had been as bad as what we had experienced that year, these mounds could have been the only dry spots in the woods for months. Our curiosity aroused, we did a little research and found out that there is a name for these oddities—pimple mounds. But no one is sure what caused them.

The term is applied to small mounds that occur in parts of the coastal plains of Louisiana and Texas. These mounds extend from southwestern Louisiana and jut south and west into Southeast Texas in a narrow band about sixty to a hundred miles wide. Their composition is identical to that of the surrounding soil, which is clay mixed with sand. The mounds occur in places with little or no drainage and with substantial seasonal rainfall.

In an article in the April 1948 *Scientific Monthly*, Frederick Koons wrote, "Some of the mounds are pitted at or near the center, usually by one, and rarely by as many as three, small pits. The mounds show no regularity of distribution and exhibit no trend. . . . In diameter, they range from 4 to about 30 feet, but a few are larger."

There are a number of theories about the origin of the mounds, all unproved, including that they were caused by the movement of glaciers, gas blowouts, wind drifts, anthills, and the ever popular root-balls. It has even been suggested that ancient pocket gophers made them to keep out of high water. If this were so, given the size of the mounds relative to those built by present-day gophers, either the ancient critters were a great deal more industrious than the modern ones or they were of gigantic size.

Similar anomalous mounds are scattered throughout the Mississippi Valley. In southern Missouri and northern Arkansas, there are mounds that are often four feet high and thirty to forty feet in diameter—similar in size to the largest ones we had found in the Big Thicket. And like the ones in the Big Thicket, they occur in wet areas, close to streams and ponds. They have been attributed to beavers, prairie dogs, gophers, and both ancient and more recent Native American cultures. One nineteenth-century archaeologist said the mounds might be "the remains of houses built of sun-dried bricks."

The theory that the pimple mounds have a man-made origin is usually countered by the lack of evidence of human remains and artifacts. But not many of the mounds have been professionally excavated and probably none in the Big Thicket. And there might be reasons why there would be no traces of artifacts. It could be the people who made them were extremely primitive or that they made them for reasons unimaginable to us. There are no artifacts remaining from the Caddo and other Mound Builders, because many of their implements had been crafted from wood, which decomposes rapidly in the damp forests where those ancient peoples lived.

The Karankawa, a tribe of ancient Native Americans who inhabited part of the region where pimple mounds are found in Texas, actually survived into the mid-nineteenth century. They were thought to have been so primitive as to have lived barely above the level of animals, with virtually no technology. Could such people have created the pimple mounds? As primitive as they might have been, the Karankawa shared a belief in sun worship with the Mound Builders. Might the Karankawa or their predecessors have also shared an earlier, more primitive form of mound building?

Visit with an Indian Girl

There is good reason to believe that the pimple mounds might have been built by ancient people who had a view of nature and the world quite different from our own. A few years ago, we happened to meet a young couple, Dan and Angie, from the town of Sour Lake, which bills itself as the Gateway to the Big Thicket and is the site of many strange occurrences. We got to talking in general about the weird things seen in that neck of the woods, and the subject of the pimple mounds came up.

It turns out that Angie's parents had owned a piece of land in the area, where they put a mobile home. There was a mound on the land that, judging from its description, was a pimple mound. Angie's parents used the mound as part of the base for their mobile home to keep it above the high water that often plagues the area. Angie was just a child at the time, but no sooner had she started living there than she began having visions.

A small Indian girl appeared in her bedroom, which was in the part of the mobile home that was directly over the mound. At first Angie was terrified, and the girl would quickly vanish. Over a period of time, however, Angie lost her fear, and the ghost of the little Indian girl would stay for longer periods of time, gazing silently at her astonished hostess. No words were ever exchanged, but if we could overcome our tendency to assume natural explanations for such things as the pimple mounds, who knows what worlds of wonder and what clues to the ancient past they might contain?

Cave of the White Shaman

For thousands of years, back in the mists of prehistory, aboriginal artists painted elaborate scenes on the limestone walls of the canyons and rock-shelters of Southwest Texas. The paintings were not done for mere pleasure, but illustrated the religious beliefs and traditions of the peoples who had populated the area while Europeans were still living primitively on their own continent. There are more than 250 of these Texas sites along the lower courses of the Pecos and Devil's rivers and at their confluence with the Rio Grande. One of the densest concentrations of Archaic rock art in North America, these are considered to be among the planet's most significant ancient rock-art finds, right up there with the ones in Europe and Australia.

The cave of the White Shaman is one of the most intensely spiritual of the sites. The following is from the description of it provided by the Rock Art Foundation, a nonprofit group dedicated to preserving the Pecos River art.

The white shaman [within the complex panel] is in his ascendancy, leaving behind his black counterpart, his mortal body. He is headless, but his clawed feet and hands betray his feline affinities. Feathers fringe his outspread arms, enabling him to fly, and, hanging from his arm, is a medicine bundle that combines human, bird, and animal attributes.... Above him is [a figure that] has been reduced to the skeletal condition, his exposed backbone being an artistic convention intended to convey the rebirth from the bones, the most durable element of the body. [Other] figures include the delicate line drawing of a deer shaman, and a number of fantastic figures that people the supernatural world. The shaman is expected to encounter unearthly beings on his ethereal transits. These drawings may inform his audience about some of the fantastic apparitions that helped or hindered his voyage.

Jim Zintgraff, a member of the Rock Art Foundation, has written eloquently of the importance of preserving and studying the ancient pictographs. Here's what he has to say about what this ancient man brings to modern man, if we have the heart to see it. (We edited Jim's words a little for space, but you'll get the idea.)

The young brave said to the old Shaman, "In my vision, I died and rose above my body in flight. Soon I was passing over the village, and I could see my friends going on their day. Suddenly I realized I had been transformed into a crow, and that is why I could fly. Was I really flying?"

"Yes," answered the old Shaman.

"Could my friends see me flying?"

The old Shaman looked at him sternly and said, "What difference does that make?"

It is the individual experience, not what we want others to see or think that is important.

What is it that so many see in the rock art of the Pecos and in the White Shaman panel in particular that draws the observer to the mystery? Regardless of our religious background, if any, there is something "sacred" left for us by the Pecos people. We are invited by the power of the vision to find out more.

Shamanism is not some bizarre pagan religion invented by Satan, but perhaps the world's first religion, and it served the Peoples of the Lower Pecos well for over ten thousand years. We know that the Pecos people lived by their beliefs; the Shaman, with the power to journey in the spirit world, often directed the entire clan to ceremony, to hunt, to sacrifice, and even to move the entire village, all based on "a trip to the spirit world." The messages of the White Shaman, other pictographs, and the desert itself are ones of spiritual quest and fulfillment.

So the Shamanism of the Pecos speaks even to those of us today who are busying ourselves with the problems of our modern world, so far divorced from anything truly "sacred." Perhaps when we journey to the Pecos and take the trail to the White Shaman, we should sit at the shelter, take off our expensive hiking boots, sink our toes into Mother Earth, and listen for the spirits. Maybe if we do, the ancient echoes of Shamanism, which originated in Paleo-Europe and echo through the Pecos people, will once again connect us with things of eternal value that our modern world has forgotten.

Visitors can view some of the famous rock art by boat at Amistad National Recreation Area. Guided tours are conducted at nearby Seminole Canyon State Historical Park in Val Verde County. The Rock Art Foundation also leads guided tours at their White Shaman Galloway Preserve, just west of Seminole Canyon. Contact them at www.rockart.org.

Wonderful Healing Powers of Sour Lake

No one knows how this ancient mineral lake was formed. One theory is that it resulted from a small meteorite that cracked the earth's crust and drew oil, sulfurous compounds, and other minerals and acids to the surface. They mixed with the water that soon filled the resulting crater, thereby forming a lake of considerable size.

Or its origins might have been something similar to the origins of the La Brea Tar Pits of California, which formed when crude oil seeped to the surface through fissures in the earth's crust. And, like the tar pits, Sour Lake might have been the grave of prehistoric animals. According to L. I. Adams, Jr., the author of *Time and Shadows,* "an object of petrified bone" was unearthed in the lake that had the appearance of the toe of a prehistoric animal. For years, it was on display at a barbershop in the town of Sour Lake.

Whatever the source of the lake, the Indians knew of the existence of its sour mineral springs and their healing properties as far back as can be determined.

Whatever the source of the lake, the Indians knew of the existence of its sour mineral springs and their healing properties as far back as can be determined. Ruth Garrison Scurlock, in Francis Abernethy's *Tales of the Big Thicket*, wrote about the legend of how this knowledge came to them. She got the tale from her grandmother, who had been steeped in the lore of the Big Thicket and whose father had been an agent here and friend of the Alabama Indians near Woodville.

The story goes that one summer a deadly plague threatened to wipe out a tribe of Indians living along the upper Texas Gulf Coast near present-day High Island. The beloved daughter of the chief succumbed to the terrible disease. That night, she appeared to the chief in a dream and said she would soon reappear to the tribe in another form and lead them to a medicine lake where they could be healed. She promised that bathing in the sacred water and drinking from the springs would make the plague disappear.

The next morning, a beautiful white doe appeared to the chief. He believed the deer to be the promised return of his daughter and urged his people to follow her. She led them northward, across the marshes and prairies, to the edge of a great dark forest. They followed her through towering trees and dense undergrowth to a beautiful glade with a small lake fed by many springs. The white doe leaped into the forest and disappeared. As directed in the chief's vision, the Indians drank the water from the springs and bathed in the lake, and soon they were well again.

However the Indians learned of the healing power of the lake—whether from a beautiful doe or from their own experience—it is widely accepted that the knowledge was common long before the European settlers arrived. The Hasinai Caddo were said to have been frequent visitors. Even the wild Karankawa came to the lake from the coast.

The warlike tribes from the north also came. Groups that were normally sworn enemies met at the Sour Lake Springs and observed a sacred truce so the place could be a healing place for all.

The white man learned from the Indians how to benefit from the mineral waters at Sour Lake. And in the 1850s, about twenty years after European settlers arrived, the first attempts were made to put the lake's healing waters to use for all mankind—at a profit.

A beautiful hotel was built at the springs, and in its heyday, people came from across Texas and from Louisiana and other parts of the South to avail themselves of its medicinal powers. Ailments such as eczema and stomach disorders were successfully treated. The fame of the healing properties of the waters spread far and wide. The following, compiled by L. I. Adams, are statements from some of the physicians of the time who were familiar with the water's curative powers.

"It possesses a combination of mineral waters of great medical value and untold commercial wealth, without rival, competitor or duplicate, as far as I know, in the world."
—R. C. Fowler, M.D., Boston, Massachusetts

"I consider the waters and baths equal, if not superior, to those of any health resort in the country. To my knowledge the use of the waters for all diseases of the stomach, dyspepsia, indigestion, all kinds of skin diseases and blood poison is followed by the most satisfactory result."
—A. W. Fly, M.D., Galveston, Texas

"They are more rapid in their effects and possess more restorative and curative powers than any waters that I know of. Their action in purifying the blood and expelling blood poisons is unparalleled."
—H. C. Watts, M.D.

General Sam Houston, venerated in Southeast Texas as the hero of the Battle of San Jacinto, visited the Sour Lake resort several times seeking aid for an ankle injury he had suffered during the battle. His war wound was said to have bothered him until the day he died. Supposedly, he had said that the most relief he ever got was from the treatment he was given at the Sour Lake Springs resort.

The original hotel was destroyed in 1883. It was rebuilt and flourished until it burned down on March 21, 1909. Attempts to revive the resort met with little success and were finally abandoned, but the strange happenings at Sour Lake were far from over.

Incredible Sinkhole of Sour Lake

In 1901, the oil industry was born in Texas when the Spindletop gusher blew outside Beaumont, not far from the lake. Leases were soon acquired to drill for oil near the Sour Lake Springs. The chances of striking oil were good. Decades before, perhaps the first oil to be discovered in Texas had been found no more than a hundred feet from the lake. Pipes were driven several feet into the ground to produce what was called a seep, from which as much as a pint of oil a day could be produced. In those earlier, less motorized days, the product was bottled and sold as medicine.

On January 8, 1903, the Texas Company, known today as Texaco, brought in its first gusher on the Sour Springs Tract. The oil boom was on, and before long, derricks were so close together on parts of the Texas Company land that their legs interlocked. In the madness of the rush for black gold, the Sour Lake Springs were all but forgotten.

For some twenty-eight years, twenty-four hours a day, untold barrels of oil and gallons of waste salt water were extracted from the oilfields near the springs. Then in early October 1929, something truly extraordinary and unprecedented in history occurred: The sink began.

On the morning of October 9, a Texas Company employee was startled to find that a piece of company land about two hundred feet across had sunk some fifteen feet and appeared to still be sinking. Within an hour, the cavity was fifty feet deep and the sides were collapsing. A little later, its depth had reached ninety feet and the hole began to fill with mud, sand, water, and oil. Derricks, oil tanks, toolsheds, and even large trees fell into it.

The initial sinking continued for three days. By the time it ended, a deep fifteen-acre lake had been created, and newspapers around the country ran the shocking headline TEXAS OIL TOWN SINKS.

The Sour Lake Sinkhole, as it came to be called, was the first known incidence in the world of land subsidence due to oil-well drilling. Geologists believe that the years of continual pumping had drained a cavity below the oilfield and that the earth's crust had collapsed. The springs feeding the old Sour Lake seemed to have been affected by the sink and slowly began to dry up. Today, virtually nothing remains of the original springs.

Many of the people who had benefitted from the jobs created by oil drilling had a feeling of remorse at the loss of the old medicinal springs. If a little more care had been taken, perhaps the springs could have been preserved even in the midst of an oilfield. But beyond this was an unspoken sense that something sacred had been violated and lost.

Some of the old-timers who were actually there when the original sink occurred wondered if one day the entire oilfield and maybe even the town of Sour Lake would be consumed by a catastrophic expansion of the sinkhole. It was not an idle concern, because the cavity continues to get bigger and deeper. The original fifteen acres has now grown to an estimated seventy-five to a hundred acres. And judging from electric utility poles that have been swallowed up, the sinkhole is at least thirty feet deeper than it was a few decades ago.

And there is another thing—the place is just plain creepy. A former Sour Lake police officer e-mailed us an account of strange feelings he had experienced there. He wrote that he and his partner "had heard strange animal noises when we would patrol the oilfields. At nighttime in those oil fields, you can hear all kinds of strange sounds. Sour Lake is spooky indeed."

If you know the full history of the lake or have ever had that creepy feeling there, you might find yourself asking some unsettling questions. Was a curse put on the place that had been revealed to the Indians by a magical white doe, only to be later desecrated by greedy white men? Had sleeping spirits in the burial mounds near the sacred medicine lake been awakened and disturbed?

Perhaps, but there is a bright and hopeful side to this story too. Years ago the sinkhole was dead and polluted, with a slimy sheen of oil floating on its surface. With its recent expansion, something remarkable has happened: The lake's water has freshened, and life has returned. There are fish now, and one half-submerged utility pole has an osprey nest perched on its top. Ospreys, or fish eagles, were considered endangered on the Texas coast not too many years ago, the victims of water contaminated by DDT. If ospreys now approve of the sinkhole's water enough to build a nest there, maybe the violated spirits have been appeased. Maybe the ancient healing waters are returning.

Wink Sinks

Way out in the almost interminably horizontal stretches of West Texas lies Wink, a tranquil burg that's home to a quiet, close-knit community. Here the streets are clean, the people are friendly, and life is good. There is, however, one problem: Wink suffers from a severe depression or, more accurately, from severe depressions.

On the morning of June 3, 1980, a contractor was performing an inspection for one of the local oil companies. He was checking pipelines just north of town, when he heard a splash nearby. Curious as to what kind of splashing there could be in a flat, dusty field, he walked toward the sound and discovered a twenty-foot-wide hole where, oddly, there hadn't been one before.

The hole, which descended four stories to a restless cauldron of water, grew within two hours to a diameter of one hundred feet. By noon, its width had doubled. The earth was caving in at an absurd pace just a few hundred yards from Highway 115 in one direction and a field of oil-storage tanks in the other. By the next day, the sinkhole had grown to some three hundred and fifty feet. Luckily, its expansion slowed before it threatened either the highway or the storage tanks. No one was injured, though the hole did swallow a water line and a utility pole before it was done.

As time passed, the mysterious crater appeared to stabilize. Over the next twenty years, the locals began to think that the hole, which they had nicknamed the Wink Sink, was just a freak occurrence.

Then it happened again. In May 2002, a second crater appeared, this time only a mile and a half from town. Dubbed Wink Sink 2, the new hole started out as large as its predecessor had ended and was twice as deep. By the end of June, it had expanded to approximately six hundred feet by seven hundred and

fifty feet, growing at a rate of roughly ten feet a day. It has continued to expand ever since, swallowing fences put up around it at least twice.

Opinions and theories as to the cause of Wink's spontaneous collapse are numerous. The area has seen continuous oil extraction since the late 1920s, so people initially thought drillers might simply be taking out too much. Not only oil, but millions of gallons of brine have been displaced over the years, which triggered images of large cavelike pockets below the surface.

A few believe the sinkholes are somehow connected with Carlsbad Caverns, less than a hundred miles to the northwest, though nobody seems very sure just exactly how, and the supposition is usually prefaced with

"You know, they say . . ."

An exhaustive investigation of the Wink Sinks has yet to be conducted, but a number of geologists have offered their hypotheses. Using expressions like "fractured anhydrite interbeds" and "cavernous permeability," they pointed their fingers at "dissolution in the middle of the Salado evaporite sequence." Basically, they weren't sure.

And it looks as though the sinkholes' expansion isn't over. There's no guarantee that Wink Sink 3 won't make an appearance. One good dissolution of the right evaporite sequence, and the town of Wink, with its treasured Roy Orbison Museum, might vanish as quickly as its name.

Odessa Meteor Crater—A Depressing Depression

What do you call a six-hundred-foot-wide hole filled with dirt? The National Park Service calls it a National Natural Landmark.

While the Odessa Meteor Crater may be one of the most significant astrogeological finds of our time, it lacks the majesty one would naturally associate with an explosive meteoric impact. Thanks to time and erosion, the hole that was created by an explosion comparable to those that ended World War II now dips belowground only about six feet.

Oddly, it's suspected to be part of the same event that formed the magnificent Barringer Crater in Arizona, a 3800-foot-wide, 570-foot-deep crater that makes the one in Texas look less like a pit and more like a pit stain. Though the Texas crater was once 100 feet deep, today it hardly looks out of place amid the surrounding terrain. If somebody hadn't put up a big sign that said CRATER with an arrow on it, you might think you were just looking at a good place to dump an old couch.

Locals have been aware of the crater's existence since the 1890s, but nobody gave it much thought. It wasn't until 1922 that a geologist realized what it was, though no one paid much attention to his discovery. Several years later, however, interest swelled after a theory was put forth that the meteor responsible for the impact was more than five hundred feet wide and was very likely buried beneath the surface. In 1939, the state, the county, the University of Texas, and the federal Works Progress Administration combined forces to locate the specimen. They thought if they could find it, they might be able to turn the site into a national park, with a subterranean elevator that could take visitors belowground to view the meteorite up close.

Once drillers believed they had pinpointed their target, engineers went about digging a 165-foot shaft to

get to it. Unfortunately, after all their efforts, they realized the drillers had come across nothing more than a particularly tenacious layer of limestone. Their valuable space rock was nowhere to be found. Scientists later came to understand that the meteor would have destroyed itself on impact.

After such a monumental disappointment, the Odessa Meteor Crater was virtually abandoned. Trash piled up,

and the county began taking limestone from the site to use as roadbed material. An effort was made in the 1960s to clean the place up and erect a small museum, but vandals robbed and defaced the site a few years later, and the area once again was abandoned

Recently, officials have made a more serious attempt at preserving the crater, adding new facilities and erecting informative signage for self-guided tours. It still takes quite a bit of imagination to understand what really went on here, but the trail makes for a nice place to stretch your legs on a long drive.

And with any luck, the county may continue its improvements and get really serious by turning the place into an awesome disaster-themed mini-golf course. *—Wesley Treat*

Do Not Pick Up

Odessa Meteorite
Iron   70 lbs.
Medium Octahedrite

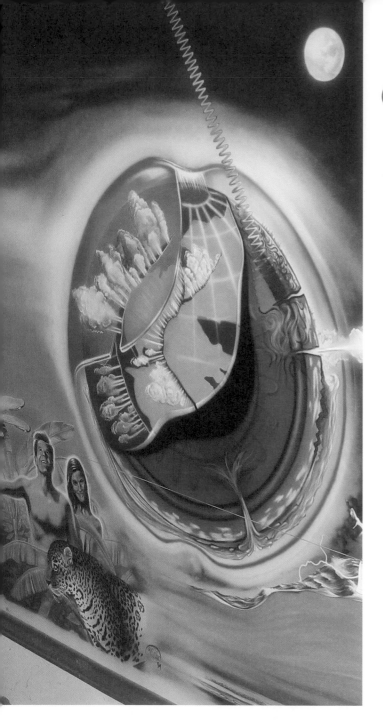

Creation Evidence Museum

Tired of the Establishment's convincing your children of its distorted view of man's origin? Afraid a trip to the museum of science and history might irrevocably pollute their minds with Darwinism? Well, fear not, creationists. You have a choice!

Only an hour outside Fort Worth, right next door to Dinosaur Valley State Park, the Creation Evidence Museum presents a godly alternative to the theory of evolution. Housed in a humble tan trailer, it showcases the lifework of the Reverend Dr. Carl Baugh, champion of "creation science."

Dr. Baugh, who, incidentally, appears to have received his Ph.D. through a branch of his own unaccredited religious school, has for years argued in favor of a biblical model of the world's development. To support his case, he cites evidence of giant men who had roamed the planet before the Flood, supposed experiments showing that eggs can't hatch outside the earth's magnetic field, and first-hand accounts of glow-in-the-dark pterodactyls flying over New Guinea. He opened the museum in 1984 to bear witness to his theories.

By way of videocassette, Dr. Baugh himself guides visitors through the museum, sharing his breakthrough artifacts: the iron cup encrusted in coal, the stone-encased

hammer, and the rock that looks amazingly like a fossil of a human finger. The real ones aren't on display, of course; they are in a safe-deposit box. But you can purchase replicas for $25.

Additionally, there's the famed Burdick Track, a fourteen-inch-long footprint preserved in stone, which supports Baugh's assertion that pre-Flood man grew to gargantuan size owing to the oxygen-rich, high-pressure atmosphere.

He also presents a device in which he re-created such an environment for experimentation. In his antediluvian hyperbaric biosphere, he has subjected fruit flies and venomous snakes to increased atmospheric pressure, oxygen, carbon dioxide, and electromagnetic radiation, which, he says, tripled the life span of the flies and turned the serpents' poison nontoxic. The electromagnetic field, he says, also unexpectedly affected the fish in an adjacent aquarium, influencing their cellular mitosis and "cellular preservation."

A sixty-two-foot-version of the biosphere is under construction in a facility next door. Reportedly, Baugh at one time figured that if increased O_2 was good, then O_3 (ozone) would be even better, and he planned to live in the biosphere and secure a physiological advantage for himself. Apparently, someone informed the doctor that breathing pure ozone would kill him, and he abandoned the experiment. Similar tests are still planned for lesser creatures.

Baugh spends the rest of the tape explaining his version of the six-day Genesis. Here, his sales pitch kicks into high gear with well-rehearsed patter articulating his theories with an almost poetic scientific idiom. He speaks

of a geocentric stretching of the fabric of space and its resultant time dilation and of a firmamental canopy of metallic hydrogen that previously assimilated shortwave radiation, kept the electromagnetic field charged, and admitted long-wave spectral radiation, "bathing the globe with benefits."

It's all very convincing, as long as you don't try to understand what he's talking about—it's like watching a commercial that extols its product for having chondroitin or retsin while saving you the hassle of knowing what that ingredient does. By the end, you're ready to cry out, "How could I have been so blind?" until you realize you have no idea what "polonium halos" are nor the slightest notion what their presence in granite has to do with natural selection.

You may as well buy it, though, because "in the evolutionary model, everything ends in despair," concludes the good doctor, exclaiming, "But in the creation model, there is promise for hope!"

Fabled People and Places

Down through the ages, man has endeavored to find mythical lands and fabled peoples. Some grand adventurers searched for the Holy Grail or for El Dorado, the fabulous city of gold. Here at *Weird Texas*, the places we pursue are far more humble than those. We're more likely to want to know who is really buried in the grave of Jesse James. We travel the back roads looking for places we have heard tell of, like the Witches' Castle, without any real evidence that such places actually exist. Risking encounters with primitive and savage phantom Indians, we light out to find answers to such questions as is there really an alien buried in the Aurora Cemetery? That's what we want to know!

We keep an open mind, just in case these fabled people and places are like Brigadoon, and must be believed to be seen and not the other way around. For we want to believe in them, even though we know they may exist only in our own collective imagination. Then again, maybe not.

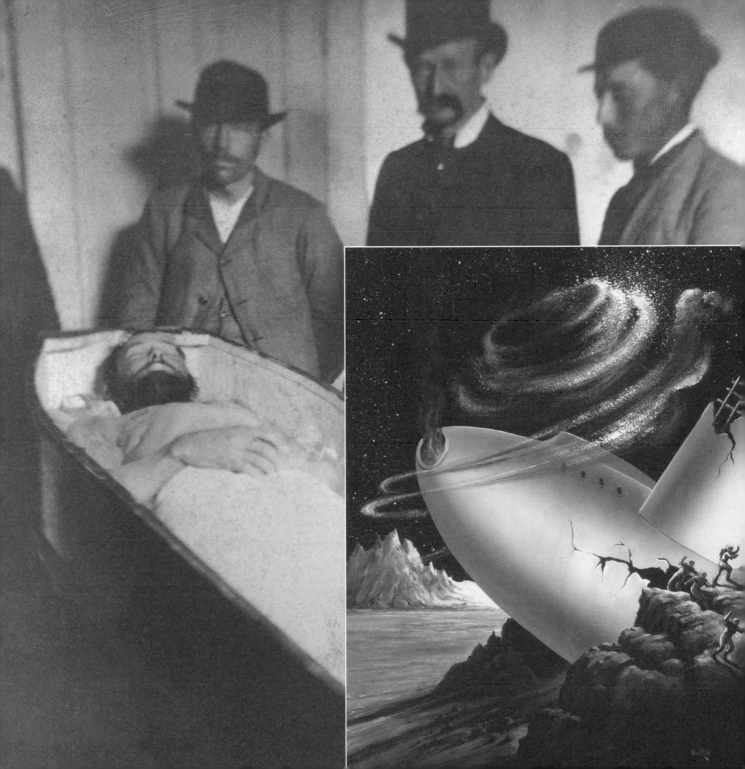

El Muerto—the Headless Rider

For the past century and a half, Texas residents have lived in fear of the mysterious specter called El Muerto—literally, "the Dead One." This lone rider patrols the deserts of the Lone Star State, bringing terror to all who encounter him. Those who lay eyes on him don't have to worry about him laying his eyes on them in return, for he has no eyes. He is a headless horseman, forever wandering the Texas deserts.

El Muerto was first seen during the 1850s, galloping throughout the Wild Horse Desert region of Texas. The cowboys who spotted him assumed he was one of the local Indians trying to terrorize them. However, when they'd send scouts out looking for his tracks or for locations of the Indian camps, they never found any. Soon the wranglers realized that they weren't dealing with Indians playing tricks. They were dealing with a genuine ghost.

As reports of El Muerto spread, his general appearance became well known. Everyone who saw him agreed that he wore the outfit of a Mexican vaquero. Most reported that his head, topped with a sombrero, was tied to the side of his horse. Many claimed to see bullet wounds in him and Indian arrows hanging off him. However, none who shot at the strange apparition ever managed to slow him down, let alone stop him.

The origins of the El Muerto legend lie in the general lawlessness of Texas during the nineteenth century. The state was then a stomping ground for bandits, most of whom operated in the southern part of the state—a no-man's-land of lawlessness. Mexican cattle thieves and Comanche bandits roamed freely, stealing tens of thousands of cattle each year from ranchers in the area. The cattle thieves were in an ongoing state of war with the famous Texas Rangers, who patrolled the territory, trying to enforce order.

One of the most infamous episodes in the history of the Rangers was their hunt for a notorious Mexican cattle and horse thief named Vidal. Creed Taylor and William Anderson "Big Foot" Wallace, two of the most respected and legendary Texas Rangers, made it their mission to hunt down and kill Vidal as an example to every other thief in the state. Vidal was in command of many of the outlaw gangs scattered throughout Texas and even had operatives in Louisiana and Mississippi.

When the Rangers finally found Vidal, they exacted one of the most gruesome punishments that Texas has ever known. Wallace severed Vidal's head from his body, then lashed the body onto a young stallion and strapped the head, still wearing a sombrero, onto the animal's side. This morbid sight became known as El Muerto. The horse rode on through the wilderness, terrorizing travelers who had no idea what it really was. They told many stories of their encounters, and El Muerto quickly became a legend.

Some Texas residents finally mustered the courage to track down the horse and its mysterious rider to a place near the small town of Ben Bolt. When they wrangled the horse, they were shocked to find that the shriveled corpse strapped to it was riddled with bullet holes and full of arrows and spears. Vidal was removed from the steed's back and buried in a small cemetery on the La Trinidad Ranch in Ben Bolt.

But a legend this good was not about to die. After the horse was found and the body removed, ghostly images of El Muerto continued to be sighted. Were the stories now so pervasive that people still told them even though the horse and its grisly rider were gone? Or was the ghost of Vidal so angry at the fate that had befallen him that in death he still roamed the desert in his discontent? Headless horseman sightings still occur frequently in Texas, and most are thought to be appearances by the infamous El Muerto.

Lost Padre Mine

In 1659, there was a mission called Nuestra Senora de Guadalupe in what is now the city of Ciudad Juárez, Mexico. According to legend, some of the mission's padres would cross the Rio Grande daily to a rich, secret gold mine in the Franklin Mountains north of El Paso. The ore was then hauled down the mountain by mules to the river, where it was melted into ingots, placed on boats, and shipped to Spain.

A four-story-tall bell tower still tops this very old mission, and it is said that the entrance to the hidden mine could at one time be seen from inside this tower. For many years, the monks of the mission mined vast quantities of gold and, to help them in their backbreaking labor, even recruited some of the local Indians, whom they had converted to Catholicism.

In 1680, the Pueblo Indians of New Mexico staged a bloody uprising against the Spanish. Several friars managed to escape and hurried south along the Rio Grande, alerting others that the Pueblo chief, Cheetwah, was on the warpath and planning to put an end to Spanish rule in the area. The friars reached the mission just in time to warn the rest that the Indians were headed their way. Legend has it that the padres loaded up their donkeys and carts with as much gold and other valuables as they could and made their way across the river, where they hid the rich treasure in the mine. Included in their stash was a king's ransom of gold candlesticks, chalices, and ingots.

Once the booty was safely stashed in the mineshaft, the monks carried silt from the river up the mountain to fill in the shaft, then covered the mine entrance with rocks, taking care to completely hide it from view. Some claim that they also left three unfortunate padres alive inside the mine to defend it against anyone who tried to enter. The remaining padres returned to their mission to defend it against the impending Pueblo invasion. They planned to return to the mine afterward to rescue the brothers they had left behind and to retrieve the riches.

Little did they know that the Indian rebellion would last until 1692 and that it would be twelve years before they would be able to return to recover their buried fortune. As peace finally settled over the area, some of the padres tried to retrace their steps to the mine and its treasure, only to find that the way had been lost in the intervening years. It didn't help that most of the original padres were either dead or no longer capable of making the arduous journey to the mountains. The monks searched the area for the lost mine, but were never able to find it. Since then, there have been a number of attempts to locate the old mine and its treasure by people from both sides of the border. Here are some of the most well-known expeditions.

In 1888, a man named Robinson declared that he had figured out the location of the Lost Padre Mine by going up into the old bell tower of the mission and studying its view of the Franklins. After an incredible amount of work, Robinson's team uncovered the entrance to an ancient mine plugged up with reddish river silt. However, a scant few days later, his financial support was suddenly revoked, and before abandoning the site, Robinson, in anger, had his men refill the mine, hiding it. It would stay hidden for many years.

In 1901, another treasure seeker, a man named L. C. Criss, claimed to have discovered the location of the mine. Criss and his team painstakingly cleared 125 feet of the shaft, finding some Spanish artifacts, including an ancient anvil and spur. At the end of the main shaft, Criss discovered yet more tunnels, and he stopped work in order to bring in more timber to shore up the dangerous passageways. One overeager worker went back into the tunnel and resumed working moments after Criss had left. As he started to dig, the shaft collapsed, burying him alive

Legend has it that the padres loaded up their donkeys and carts with as much gold and other valuables as they could and made their way across the river, where they hid the rich treasure in the mine.

with dirt and rock. Criss was unable to obtain further financing, and excavation was halted. He left El Paso, never to be heard from again.

To this day, many treasure hunters still believe that the golden treasure of the Lost Padre Mine is still waiting to be found, nestled in the rocky peaks of the untamed Franklin Mountains, still guarded by souls of the monks left behind to defend it so many years ago. –*Shady*

Dead Man's Hole

The world is full of so-called Dead Man's Holes—treacherous natural fissures in the landscape that can snare a careless hiker. Some appear to have a history of actual dead men, while others may be so nicknamed just to intrigue tourists.

In Texas alone, there are no fewer than four Dead Man's Holes. Three aren't exactly holes, just hollows of some kind, and there are no known stories involving the deceased. The name just sounded good to someone. Number four, however, meets the sinister title's criteria in full: It's a hole, and it has had a dead man in it—several, in fact.

This place, located a few miles west of Austin, just south of Marble Falls, has been known about for nearly two hundred years. It was discovered in 1821, when an entomologist, while studying nocturnal insects, was lucky enough not to fall in, and personally gave the chasm its new name. But the hole wouldn't earn its dismal moniker for a few more decades. It was during the Civil War, when Americans were pitted against one another, that people began throwing their enemies into the pit. Staunch Confederates, apparently looking to sway the vote for secession, murdered Union sympathizers and dumped the bodies down the hole. Legend has it that the limb of an oak tree that once shaded the opening was scarred by the weight of

a noose—part of an all-in-one human Disposall®.

Years later, those brave enough to descend into Dead Man's Hole began bringing up the bodies—or what was left of them. In all, the remains of seventeen men were recovered. Only three, however, were officially identified: a settler named Adolph Hoppe, who opposed the war; Judge John R. Scott, the first Chief Justice of Burnet County and a pro-Union voter; and Ben McKeever, who had had a run-in with local freedmen soon after the war. Some of the others were believed to be carpetbaggers who had simply disappeared in the night.

Further exploration of the cave wouldn't take place for several more years. Dead Man's Hole is apparently a gas fissure, fumes from which prevented anyone from spelunking very far. Finally, though, the geological orifice was thoroughly mapped and measured in 1968, when cavers recorded its depth at one hundred and fifty-five feet and discovered two branches—one that stretched an additional fifteen feet and a second that extended another thirty feet. Today, the hole's seven-foot aperture has been sealed off, with only a small, barred entryway to allow anyone a look-see. And the only things you'll see down there nowadays are bottles, cans, and maybe a few coins. A caver did, however, once unearth a stolen wallet, with a driver's license that had expired five years earlier.

Unfortunately, it's hard to tell just how deep Dead Man's Hole is, but if you drop a rock in just the right spot, you can hear it tumble for several seconds. Try not to sink too many down there, lest we collectively turn it into Dead Man's Indentation.

TEXAS

DEAD MAN'S HOLE

ENTOMOLOGIST FERDINAND LUEDERS MADE THE EARLIEST RECORDED DISCOVERY OF THIS CAVE IN 1821. NOTORIOUS IN THE CIVIL WAR ERA, THE HOLE IS BELIEVED TO HAVE BEEN THE DUMPING GROUND FOR UP TO 17 BODIES, INCLUDING THOSE OF PRO-UNION JUDGE JOHN R. SCOTT AND SETTLER ADOLPH HOPPE. SEVERAL RECONSTRUCTION-ERA GOVERNMENT OFFICIALS AND COUNTY McKEEVER, WHO HAD A CONFLICT WITH LOCAL FREEDMEN. AN OAK TREE WHICH ONCE STOOD OVER THE CAVE WAS SAID TO HAVE HAD ROPE MARKS CAUSED BY HANG-INGS. POWERFUL GASES PREVENTED THOROUGH EXPLORATION OF THE SITE UNTIL 1951. THE HOLE WAS PLATTED IN 1968 BY THE TEXAS SPELEOLOGICAL SOCIETY AND WAS FOUND TO BE 155 FEET DEEP AND 50 FEET LONG.

(1968)

DEADMANS HOLE

It was during the Civil War, when Americans were pitted against one another, that people began throwing their enemies into the pit.

Will the Real Corpse Please Stand Up?

Jesse James is arguably the most infamous Wild West personality in history. He became a legend staging daring holdups and train robberies that are still inspiring stories and films. Together with his brother Frank and their band of ex-Confederate outlaws, James left a trail of blood and money from Iowa to Texas.

On April 3, 1882, the history books tell us, Jesse James's renegade lifestyle finally caught up with him. Seeking a $10,000 reward for James's capture, Robert Ford, a member of the James Gang, entered Jesse's home and shot him in the back of the head. At the age of 34, Jesse James was confirmed dead and laid to rest in Kearney, Missouri. But then he was also confirmed dead at age 95 and buried in Blevins, Texas, then again at 103 and buried in Granbury. You can visit his grave at the location of your choice.

According to the folks in Granbury, James wasn't actually killed in 1882. Instead, he faked his death and relocated to North Texas. There, he worked as a railroad contractor under the name J. W. Gates, though he was more widely known as J. Frank Dalton. Near the end of his life, Dalton revealed his true identity to Granbury's sheriff at the time, Oran Baker. According to Baker, Dalton spent his final days recounting for the sheriff the adventures he had shared with his brother Frank and the rest of the James Gang.

On the day of Dalton's passing, Sheriff Baker conducted an examination of the body. He observed several scars that appeared to be from bullet wounds, a mark around the neck that resembled one left by an unsuccessful hanging, burns on the feet, left by Union interrogators, and a missing tip from an index finger, all of which, Baker said, were consistent with incidents known to have occurred in James's life.

Granbury is so convinced Dalton was telling the truth that they have placed signs in their cemetery leading the way to his gravesite, where his headstone bears the name Jesse Woodson James. Below that, it reads SUPPOSEDLY KILLED IN 1882.

Meanwhile, farther south, in Blevins, Betty Dorsett Duke has been picking a fight to have her great-grandfather James Lafayette Courtney recognized as the true Jesse James. According to Duke, when she was a child, her parents repeatedly told her that Courtney was the notorious outlaw, but she never believed it. Recently, however, she began to notice similarities between the photographs of James's mother and those of Courtney. Moreover, when

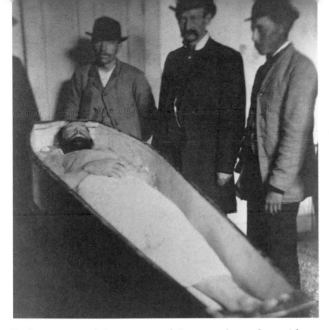

Duke compared the images of Courtney's mother with those of James's mother, she was certain they were of the same woman. Then Duke recalled the exceptional skill her great-grandfather had demonstrated with guns and the fact that he had always paid for everything in cash.

Duke now believes that the man buried in Missouri is actually Wood Hite, a member of the James Gang and Jesse James's cousin. She argues that James and Robert Ford, the man who supposedly killed James, had conspired to murder Hite and bury him in James's place. The real Jesse James is her grandfather, now resting more or less at peace in Blevins.

So how does a person know who is really sealed away in each town's casket? Well, the same way you find out which chocolate is filled with the raspberry cream—you cracks 'em open and you sees what you gets. In 1996, folks in Missouri did just that. After digging up Kearney's Jesse James, experts performed a DNA test using samples taken from two descendants of James's sister. The results indicated that, with very little chance of error, everybody else was hopped up on goofballs—Kearney had the real Jesse James.

Betty Duke, however, didn't buy it. She claimed that no DNA had actually been extracted from Kearney's disinterred body and that the DNA used for comparison came from a tooth retrieved from the James Farm Museum, a tooth that had never been documented to be Jesse's. Besides, since the man buried in Kearney happened to be Jesse's cousin, any DNA taken from the body would have shown a match anyway.

Duke petitioned to have her own DNA test performed on her great-grandfather. The judge who heard her case, however, determined that the evidence simply wasn't strong enough and ruled in favor of opposing family members, who wondered why she would want to associate them with such a dreadful criminal.

Then it was Granbury's turn. Bud Hardcastle, a used-car salesman and an avid Jesse James enthusiast, volunteered to represent three of James's supposed grandsons in a search for resolution. Together they hoped to unearth Granbury's Jesse James, a.k.a. Frank Dalton, and prove his alleged identity. After years of legal wrangling, Hardcastle was finally granted permission for an exhumation in February 2000. But when workmen moved Dalton's headstone aside and dug up the casket, it turned out that they'd disinterred the wrong man. Dalton's earlier grave markers had been stolen enough times that the exact location of his body had been slightly misplaced. Another attempt to disinter him would have required a second exhumation order, and having spent all his funds the first time around, Hardcastle has been unable to organize another effort.

So in the end, we're right back where we started. We have a probably, an unknown, and a maybe. And to top it off, there's a banker buried in Brownwood who might also be the man in question. Let's just hope he has a descendant somewhere with good DNA, a convincing lawyer, and a better idea where his ancestor's body is located.

Witches' Castle of Cameron Park

A friend and I had heard that there was a legendary place called the Witches' Castle in a wooded area known as Cameron Park in Waco. It was rumored to be a sinister spot where satanic activity takes place, and one person had even told us that there was an altar in the castle. But without the greatest directions to go on, it was another one of those places that many people seemed to know about, yet few could tell us how to get to.

The descriptions mentioned a hidden spot that resembled a castle, with stairs and turretlike walls and moatlike pools of water. There is also rumored to be a horrible stench emanating from the place, said to be the scent of the decaying bodies of the many victims of the evil witches. Some said that if you lingered here after dark, you could hear strange noises, such as screams, gasps, sobs, and a terrible banging.

Needless to say, we really wanted to see this place. But the only semigood directions we had said that it was "off to the right" in relation to the park entrance. We tried to search everywhere on that side, but we didn't see anything. We were actually going to give it up for the day, when I wandered up a small hill to get a few shots of the

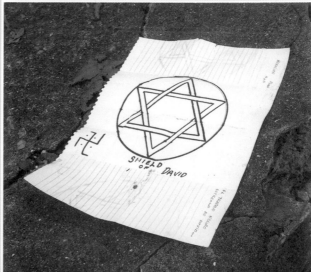

park before we left. It was then that I first noticed the trail. It was very faint and seemed to lead right into a patch of dense brush. I couldn't imagine what it led to, and of course, that piqued my curiosity even more.

I signaled to my friend that I had spotted something. We headed for the trail, following it until it led into a narrow little valley between two wooded hills that had not been visible to us before. It was at that point that I did a little spastic insane jerky FREAK-OUT dance, because I unknowingly walked full-on into a humongous spiderweb that had been

stretched across the path, and was instantly draped in the sticky awful mess from head to foot—a pretty horrid experience, lemme tell you. So as I rounded the rest of the corner and moved deeper into the little canyon, I was pretty jumpy.

That's when I saw the first set of stairs on my left and started to get excited. Could this be it, I wondered? We kept on going and came to the head of a dark pool of water, where we stopped and found ourselves looking down at a series of stairways and ledges and pools of water. There was even an altarlike formation that was part of a strange structure of castlelike appearance! And yes, there was a terrible smell rising up from below. This HAD to be the Witches' Castle.

We both had to wonder how this could have been right under our noses, and we almost missed it. As we inspected the "altar," we found a piece of paper lying there. It was a thick yellowish parchment with a swastika, a Shield of David, and the words El Trabajo Negro (the Black Work) and Estrella de David (Star of David) scrawled on one side. On the other side was the word *natas* (Satan spelled backward) written with an inverted cross for the T. So obviously, someone was definitely taking the satanic aspects of the place seriously. We left the paper where we found it and explored some more.

The source of the bad smell became apparent as we neared the upper pool, which was quite stagnant and, oddly enough, had a bunch of Cheerios floating in it. On the other side of the pool, I happened to find a roach (not the insect kind) left behind on a leaf. We also found a sign saying that the name of this place was Proctor Springs. The mouth of the spring comes right out of the ground and almost looks like a real mouth, complete with moss-covered Rolling Stones–style tongue.

This was a really exciting find; it was great to finally unearth this strange and unusual place, and finding that sinister paper on the "altar" added a memorably creepy note to the experience. I almost expected to hear a witch's cackle from the dark and shadowy woods at any second. And I guess it might be noteworthy to mention that some people sitting at a picnic table farther out in the park looked at us as if we were crazy when they saw us emerge from the place after checking it out for a bit. And that's always good. Right?—*Shady*

Alien Plane Crash in Aurora

Texas is known for its tall tales, and whenever a small town is lucky enough to be associated with one, the residents will usually do their best to run with it, be it true or not. After all, publicity means tourists, and tourists mean dollars. The town of Aurora, just north of Fort Worth, seems to be an exception, however. Locals there were long ago blessed with a shot at the easiest dollars of all: UFO dollars. Strangely, they've never grasped the opportunity.

The tale in question dates back more than a hundred years to the spring of 1897.

In an April 19 story published by the *Dallas Times Herald,* reporter E. E. Hayden wrote of a strange airship seen flying over town early that morning, just before it crashed on the property of Judge J. S. Proctor. The unidentified craft "went to pieces with a terrific explosion," destroying Proctor's windmill and, tragically, his flower garden.

At that time, airship sightings were not uncommon. In the fall of the previous year, West Coast residents began describing a cigar-shaped craft drifting under cover of darkness across the California skies, which was unusual, since the first successful American dirigible wouldn't be tested for several years. The reports continued for months, spreading eastward to other states, including Texas. Many accounts surfaced simultaneously from distant locations, suggesting the existence of more than one craft. The incident, still unexplained, has become known as the Great Airship Mystery of 1896–1897.

TEXAS HISTORICAL COMMISSION

TEXAS

AURORA CEMETERY

EST KNOWN GRAVES HERE, DATING FROM AS E

OSE OF THE RANDALL AND RO

Surprisingly, nowadays the legend has simply been brushed aside. Most Aurorans appear uninterested in the tale, with many refuting it as a hoax. They'll tell you that Judge Proctor never had a windmill and that it's likely he had cooked the whole thing up with E. E. Hayden, who was from Aurora and may have been looking to revive his declining hometown. If it weren't for the historical marker outside the cemetery, which briefly mentions the alleged incident, Aurora wouldn't offer any evidence of the event at all.

If the townsfolk had any entrepreneurial spirit, of course, they'd take a cue from Roswell and make the most of what they were handed. All it would take is a couple of green buildings, a few businesses with "UFO" in the title, and maybe an annual parade, and the geeks would line up, every one eager to shell out cash for all the foam-rubber aliens and little broken windmills they could carry.

Hundreds claimed to have seen the vessels, but the most unusual report continued to be that from Aurora. Not only had the airship crashed, but according to Hayden's article, a small humanoid body was recovered from the wreckage. The being was said to have been disfigured by the accident, but it was clearly "not an inhabitant of this world."

Those who arrived on the scene, being the considerate folks that they were, buried the creature in the Aurora Cemetery. A small grave marker was erected, which was said to have been carved with an image resembling the visitor's spacecraft. Unfortunately, when the story resurfaced in the 1970s, vandals made off with the marker.

Phantom Indians of the Swamp

Some things that we witness under weird circumstances force us to examine our assumptions about the very nature of time and space. What we have come to call Phantom Indians, reported from the strangeness that is the Trinity River swamp, certainly fit that category.

It is known that strong magnetic anomalies can produce a bleed-over effect in radio reception in a given area. We've all run into it while driving long distances. The frequency band may temporarily bleed over into another, or a radio receiver may also pick up signals from far beyond its normal range. When strong anomalies occur, they could theoretically produce little-understood conditions, during which, as bizarre as it may sound, aspects of a reality or dimension at one frequency could temporarily bleed into another.

If this can be said about dimensions of space, what can be said about how such weird energy conditions could affect the dimension of time? There is a theory of modern physics involving what are called time lines. According to this theory, the past does not simply disappear, but remains on a time line other than the one we are consciously experiencing. It is within the terms of such a theory, in which time-line bleeds occur corresponding to radio-frequency bleeds, that we can begin to account for the patterns suggested by the Phantom Indian stories below. They seem to tell of manifestations of beings as much from another time as from another dimension. Interestingly, the stories come from several independent sources, and the teller of one tale was unaware of the experiences of another.

Let's start with Rick, a professional treasure hunter from the Texas Gulf Coast. Rick has spent years exploring the Gulf of Mexico and the Caribbean and has been successful in finding lost Spanish gold. He flies over an area in an airplane equipped with a magnetometer—a device resembling an oversized metal detector—that picks up anomalies in the magnetic field. Large deposits of metal, such as would be contained in a buried treasure, can cause such anomalies. This technique works especially well in such swampy areas as those of the Texas Gulf Coast, which contain little or no natural metal-bearing stone.

One day, as he was surveying a section of the lower Trinity River swamp just off Trinity Bay, he came across a spot with just such a magnetic anomaly. Rick knew that this particular stretch of the bay was the subject of legends about pirate Jean Lafitte's buried treasure, so he was encouraged by the magnetometer's reading. He excitedly set out to explore the site on foot, but when he approached the area, he met a game warden. The warden, a little suspicious of Rick because he wasn't carrying hunting or fishing equipment, asked him where he was going. When Rick told him, the warden surprised Rick by advising him not to proceed.

The game warden said that a number of hunters and

fishermen had reportedly been attacked by strange people in the area Rick wanted to investigate. The warden believed the reports because he had also been accosted. Naturally, Rick asked who would be hostile enough to attack innocent sportsmen and a park official. The warden looked at Rick as if trying to decide whether to go on with his story or whether Rick would think he was nuts if he told the truth. Rick must have looked okay, because the warden told him that an "Indian" had attacked him and barely missed hitting him with an arrow. At least he thought the dark and practically naked figure who had assaulted him was an Indian. It couldn't possibly be anyone else.

Rick couldn't help but wonder what kind of weirdo would be wandering the swamp apparently playing a serious game of cowboys and Indians. The game warden claimed that he had retrieved the arrow that had been shot at him and that he had examined it closely. It appeared to be handmade, with a rough and primitive appearance. The Indian was also quite strange-looking, the warden said, and seemed so primitive that it was as if he were from another time.

At the time, Rick merely thought the incident to be curious, but he believed the story enough to heed the game warden's advice and not enter the swamp on foot. There's no way to know whether the arrow in question even existed, but there is an element to the story that prevents us from dismissing it as hearsay. What had attracted Rick to that particular spot in the swamp was a strong localized magnetic anomaly, the kind that theoretically could be associated with a time-line bleed.

Rick's experience is not an isolated one. A possibly corroborating incident comes from the mother of a Beaumont man named Eddie. Eddie's mom had a cabin in a fishing camp near the lower Trinity River near Trinity Bay, the same area where Rick's treasure-hunting

experience occurred. An old man who ran a small store and bait shop there told her the following story.

A lineman had been sent to make repairs to an electric utility line in a remote area on the margins of the swamp. When he finished making the repairs, he looked down and was startled to find that he was surrounded by what he described as several "Indians" who had gathered around the base of the pole. After they had stared at him threateningly for a few minutes, they disappeared into the surrounding woods. The lineman said they were practically naked and remarkably primitive in appearance. They brandished bows that seemed equally primitive. Why the supposed Indians hadn't shot the astonished lineman is anyone's guess.

Yet again, elements in this story suggest the same patterns we have seen. Could it be that the lineman was sent to make repairs because there was a localized power outage caused by an intense local magnetic anomaly that had attracted Rick to the area in search of buried treasure?

The old man at the bait shop tried to investigate the region after he had heard the lineman's story, but he was quickly discouraged by a horrifying discovery: He found what was left of a human skeleton strapped to the base of a tree not far from the pole where the lineman said he had seen the Indians.

There actually had been a tribe of particularly primitive Indians on the Texas Gulf Coast that had roamed the area where both these events took place. They were known to perform a brutal ritual on their captured enemy: They strapped the unfortunate victim to a tree and stripped pieces of flesh from the body. They then roasted the flesh in a bonfire before the captive's eyes and frenziedly danced around the fire in a drugged stupor induced by drinking an intoxicant made from fermented yaupon berries. That tribe was the Karankawa.

The Karankawa—Brutal but Stinky

Tom, a Houston businessman and amateur treasure hunter, provided yet another story about what could be sightings of the Karankawa on the Texas coast. Tom was beachcombing near the mouth of Trinity Bay with his metal detector, when he had a chance meeting with a treasure hunter he knew from previous outings. Tom told him that he would like to take an airboat into the bayous that empty into the Trinity River to look for the legendary treasure of the pirate Jean Lafitte.

The treasure hunter advised Tom against it, because he knew of people who had been attacked by Indians in the bayous at the upper end of the bay. Tom asked why the people thought they had been attacked by Indians and not by, say, a bunch of gung-ho, drug-crazed survivalists. Because the attackers had used bows and arrows, the man said, and because the arrows and the Indians themselves were very primitive-looking.

There was also the stench. The attackers reeked so badly, apparently from smearing themselves with putrefied animal fat, that they could be smelled from some distance. Tom knew enough about the Karankawa to know that they were said to have covered themselves in alligator or shark grease for protection against the clouds of mosquitoes infesting the swamps and that they were known for their horrible smell. Tom told us his story before he heard the two other accounts of the Karankawa possibly being seen near Trinity Bay.

So what are we to make of all this? Could there possibly be surviving bands of primitive Indians patrolling their ancient swampland and coastal territories? According to historians and archaeologists, the Karankawa vanished almost two hundred years ago, leaving virtually no trace of their existence.

When we at *Weird Texas* first heard these tales, we thought that the Indians were perhaps ghosts or phantoms. But could mere specters fire solidly real arrows at those who unwittingly violate their boundaries? In an area known for a range of bizarre phenomena associated with anomalous magnetic episodes, we have to at least consider that sometimes elements of the past can bleed into the present. For the sake of anyone venturing into the primordial wilds of the Trinity River swamp, we hope that that process does not work both ways.

Unexplained Phenomena

Here in Texas, the unknown sometimes makes profound intrusions into the comfortable routines we take to be reality. Mysterious ghost lights act like conscious beings and chase carloads of astonished witnesses down lonely country roads. Giant fireballs streak through the late-night skies, leaving thousands of homes without electricity. Freakish winds of unknown meteorological origin devastate thousands of acres of forests. Glowing spacecrafts emitting intense radiation cause severe injuries to those unlucky enough to be caught in their paths and stop moving vehicles in their tracks. These unexplained phenomena defy our commonsense notions of what is real and possible. They confound attempts at scientific explanation and challenge us to take a closer look at them. So come along, if you dare, for a wild tour through some of the Lone Star State's weirdest mysteries. You might emerge with a deeper appreciation of the subtle links between the forces of nature, the energies in the earth, and the human mind.

Texas Ghost-Light Mysteries

The two best-known mystery lights in Texas are the Marfa Lights, out in West Texas, and the Bragg Light—also known as the Big Thicket Ghost Light—which is in East Texas, in the vicinity of Bragg Road, near Saratoga. What is particularly intriguing about these ghost lights is the vastly different conditions under which they occur. The two locations are extreme opposites in terms of climate, geology, and vegetation. The city of Marfa is situated in the desert and receives only a few inches of precipitation annually. It lies in a rocky basin nearly a mile above sea level, with the peaks of the nearby Chinati Mountains rising to an elevation of over eight thousand feet. Vegetation is sparse except in the highest elevations. Bragg Road, on the other hand, is only about a hundred feet above sea level, with

an average rainfall of more than an inch per week. It is surrounded by the green, swampy lushness of the Big Thicket—the only place in America other than the Everglades that botanists classify as jungle.

West Texas's famed Marfa Lights have been seen regularly for more than a century. The first recorded sighting was reported by a local rancher, Robert Ellison, in 1883, but in the ensuing years, sightings became so common that years ago, the highway department put up a sign at a paved turnout off Highway 90, about nine miles east of Marfa toward Alpine, indicating the best vantage point from which to view the lights. In 2003, the Texas Department of Transportation made significant improvements to this spot, which has become known as the Marfa Lights Viewing Area, by adding such amenities as a viewing shelter, restrooms, information plaques and

displays, park trails, and coin-operated telescopes.

Not to be outdone, Bragg Road, which is more commonly known as the Ghost Road, has recently been designated a public park by Hardin County. Although there are no facilities here comparable to those at the Marfa Lights Viewing Area, the county has committed to maintaining Bragg Road to make it more accessible to visitors and to preserving the sandy road's atmosphere by protecting the trees that line its entire length.

The way the two sets of lights manifest themselves is quite different. The Marfa Lights most commonly appear low on the horizon, several miles from the highway, in a basin near the foothills of the Chinati Mountains. Typically spherical in shape, they move in unpredictable directions for perhaps a minute before disappearing just as mysteriously as they had appeared. Varying shades of yellow, white, and orange (sometimes transitioning to red) are the colors commonly reported. Less frequently, the lights are seen to appear above the horizon and then dive below it; sometimes they approach within several hundred yards of the viewing area.

In contrast, Bragg Light usually involves the appearance of only one light at any particular time. It is most frequently described as a very sharply defined bluish-white sphere about the size of a basketball. However, occasionally there have been reports of a smaller light, roughly the size of a tennis ball. Sometimes Bragg Light is seen as a vaguely defined bright spot in what appears to be a small luminous fog bank. Because Bragg Road is surrounded by the dense woods of the Big Thicket, it is not possible to view the light from several miles away, as is the case with the Marfa Lights. Sightings are limited to open areas, like Bragg Road itself.

What would a ghost light be without a spectral tale or two? Not surprisingly, these famous Texas lights have inspired their fair share of local folklore. The Marfa Lights are romantically linked with the spirits of various Native American chiefs, particularly that of Chinati, whose name was given to the small mountain range south of Marfa. And the most common legend regarding Bragg Light is that it is the spectral lantern of an old railroad brakeman who still roams the road looking for his head, which he lost in a railroad accident back when the road was the bed of a railroad that served an old logging mill. As hokey as these legends are and despite the fact that the ghost lights have been scientifically shown to be real phenomena, there might be a reason other than mere superstition that these lights have always been called ghost lights.

Skeptics of the Marfa Lights claim that the lights seen from the official vantage point established by the Texas Department of Transportation are nothing more than car lights from the distant Presidio-to-Marfa highway. They hold that the movement of the lights and their fluctuation from bluish-white to red are nothing but alternating headlights and taillights going up and down the hills, coming from and going toward Presidio. A careful observer would have to admit this would probably account for the majority of the Marfa Light sightings from that location. But there is another category of sightings that is not so easily dismissed.

Researcher James Bunnell, whose excellent work is documented in his book *Night Orbs*, estimates that viewers have about a 15 percent chance of seeing what he calls a genuine mystery light at the Marfa Lights Viewing Area. His book, a must-read for anyone interested in this ghost-light phenomenon, contains convincing time-exposure photographs and documentation that compare genuine mystery lights with automobile headlights and other artificial light sources that could be mistaken for them.

Scoffers of the Bragg Light similarly claim that the light is nothing more than headlight beams. Admittedly, this may indeed be what many people are actually seeing when they think they are seeing the genuine mystery light, but close-up encounters with Bragg Light are not so easily explained.

Other cynics claim that ghost lights are actually foxfire, a phenomenon in which high concentrations of methane gas generated by rotting vegetation are ignited by natural combustion. Foxfire is also referred to as swamp gas, and those with intellectual curiosity often cite it as the explanation for a range of mysterious luminous phenomena, including both ghost lights and UFOs. Although swamp gas might be expected to occur in the vast wetlands of the Big Thicket, it is difficult to imagine it in the West Texas desert. As James Bunnell points out, the gaseous origin of ghost lights, given their brightness, is further suspect because it does not account for how the gases are ignited to produce the lights. And if the lights were burning gases, he notes, why would they not start brush fires. The Marfa Lights have never started such fires, and as far as we know, neither has the Bragg Light.

Although the Marfa Lights have been witnessed by about as many generations of West Texans as the Bragg Light by East Texans, it is a surprise to most Texans to learn that there are literally hundreds of locations around the world where similar lights have been documented. Whether they are called fireballs, ghost lights, spook lights, earth lights, mystery lights, or anomalous light-form phenomena, increasing numbers of investigators have come to regard these lights as a global phenomenon of potentially great significance. The consensus is that the lights constitute a little-understood discharge phase of the earth's electromagnetic energy field.

However, genuine ghost lights may not be mere electrical discharges. We might have to resort to more than current scientific theories to be able to comprehend what these lights truly are.

The details of some of the encounters that you'll read about in the following pages may be hard to believe unless you've had such an experience yourself. But for many ghost-light witnesses, all scientific theories fall short of even describing the lights, much less explaining them. Even to call them weird might not be adequate.

The Rancher and the UFO

A fascinating account of the Marfa Lights comes from a local rancher who shall remain unnamed to protect his privacy. He told *Weird Texas* that one of the astronauts from the moon missions had made numerous trips to his ranch and was convinced that the energy involved with the Marfa Lights was somehow related to UFOs. The rancher who volunteered this information was not a Star Trekkie type of fanatic, but a God-fearing, salt-of-the-earth, slow-talking Texas cattleman. He told us an amazing story of an unusual craft he had seen one night in an arroyo on his ranch. The craft was cylindrical, not saucer-shaped, and was maybe fifteen feet long. It was metallic, shiny-looking, and solid, not just a light. The rancher seemed almost apologetic as he described it. Still, he seemed relieved to be able to talk about it to people outside Marfa, who wouldn't go blabbing the story to the locals and risk subjecting him to ridicule. It was impossible not to believe him.

Extraordinary Encounter on the Bragg Road

The look on Jim's face and the conviction in his voice told us he was extremely disturbed by what had happened to him on the Ghost Road. This Beaumont man was also struggling to come to grips with something that conflicted with his most basic beliefs and that made him doubt his own sanity. His encounter had haunted him for over thirty years; it was something he didn't even want to think about, much less talk about, and he was sure no one would believe him anyhow. So he'd kept the story to himself all those years, not even telling his wife, Mary, about it. Mary knew Jim had a fascination with the Bragg Light, but she had no idea that there was such a trauma attached to it. It was Mary who had urged Jim to talk to *Weird Texas* about his interest in the lights. Jim seemed relieved when he told us his story. He finally had people

to talk to about his experience who would not doubt his sanity and who might even help him deal with the genuine encounter with the unknown that had shaken him so deeply.

As remarkable as Jim's story is, it is also remarkable to us that he'd been reluctant to tell anyone about it. His experience did not occur in an atmosphere of ridicule or disbelief. There are hundreds, if not thousands, of Texans who claim to have seen the ghost light on Bragg Road. For generations, carloads of curious would-be witnesses have made the trek to the Ghost Road to seek out the very thing that had so traumatized Jim. In fact, to this day, it is widely considered a wholesome family activity to go looking for the ghost light. Why, then, would Jim feel that no one would believe what he saw? The simple answer is that he'd had the daylights scared out of him there.

Many light sightings on Bragg Road are questionable, but Jim's encounter was in your face, up close, and personal—the real thing. There are those who claim to have seen the light and who go back time and again for the fun of it. What Jim saw was no fun at all; on that fateful night, something he could not wrap his brain around rudely destroyed his assumptions about the nature of physical reality.

The encounter began around midnight, when Jim and two buddies arrived at the Ghost Road and drove north for about five miles. No sooner had they stopped their car and turned off the headlights than they were shocked by the sudden appearance of an eerie orange glow that came from the pitch-black woods to their right. Jim described the glow as being "like what would precede a lantern entering a dark room." It was cast by a six-inch-diameter sphere of brilliant orange light that approached them and hovered at about car-top level less than twenty feet in front of them.

Astonishment turned to abject terror as the light

approached even closer. It finally came to a stop just to the right of the car. Then it moved slowly across the hood, causing the car's engine, which had been left idling, to stall. When the light came to rest again on the other side of the car, the boys, who by now were in a panic, were able to restart the engine. They took off down the road as fast as its unpaved, sandy surface would allow. The light came right after them, easily keeping pace at speeds approaching fifty miles per hour. After about two miles, the light, like a cat that was tired of playing with a frightened mouse, made an abrupt ninety-degree turn to the left, rose above the treetops, and disappeared in a flash of unimaginable speed. The entire episode took about five minutes.

You can see how this would be enough to leave anyone with a lifetime of recurring nightmares—swamp gas and car-beam reflections don't knock out automobile engines. Naturally occurring electrical plasmas that might cause cars to go dead last for only a few seconds or even a fraction of a second and do not maintain a sharply defined form for as long as this light did. For that matter, nothing known to science acts like this light did. Jim's sudden confrontation with something so totally outside the range of normal experience makes his reaction understandable, but what really plunged him into a thirty-year silence and what he struggled to sort out in his mind was the behavior of the light and how it had interacted with him and his friends.

When the light moved across the hood of the car and knocked out the engine, the terrified boys were convinced that the thing was moving deliberately, watching them intently, like a predator stalking its helpless prey. There was no question in the boys' minds that the glowing glob was conscious of them and knew what it was doing. As Jim put it, still trying to sort out the experience in his mind, "That damn light was alive!"

Jim's experience and the conclusion he has drawn are not isolated. Other witnesses and researchers have frequently observed that the lights' movements do not seem to be mere responses to physical or electromagnetic forces. In fact, the lights' acrobatics and dancelike game of repeatedly approaching and then retreating from observers, even chasing them, are highly suggestive of curiosity or playfulness. The lights seem to have a personality! Their behavior is similar to that of impish fairies in Celtic folklore and of trickster spirits in Native American stories. At any rate, after lengthy sessions of such behavior, the lights will suddenly streak away, leaving astonished witnesses with the unsettling feeling that they have been played with and suggesting the unthinkable—that the lights are conscious entities. No matter how hard it might be for anyone who has not had this experience to accept this observation, Jim would not argue with it.

After reading this account, you might decide to go check out a ghost-light location for yourself. You've now been warned about the possibility of running into something that you might not be ready for. If that's not enough to persuade you to be cautious, consider this: If you do seek out the Bragg Light, you should not assume that you will return with your sense of reality or your sanity intact. The long-displaced Native Americans of southeastern Texas are said to have avoided the depths of the Big Thicket, especially that part where the ghost light has been seen for so many years. They believed those ancient shadowy woods to be haunted by evil spirits and demons. But if you give no credence to their version of reality and if you will not heed their foreboding, remember Jim's testimony: His personal reality map was altered so severely by what he felt had no doubt been a living thing that he went more than thirty years before he could bring himself to talk to anyone about it.

On a Dark, Unpaved Road That Is Pure Legend

I live just down the highway from the town of Saratoga. There is a phenomenon that has been happening here for generations that I think you folks at *Weird Texas* would be very interested in knowing about.

There is a dark, unpaved road outside Saratoga, just off of 787, that is pure legend in these parts. Some call it Ghost Road, but true locals refer to it as Bragg Road. I have heard many stories about why the road is haunted. The one I've heard the most—and that I believe—is that a young bride was killed while walking on this road shortly after getting married. The recent groom left the nearby hotel they were staying in and began wandering the woods with a lantern looking for his wife. He never found her, and he never came back. To this day, people see his lantern roaming the woods.

Unlike most ghost stories, this one is unquestionably true. I have been down Bragg Road and can vouch for the existence of a light that appears there. It only happens at night and only when you turn off your car's lights. At this point, roughly sixty percent of the time, a white ball with blue edges will appear in the distance. It will come towards you. Going down the road towards the light does not get you closer to it, however—it retreats when you approach it.

I have seen this light come within thirty feet of the car, then turn bright yellow and disappear. I have also seen it shoot straight into the sky. These could not have been car lights or pranksters. It happens too consistently and with too many variables to be either of those things. I have absolutely no explanation for what I have witnessed. Seeing the lights on Bragg Road is one of those experiences that make you question your grip on reality. If you want to encounter a true mystery, and one that will erase skepticism from your mind, make your way to Bragg Road.
—Doug St. Clair

Bragg Road's Playful Ball of Light

I have seen the light a few times. I don't feel like it's spooky, but it can be playful. The first time I saw it, I was driving down the road and it was coming from behind us, where the main road is. It was small and bright, so I passed it off as being headlights, except it stayed there for quite some time. It went away before it got close. Shortly after that, we saw it in front of us, but this time it was a dim glow, pale green in color and about the size of a basketball. It came at us very fast and whizzed right over the front windshield and hood. It didn't look like a lantern or anything. It stayed about thirty feet behind us after that, even when we got out to look at it. We walked towards it, and it maintained its distance and was approximately ten feet off the ground.

We turned around at the end of the road, and it flew back over us and stayed behind us the whole way back to the main road. That was my first trip. My last trip was made with a lot of friends in two cars, and we drove down the road all the way to the railroad tracks. We got out. We had flashlights and kept our car headlights on. It was a fairly clear night, and I brought along my camera. Only two pictures came out of the twenty-four-exposure roll, and the two that came out have some strange mist floating about that I cannot remember being there. We say "Saratoga" when we refer to the road. It is a very beautiful place to be. I don't think there is anything to be afraid of except a playful ball of light.*—Claire Adaway*

Those Marvelous Marfa Lights Don't Disappoint

For my entire life, I've lived near the border of Texas and Louisiana. Even living all the way in East Texas, I heard the legends of the Marfa Lights. Supposedly, around the Chinati Mountains, all the way to the west of my home state, was a desert where ghostly lights appear on clear nights. People come from far and wide to view them, the best vantage point being on Highway 90.

Marfa is a long haul from where I live, but I've wanted to see the lights ever since I first heard of them as a kid. I heard so many tales trying to explain their existence—that they were the ghosts of Indian braves and Mexican bandits, that they were the wandering lost souls of travelers who died trying to cross the desert, etc. Apparently, the lights had been seen for decades, even before electricity was used in that area.

When I was twenty-two, I finally got a chance to see the lights for myself. I had gone to school at UCLA and decided that after graduation, I would drive from Los Angeles to Louisiana. I made a point to make my way down to Marfa to finally lay eyes on the legendary balls of light.

I was surprised to see that there was an officially marked Marfa Lights Viewing Area, filled with people. Apparently, this place fills up on every clear night. The night I was there, I'd estimate there were between sixty and seventy people. And I have to tell you, none of them went home disappointed!

There was a radio tower in the distance, and people were pointing towards it and commenting about what they saw. I made my way to the front of the crowd, and, man, was I blown away. Just as the stories said, there were balls of light bouncing around out in the distance. Most of them were white and yellow, but I saw a few reds and even a blue one. There was a steady stream of the lights, and they definitely had a strange, intimidating aura about them. They moved haphazardly and would come and go at random. There's no explanation that I can fathom for these lights. Some say they're actually swamp gas or car headlights, but I don't buy it—they both seem like easy explanations for something that seemed much more mysterious.

I came into the night expecting to be underwhelmed. After all, I had heard about these lights my whole life and had even seen television stories about them. I didn't think the experience would live up to the high expectations I had set. Seeing those lights with my own two eyes was a real trip, though, and I don't think I'll ever be able to explain what they were.—*Dave Gorman*

Stalking the Elusive Illuminations

Many Texans believe Hardin County's Big Thicket, with its vast stretches of lush vegetation, has plenty of suitable habitats for the wild, apelike creatures that have been sighted in East Texas for several years. Some claim that there is a connection between the sightings of such creatures and the ghost-light phenomenon. Indeed, there have been a number of Big Thicket Wild Man sightings on Bragg Road itself. There are even those who reported seeing the ghost light immediately before the mysterious hairy creature showed up. One interesting theory holds that the Wild Man appearances may somehow be related to the same unknown energy sources that produce the ghost lights.

Cajun Jim: Ghost Lights Along the Neches River

Weird Texas received a phone call from a man who identified himself only as Cajun Jim. He said that he had grown up in East Texas and that he wanted us to know that there are other places in the Big Thicket besides Bragg Road where strange lights are seen. His family owned a fishing camp on the Neches River about thirty miles north of Beaumont, near the river's confluence with Village Creek. It's an area that's known as having one of the nation's finest stands of virgin swampland hardwoods, and Cajun Jim was in the habit of hunting rabbits there, using the old-fashioned night-hunting technique known as shining up game. The process involved cruising at slow speed in a flat-bottomed boat close to the riverbank and shining a bright flashlight on the bank. If a rabbit was caught in the beam, the reflection of the flashlight would light up the rabbit's eyes. Jim would then fire a light-gauge shotgun at the eyes. He admitted that he was not too particular about what he shot. If he shined up raccoons or possums, he would just as soon take them as rabbits.

One night, while he was hunting, Jim happened to look back about a hundred yards upstream, only to see a spherical red light floating in the air directly above the middle of the river. His initial amazement gave way to overwhelming curiosity, and as the light hovered motionless, he had time to judge its size and height.

He could see that it was just below the tops of the highest trees along the riverbank, because he could see the tree line behind the light. That told him it was hovering about a hundred feet in the air. Judging from the light's distance from him and the height at which it was hovering, he guessed it was about the size of a basketball. It was bright scarlet red and shone with a brilliant intensity.

After several minutes, he decided to turn back upstream and see if he could get right under it and determine more closely what it was that he was seeing. He stayed as close to the bank as he could to lessen the resistance of the current, and he kept his outboard motor at low speed to lessen the noise of his approach. Just as he pulled up even with the red, spherical light and was about to cross the river to pull up under it, he had second thoughts. There was no telling what he was dealing with, he decided. That damn thing could be dangerous. His hunter's instincts took over, and he reached slowly for his shotgun. "I'm not lying," he said. "The very instant I had the thought to reach for my gun, that thing streaked off in a flash and was gone in an instant. It was like it read my mind."

Cajun Jim's sighting of a weird light on the Neches was not an isolated account.

A woman from Beaumont who identified herself only as Alison contacted *Weird Texas* and said she knew a place, also in remote woods along the Neches River, where an unexplained light had been seen for years. Both of these locations would have been on the eastern edge of the Big Thicket, about twenty miles from Bragg Road. There have also been reports of mystery lights in other parts of Marfa's Presidio County, and in adjoining Brewster County. These sightings argue against the mystery lights being caused by localized hidden geological forces.

Streaking High-Speed Ghost Light of Route 201

I'd heard of them but had never seen a real, honest-to-goodness Texas ghost light. This whole ghost light concept had always seemed a bit out near the edge of reality for me, although I certainly trusted a couple of people who claimed to have seen the lights in the Big Thicket's famous Bragg Road area. Those folks were good, honest teetotalers, so I did allow myself to have an open but skeptical mind.

On Monday afternoon, June 21, 2004, my wife, Sharon, and I were returning from visiting relatives near Toledo Bend Reservoir, which separates Texas and Louisiana. The reservoir is near the Big Thicket's north edge and is surrounded by Sabine National Forest. Sabine's dense swamps and forests are loaded with wild pigs, deer, cougars, snakes, alligators, coyotes, old graveyards, ancient Indian mounds, descendants of Cherokee Indians, retired folks, missing astronauts, and who knows who or what else. Toledo Bend's biggest "town," Hemphill (population 1,036), is an old-fashioned East Texas town. It was also the main crash site of our recent space-shuttle disaster.

Sharon and I left Toledo Bend at around four p.m. and headed north on Highway 87, turning west just before Hemphill. We were about five miles down 201, on our way to Jasper, when suddenly out of nowhere a bright ball of light, perhaps a soccer ball-size, came barreling and flashing down the highway straight towards us at a very high speed. It was moving so fast, it appeared to be leaving a trail of light behind it. It streaked right over our hood and windshield, swerved up a bit, probably twenty feet above us, and headed off down the highway somewhere behind us. The ball of light's brightness hurt my eyes, and even days later, when I thought about it, it still gave me a slight frontal lobe headache. I looked over at Sharon and said, "Did you see that?" She answered, "You saw it too? The streak of light? Weird, wasn't it? I'm glad you saw it, because I thought I must be crazy. There was no way it could be a plane or anything else that could move so fast and so low, maybe a few hundred miles per second.

Seriously, it was QUICK!" Then she laughed nervously and said, "Maybe it was a UFO—a little one."

I'm a Houston computer engineer and businessman who has held high government security clearances, and Sharon is a practical-minded bookkeeper. We are both pragmatic, sensible people. Do I have a scientist's explanation for this high-speed ball of bright light? No, I really don't.

My first thoughts were of a daylight "meteor" or "shooting star," but I rejected this concept because of its flat trajectory coming straight down the highway until it "intelligently" swerved acrobatically up and over our car.

Secondly, it could have been a hovering light we approached and passed under. The only problem with this concept is that Sharon and I both saw a streaking trail of light behind the zooming light ball as we approached it on our collision course. Further, a hovering ball of light in broad daylight could pose as many questions as a streaking one. No, the light ball and our car were both independently moving objects, with the light ball traveling much faster than our car. The whole event was over in a few split seconds.

I never stopped, and I could not spot the streaking ball of light out of my rearview mirror as I headed on down Highway 201 towards Jasper. In fact, I stepped on it to get the heck out of there. I don't know if the light had anything to do with ghosts, but I know for sure I've finally encountered what so many people call a Texas ghost light.—*Tom Dillman*

Anson Ghost Lights

Anson is a small town located twenty miles north of Abilene on Highway 83/84. It is the home of a well-known yet unexplained phenomenon that has simultaneously delighted, terrified, and baffled visitors for decades—the Anson Ghost Lights. Hundreds of people have traveled from far and wide to witness these strange illuminations, and the process for conjuring the lights seems to be unanimously agreed upon.

When entering Anson, turn right at the Alsups and continue until you come to the graveyard just outside town. Turn right down the dirt road next to the cemetery. At the crossroads, turn your car around so it is facing back toward the main road. Turn off your engine and flash your headlights three times. Within a few minutes, you will see the lights.

Most people describe the phenomenon as a slow-moving white light that travels down the road toward their car. Some have seen it swing wildly from side to side; others have seen it dance among nearby treetops. It is never accompanied by any noise. Sometimes it changes colors—some say that if one disrespects the light by taunting or cursing it, it turns red. It ranges in size from that of a flashlight to that of a motorcycle headlight. Some have seen it start at its usual size, then grow to immense proportions as it travels down the lonely unpaved road. If one travels toward the light in an attempt to touch it, it fades away and disappears. Usually, it appears not as one light, but as several small lights.

The Anson Ghost Lights tend to occur on warm, clear nights. They never appear in the rain, and they tend not to show up when it is cloudy. The lights, stories say, are caused by the ghost of a woman who had lived in Anson in the nineteenth century. She is forever wandering the road where the lights now appear, looking for her three sons. They were sent outside to chop wood one night and were told that if they encountered any trouble, they should flash their lanterns three times. They did just this, but by the time their mother managed to get to them, all three boys had been killed. So now when visitors flash their car lights, the woman's spirit emerges, carrying her own lantern in the hopes of finding her sons.

Baffling Beaumont Blackout

The areas where ghost lights occur can extend twenty miles or more in any direction from the specific spots where the lights are most frequently observed. Interestingly, these areas have been associated with recurrent electrical disturbances. In some rare instances, the areas may extend to hundreds of square miles, and hundreds of thousands of people may be unknowingly subjected to the same unusual energies that produce the ghost lights. For this reason, it is vitally important to understand the forces involved in mystery-light phenomena and the means by which these forces interact with living organisms. It is clear from the meager research that has been done that these energies may have a disturbing impact on the human mind.

To illustrate just how widespread the effects of these disturbances can be, let's consider an article by Kevin Carmody in the May 3, 1985, edition of the *Beaumont Enterprise*. Carmody, who reported on the environment for the newspaper, speculated about the causes of a blackout that had occurred in the early hours of that morning, leaving 132,000 people in the Greater Beaumont-Southeast Texas area without electric power.

Officials of the local electric company, Gulf States Utilities, blamed the blackout on a lightning storm in Arkansas, about a hundred miles north of Beaumont, claiming that it had blown out a transformer and tripped a relay, resulting in a domino effect of failed transformers, which led to the blackout. But Kevin Carmody didn't buy this theory.

In his article, he ruled out UFOs as the cause of the blackout—he obviously wasn't willing to go that far—and surmised that the only possible explanation was an "electromagnetic disturbance of incredible proportion." He quotes an engineer with the American Public Power Association, who said, "It is rare and it's unlikely that an electromagnetic interruption could be of that magnitude, but it is theoretically possible."

Carmody, however, believed that just such a massive disturbance might have indeed occurred around twelve-thirty a.m. to one-thirty a.m. that morning in the Greater Beaumont-Southeast Texas area. He further reported that some residents whose homes hadn't experienced blackouts reported picking up Houston television stations that would not normally be in their range of reception. Others noticed strong fluctuations in radio reception. As Carmody commented, "All that would be consistent with a localized disturbance in the electromagnetic field surrounding the earth."

Most compelling of all was his description of his own weird experience at the time of the blackout. He had worked late at the paper that night and was in his car in the ATM drive-through lane of his bank, waiting to make a withdrawal. It was about one a.m. He was sitting in his car with the engine running and the lights on at precisely the time the blackout hit Beaumont. It was not raining. There were no thunderstorms, and there was absolutely no lightning in evidence anywhere in the vicinity. Suddenly the entire neighborhood was plunged into an eerie darkness, and for as far as he could see, building lights, streetlights, traffic signals, and lights in homes had gone out.

No sooner was Carmody aware of what had happened than his car engine stalled and the headlights went out. For a brief moment, he tried unsuccessfully to restart the engine, but the battery was completely dead. After a few minutes, the battery came back to life enough to restart the engine. The car radio, which had also gone dead, also came back on, but it crackled and hissed from interference.

From these details, it is easy to understand why Kevin Carmody was not persuaded by the utility company's explanation that lightning had caused the blackout. He knew that it was not a coincidence that his car had gone dead at the same time as the blackout. He could only conclude that whatever had knocked out the utility grid had also knocked out his car, and it was obvious that an electrical storm a hundred miles away would not have affected his car.

People reported mysterious fireballs in the sky above Beaumont while the city lay in darkness, but Carmody couldn't bring himself to blame these ghost lights on UFOs or other paranormal phenomena, even though something weird was clearly taking place.

Big East Texas Blowdown

A *strange* and astonishing meteorological incident of quite a different sort occurred in East Texas in 1998. What was described as a "freak wind" blew down an estimated four million trees. Yes, that's right—four million trees. Wind speeds were estimated at between 70 and 120 miles per hour, with isolated gusts of up to 150 miles per hour. Winds of that strength occurring over an area vast enough to contain four million trees are generated only by hurricanes and tornadoes, which have circulating winds. Since the path of destruction in this Texas blowdown was virtually straight and since the trees were all left pointing in the same direction, it can only be deduced that these were straight-line winds.

Amazingly, even though a small number of mobile homes were crushed by falling trees, no one was killed. As fate would have it, the storm path extended over a hundred miles through sparsely inhabited areas of woodlands. Starting from a point northeast of Conroe, in the Sam Houston National Forest, it raged in a northeasterly direction through Angelina National Forest, past Sam Rayburn Reservoir, to terminate in the Sabine National Forest a few miles short of the Louisiana border. Had the freak wind occurred in a more populated area, it could have been a disaster of biblical proportions. As it was, the event went virtually unnoticed outside East Texas.

It is not known what meteorological elements could produce winds of such an unprecedented strength and extent. However, it is speculated that somehow the jet stream had temporarily dipped to the surface of the earth. Jet-stream winds normally occur at altitudes of 18,000 to 30,000 feet and vary in strength from 70 to 150 miles per hour. What colossal, unimaginable force would be required to drive a hundred-mile length of the jet stream downward a distance of some three miles?

The jet stream had to have been responding to some outside force. It is known to react to fluctuations of the earth's electromagnetic field and to solar magnetic storms. Could there have been a magnetic disturbance immense enough to so drastically alter the jet stream's normal course and cause it to inflict such destruction?

There were rumors that connected the blowdown to UFOs, but whether you believe them or not is up to you. You should know, though, that the testimony concerning UFO sightings in Texas is strong.

The Texas Piney Woods UFO Incident

Mysterious black helicopters of unknown origin pursuing unknown purposes have been reported in the United States for some fifteen years. They are usually said to be Hueys and Chinooks, which are favored by the U.S. military. In a typical sighting incident, the very existence of the helicopters is routinely denied by the military installations nearest to where the copters have been seen. From this fact, and because it is alleged that the helicopters do not show up on radar, it is widely assumed among conspiracy buffs that the crafts' black color comes from a surface coating that employs radar-reflecting stealth technology. This alleged technology is reputed to be so advanced that it gives the mysterious choppers the ability to appear virtually out of nowhere and to vanish just as suddenly without leaving a trace.

Speculation about who or what employs the black helicopters has become a favorite pastime among conspiracy buffs. Naturally, there are as many theories as theorists, but some of the most popular are: The copters are being used by the U.S. government for secret surveillance purposes; they are an alien life-form; they are being used by sinister extragovernmental agencies intent on imposing an evil new world order. Reportedly, the helicopters are seen most frequently in the West, particularly in the skies over California, Nevada, New Mexico, and, wouldn't you know it, Texas. In California and Nevada, it is assumed that these helicopters are involved in the transport of goods and personnel to and from Area 51, the semimythical, supposedly top secret UFO research facility in the Nevada desert. In New Mexico, they are said to belong to some unknown agency that's monitoring the U.S. government's nuclear weapons facilities or even the Roswell UFO crash site. But what are the helicopters doing in the Lone Star State?

Well, for starters, part of the "black helicopter" lore is that the choppers are known to harass UFO witnesses. Could the frequent appearances of these black helicopters in Texas be related to the high incidence of ghost-light sightings in the state? Of course, this sounds suspiciously like the Men in Black (MIB) phenomenon. Well-known paranormal investigators John Keel and Ted Holiday were among the first to write about these spooky hombres, and both Keel and Holiday actually had run-ins with MIB in the course of their investigations of UFO events. A typical MIB occurrence goes as follows: Swarthy men in black suits claiming to be government agents show up in black Cadillacs to threaten and harass recent UFO witnesses, they tell the terrified witnesses not to speak to anyone about their experiences, they are observed by a number of witnesses, and then they simply vanish into thin air.

Because the black helicopters have the ability to suddenly appear out of nowhere and to disappear without a trace, those who are familiar with the extreme strangeness of UFO and MIB encounters consider mysterious black helicopters to be an extension of the MIB phenomenon. There have even been witnesses who claim that unmarked black helicopters are actually projected images, a form of disguise that UFOs use to conceal themselves. These witnesses also claim to have seen typical saucer-shaped crafts morph into black helicopters. And wouldn't you know that the most famous documented encounter with unmarked black helicopters, combined with one of the most significant UFO sightings in U.S. history, happened right here in Texas. It's known as the Piney Woods, or Cash Landrum, Incident.

As the *UFO Casebook* puts it, "An extremely haunting UFO sighting which has well stood the test of time took place in the Piney Woods of Texas, near the town of Huffman. On the chilly night of December 29, 1980, two women and one child encountered a craft of unknown origin, and all three suffered not only emotional trauma, but severe physical injury as well."

The *UFO Casebook* goes on to describe how Betty Cash, who was fifty-one at the time, was driving from New Caney to Dayton on Farm-to-Market Road 1485, accompanied by her friend, fifty-seven-year-old Vickie Landrum, and by Vickie's seven-year-old grandson, Colby Landrum. The area they drove through was densely forested with pines and oaks and included occasional swamps and small lakes. The three of them saw a light in the sky in the distance, which they assumed to be an airplane or helicopter. As they approached it, the light loomed larger and crossed the treetops. Suddenly the three of them were confronted with a diamond-shaped craft of huge dimensions directly above the road and right ahead of their car. As if the mere sight of the thing weren't horrifying enough, the craft was also intermittently belching out reddish-orange flames and emitting a continuous beeping sound.

Betty stopped the car to keep from driving directly under the flame-spewing craft. The interior of her car heated up, and suddenly the sky filled with unmarked black helicopters. To Betty, Vickie, and Colby, it seemed as if the copters were trying to encircle the strange craft. The UFO ascended and headed southwest, pursued by the black helicopters. Betty and Vickie claimed to have counted twenty-three copters, and from their descriptions, the choppers were identified as Hueys and Chinooks, which are seen in most such events.

The *UFO Casebook* account further states that there were corroborating reports from an off-duty Dayton policeman and his wife, from a Crosby man, and from a Dayton oilfield worker. As in most incidents involving mysterious black helicopters, the local air bases, military installations, and government agencies all denied any knowledge of the strange craft or the deployment of any government helicopters.

The full significance of the Cash-Landrum encounter came from what happened next. Vickie, Betty, and Colby became violently ill within a few hours of returning home to Dayton. Their symptoms included hair loss, swollen eyes, skin burns, and radiation poisoning, considered life-threatening by the doctors who treated them. Their severe maladies offered definitive proof, rare in UFO sightings, that their encounter was with something real and tangible. What they saw was not the subjective misinterpretation of a known object or meteorological phenomenon. This was not the planet Venus shining bright and hanging low on the horizon. This was not ball lightning or swamp gas. This was something else.

Significantly, the same types of burns suffered by the three Piney Woods victims have been reported by other UFO witnesses, although the burns have rarely been as severe as in the Texas event. Even more bizarre, witnesses of other types of paranormal encounters, including mysterious creature sightings, have also suffered similar injuries, particularly reddened and swollen eyes.

Uncle Jessie's UFO Sighting

One day while we of *Weird Texas* were having lunch at Hao Hao, our favorite Asian restaurant in South Austin, we happened to overhear an interesting conversation at an adjoining table. Two women and a man were talking about picking up magnetic anomalies with field magnetometers. Curiosity overwhelmed us, and we asked them what kind of research required them to use such equipment. It turned out they were amateur paranormal investigators—ghost hunters to be exact!

We got to talking about the curious mystery-light phenomena on the Ghost Road and elsewhere in East Texas. We mentioned that we found it interesting that these anomalous luminosities, as well as such paranormal activities as entity hauntings, also seem to be associated with highly localized magnetic anomalies.

One of the women, Renee Gibson, took a particular interest in the conversation. Her uncle Jessie, who had retired and moved from the Houston area to Arkansas, had a story she thought *Weird Texas* ought to hear about.

A few weeks later, we met with Renee at her apartment, and we called her uncle. Sadly, Jessie had been diagnosed with congestive heart failure and had been told he had only a short time left. Renee had telephoned him beforehand to arrange our conversation, and Jessie seemed eager to talk about his experience to people who would take it seriously. He seemed relieved that he might be able to leave the incredible story of his experience to posterity.

Jessie told us that early one morning in 1982, during the wee hours after midnight, he was on his way back to Texas City from a business trip to Lake Charles, Louisiana. He was approaching the Baytown exit on Interstate 10 when, to his utter astonishment, he saw what he could only describe as a glowing saucer-shaped craft land a short distance from the freeway in a swampy area surrounded by woods. The shock of the sighting had barely subsided

when, to his dismay, his truck went dead, its electrical system completely shut down.

"I don't give a damn if you believe me or not!" Jessie exclaimed with a gruffness that came, no doubt, from the frustration of having tried over the years to communicate his extraordinary experience, only to be met with blatant disbelief or polite head nodding. "But it damn sure did happen. That damn thing ruined my truck's electrical system, burned out all the points. And I've got the bill I can show you from having to have my truck towed all the way from there to Texas City."

The thing didn't stay on the ground for long, taking off right after Jessie's truck had died. Another car, going in the opposite direction, had also died. Jessie said he actually talked to the driver, a man from Beaumont who was on his way home. "We agreed that there was no point in reporting what happened to the news or to the authorities," Jessie said, "because no one would have believed us anyway."

We thanked Jessie for telling *Weird Texas* about his sighting. "We believe you, Jessie," we said. "And believe it or not, what you saw actually fits in with a lot of weird things we've heard about. They happen, probably more often than anybody would suspect, down in those swamps and woods."

Thirtieth Parallel Mystery

One of the most fascinating aspects of ghost-light sightings is that witnesses consistently mention that the lights seem to exhibit signs of intelligence. This certainly puts these witnesses way out in UFO land. However, before accepting a paranormal explanation for all the mysterious luminous phenomena observed in Texas and elsewhere, many people search for a scientific explanation. After all, mystery lights seem to appear in the same areas year after year. What unique qualities do places like Bragg Road and Marfa possess that cause the lights to be seen there on such a consistent basis? And what is the outside energy source that, according to some experts, temporarily intensifies local geomagnetic fields in ghost-light locations?

Some researchers have suggested that mystery lights are related to sunspots and solar magnetic storms, and there does appear to be a correlation. But if sunspot activity were the only factor determining the locations of these lights, shouldn't we expect that ghost-light appearances would be more evenly distributed on the earth's surface? And if such geophysical factors as fault lines, mountain ranges, and mineral deposits do not account for ghost lights and related phenomena clustering in specific areas (as we know from a comparison of the Bragg and Marfa locations), what, then, does account for the clustering? In other words, if the sites do not have geophysical features in common, what features do they share that would provide a possible explanation for the manifestation of the lights?

The one thing the Bragg and Marfa lights do have in common is that they occur at almost exactly the same latitude, within a range of fifteen to twenty miles to the north of latitude 30 degrees N. And this is no isolated coincidence. There's another ghost light along the same latitude that occurs near Llano, which has earned the name Six-Mile Light because of its proximity to a nearby creek of the same name. In addition, there are well-known ghost-light locations along this same general latitude in Louisiana, Florida, Algeria, and Egypt.

The alignment of these mystery lights suggests the possibility of there being a trans-global line of geomagnetic force. Could there be such lines of energy that perhaps somehow attract the magnetic disturbances of the sun, creating localized high fluxes of the magnetic field and causing the ghost lights?

In the end, though, geological, seismological, and meteorological explanations do not fully explain the mystery-light phenomena. There must be other factors involved, and some of these may stretch the envelope of our most basic assumptions about how the universe works and about the structure of reality itself. The lights may be just the tip of the iceberg of a profound mystery. The apparent alignment of the light locations suggests that they are connected in ways we do not understand. It may be that we are also connected to one another, to nature, and to the cosmos in ways that we are only beginning to comprehend.

Bailey Ghost Light Is Looking to Wet Its Whistle

I wanted to let you know about a surly old ghost that haunts Brazoria County. There is a stretch of land known as Bailey's Prairie, near Angleton. It is named for the mean old man who owned the land back in the days before this area was even part of America. He did whatever he wanted, often disobeying orders from the government. He was a slave owner and was incredibly brutal to his slaves. When he died, they got their revenge on him, not knowing that it would cause him to come from beyond the grave to haunt them forever.

Bailey asked to be buried standing up, facing west, with his gun and a jug of whiskey at his feet. Well, before they filled in his grave, those slaves figured he owed them something for all the abuse he dished out to them over the years. They stole his jug of whiskey and drank it.

Ever since, people have seen a strange ball of white light bouncing around in Bailey's Prairie. They say it's Old Man Bailey, carrying a lantern, still roaming his old stomping grounds, searching for his whiskey jug.

When I was thirteen, my cousin took me out there to see the lights for myself. She and her friends were older and had seen it many times before. I was completely terrified by the story of Old Man Bailey's ghost. My cousin greatly enjoyed seeing me so scared.

We drove out near West Columbia. She took me to a specific area—I can't remember exactly where—and we sat and waited. I begged her to go and was greatly relieved that after a few minutes nothing had appeared. She seemed to be getting bored and disappointed. She started the car and started to back up. I was elated.

"Wait, look!" she said, and put the car back into park. Off in the distance, an intense white light was moving around. It started heading right towards us. I began screaming.

She put the car in drive and got out of there. The thing got within a few hundred yards of us and then disappeared as abruptly as it had appeared. I don't know what it is—I've tried to think of rational explanations for it but still can't think of anything that explains it away. I guess Old Man Bailey was just thirsty that night.—*Greg D.*

Bizarre Beasts

A legitimate Bigfoot sighting in Texas might seem about as likely as a sighting of a polar bear in the Amazon jungle. The Hollywood image of Texas as a vast treeless expanse of wide-open spaces makes the very idea ridiculous. That image is the only one known to most non-Texans and even to some Texans living in the parts of the state that have inspired the stereotype. But there is a side to the Lone Star State that is not familiar to those who rarely venture east of I-45.

Texas is not thought of as a forested place, but the sixteen-million-acre area occupied by the East Texas woods is greater than that occupied by the forests of Oregon. In these deep woods and swamps are many places that have long been thought to harbor hairy, apelike creatures. But as you will see, Bigfoot is by no means the only bizarre beast that roams the wilder regions of our state.

Something's Big, Wild, Hairy, and Naked in the Big Thicket

Documented sightings of Bigfoot-type creatures in the Big Thicket—the swampy southern end of the Pineywoods, where the Louisiana bayou bleeds into Texas—date back at least fifty years. Typically, those sightings, of a naked, hairy wild man, were brief glimpses caught from a car moving along a remote country road before the creature-man quickly disappeared into the dense woods. Eyewitness accounts varied regarding the man's appearance, but there was general agreement that, as reported by the *Kountze News* on August 14, 1952, he "had a heavy beard and a hairy body."

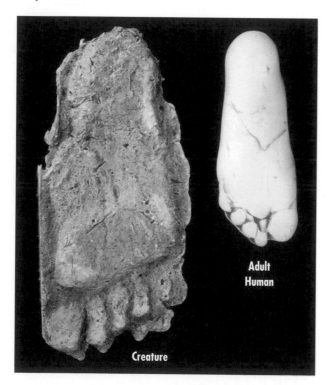

Adult
Human

Creature

It tells you something about the mystique of the Big Thicket that the sightings were not summarily dismissed as hoaxes. They were taken seriously enough that the Hardin County Sheriff's Office investigated several. Some of the results of these investigations were noteworthy, because the 1952 article also mentioned that the sheriff had said that "the barefoot tracks were plain in each case."

Bigfoot was unheard-of back then. The name did not even originate until some five or six years later, when the creature was seen in the Pacific Northwest. So there was no chance that people's imaginations had been influenced by stories from other areas. Rational attempts to explain the wild man included theories of an escaped convict or mental patient who had managed to survive in the wild or of a crazy old hermit or derelict Indian who delighted in startling astonished witnesses.

But the experienced woodsmen and hunters who reported the sightings doubted those explanations. They'd been in the woods long enough to know when they were seeing something unusual. And the wild man was always reported as being barefoot and naked. No human being, no matter how crazy or desperate, could last long running around naked in those woods. It had to be some kind of unknown animal, no matter how weird or manlike it might be.

Weird Texas wondered whether any of our readers would remember the wild man stories that had circulated in the 1950s. We also wanted to know if there had been any subsequent sightings, especially in more recent times. We invited people to let us know of any unusual things they may have seen in the woods of East Texas. The invitation was vaguely worded and made no specific reference to the earlier sightings so as not to influence the responses. The answers we received far exceeded our expectations and were weirder than anything we could ever have imagined.

Rat Finks Meet Booger Man

In 1965, Sharon Gossett belonged to an informal club of kids at Kountze High School who called themselves the Rat Finks. They amused themselves by going, in their words, "booger hunting," which is sort of like looking for a boogeyman. On one particular visit to a favorite booger-hunting ground, however, they got more than they had bargained for.

There is a gravestone in the cemetery at Old Hardin, just outside Kountze, that has a statue of an angel pointing at the heavens. The Rat Finks called it the Talking Angel and would take new members to the cemetery to ask it questions. The legend they made up was that if the angel did not answer you, you were doomed. (Personally, we would have felt even more doomed if the angel had talked.) During one such occasion, their ceremony was disrupted by a shadowy form racing across the cemetery. It ran into a maintenance shed, turning over cans, tossing about equipment, and making a noisy ruckus.

The kids got out of there as fast as they could. But before they could leave, they all got a look at the so-called booger man, and to their horror, it was a huge, hairy apelike creature. They knew that if they ever told anyone about their experience, they would be accused of having overactive imaginations, so they persuaded an aunt of one of the girls to return with them to the cemetery for another look and to verify their sighting.

They saw the creature again, noting that it was about seven feet tall and covered with hair, like an ape. It followed them as they ran to the car, loping on all fours alongside them. One would think that would have been enough for one night for the Rat Finks, but not so. They left the horrified aunt at her house and found an adult male volunteer to take along for another look at the beast. When the beast emerged again, their brave protector passed out on the spot from sheer fright!

Sharon reported to us that the grandmother of one of the Rat Finks told the kids that she could remember hearing of similar sightings near Old Hardin in the Cypress Creek bottoms when she was a child. The evidence is frighteningly clear: There's a long history of the creature's presence in northern Hardin County.

Suddenly a creature—big, hairy, and screaming—pounced on the hood of their pickup and glared menacingly at them through the windshield. The couple was shocked and terrified. Luckily, the man, like any good East Texas outdoorsman, just happened to have his shotgun with him.

A Howling Hairy Thing on the Ghost Road

We were told a tale even more bizarre than the Rat Fink story. It involved both a big hairy creature and the Ghost Road, also known as Bragg Road, deep in the heart of the Big Thicket. A young couple drove to the road to look for the ghost lights that are supposed to bounce along that dark stretch in the dead of night. They thought that with two of them together, there was little risk of the ghost lights getting them. But something else did. Suddenly a creature—big, hairy, and screaming—pounced on the hood of their pickup and glared menacingly at them through the windshield. The couple was shocked and terrified. Luckily, the man, like any good East Texas outdoorsman, just happened to have his shotgun with him. Without hesitation, he pulled it down from its rack and emptied both barrels through the plate glass at the howling monstrosity.

The woman who told us the story said the couple was so badly shaken by the incident that they had told only her and a few other friends about it, for fear of being ridiculed. She assured us, however, that she had seen the damaged windshield. And there was another compelling reason she believed her friends' story: There were two sets of claw marks scratched deeply into the pickup's hood. The wounded creature left them as it leaped off the pickup and ran screaming into the woods.

An almost identical story came to us in a phone call from a man who identified himself only as Steve. He said that he lived in the Beaumont area but that he and his fiancée sometimes attended church services in Batson. After evening services one night, he suggested to his fiancée that they make the short detour to the Ghost Road and look for the ghost lights for the fun of it. After sitting for quite some time, they saw what they thought might be the ghost lights not far from them. Shortly after, Steve needed to step outside the car to answer nature's call. As he entered the fringes of the dark woods, something big and hairy emerged without warning. It grabbed the rear bumper of the car and began shaking it, bouncing the car violently up and down while howling so loudly that Steve could barely hear the horrified screams of his fiancée. He made a mad dash back to the car, and the couple was able to get away.

The Ape Critter at the Bayou Bridge

Weird Texas attended a Halloween spook house in Saratoga for a fund-raiser sponsored by the Big Thicket Association. The event was a great opportunity to interview people who live in the very heart of the Big Thicket and who might have witnessed unusual phenomena. Among those present were three teenage boys who listened intently to the stories being told. Finally one of them stepped forward and said that he and his two friends had seen what they called an "ape-looking critter" in the nearby woods on at least three different occasions.

The first time was from a distance across a rice field as the three boys were riding in the back of a pickup between the towns of Saratoga and Sour Lake. They initially thought the critter was a black cow or a large calf, since it was running on all fours. But its lope and gait were wrong, and the hair was too shaggy. Just when they realized it had to be something unusual, it disappeared into the woods bordering the field.

The second time, the boys saw it at much closer range, near a bridge that crosses a bayou close to the boundary of the Big Thicket Preserve. They assumed that the apelike beast was an escapee from a circus or zoo.

Their most remarkable sighting was in the same area, just before dusk, near a sludge pit that was part of an old abandoned oilfield. Even in the gathering darkness, they could see that the beast was similar to the ape, if not the same ape, they had seen earlier at the bridge. When the hairy creature saw the boys, it howled at them menacingly before disappearing into the woods. It was an unforgettable sound, they assured us, so loud that it could not possibly have been produced by human vocal cords.

Hairy Man Walks the Pipeline

Ann Bazan is from one of the Louisiana Cajun families that first settled Southeast Texas many years ago. Back in the 1920s, before airplanes took over the work, her father rode on horseback to check the first oil pipelines laid in the woods and do maintenance work on them. Much of that part of the county had no roads then, and these pipeline right-of-ways ran for miles through virtually uninhabited woods and swamps.

One day, while on patrol, her father was viciously attacked by something big, humanlike, and hairy that tried to wrestle his horse away from him. At first, in the frenzy of repelling the attack and making his escape, he assumed that the assailant was a deranged lunatic living wild in the woods. But that didn't seem quite right, since the thing was naked and extremely hairy, and the eyes and face were not quite human. Understandably, the incident haunted him throughout his life, Ann told us, and he was never quite sure what exactly had attacked him.

Her father's story pushed back the earliest eyewitness account at least another thirty years from what we had known previously. It is also consistent with other recent sightings of the Hairy Man along the pipelines. A fellow from Orange County had seen one when the country road he was on crossed a pipeline. And some kids who were out rabbit hunting one night near a pipeline near the town of Pinewood told us that their flashlight, which they used to spot rabbits by catching the reflections of light in the animals' eyes, caught the reflection of an unexpectedly large, wide-set pair of eyes. When they went to investigate, they were horrified to find a huge, naked manlike thing, its beard and hair scraggly, bent over on all fours with a bloody dead rabbit hanging from its mouth and a wild look in its eyes.

It seems that these hairy beastlike creatures use the right-of-ways as thoroughfares for quicker travel through the dense woods. Judging from Ann's story, it didn't take them long to figure this out after the first pipelines were built.

A Brush with the Brazos River Booger

I would like to tell you about the closest I ever came to encountering something truly weird myself. In all honesty, I consider myself lucky to be alive. After hearing my tale, you'll surely understand why.

I spent the majority of my life living in Robertson County, which is known by those who live there as Booger County. Growing up in the late '70s, I had heard stories about the

along the riverbank, but I felt no sense of peace. Instead, it was replaced by a real paranoia and a feeling of not being alone. I decided to get the hell out of there.

I turned back the way I came when I noticed something incredibly strange. There was this stench that I can only describe as a mixture of spoiled food, rotten garbage, and the worst body odor you've ever imagined. It seemed to come out of nowhere, and as soon as I smelled it, it felt like it hit me

monster. This beast resembled a man but was hairier, more muscular, and more animalistic in general. It scared a lot of farmers, and killed its fair share of farm animals. Supposedly, this creature hung out around the Brazos River, which bordered our family's property, and the thought of this monster lurking there, waiting for its moment to kill, chilled me to my core.

My personal stake in the story happened either in 1977 or 1978, making me either 11 or 12 years old. I had hit that "woe is me point" in my preteen life, when I didn't want to deal with anyone, and became a real loner. I often found myself hiking down to the Brazos. I loved how the peace and quiet allowed me to just relax and think.

Well, one hot, hot July day, I was walking my regular route

dead in the face. I took off running back towards home. Behind me, I swear to you, I heard a cry. It was completely chilling.

I ran in a flat-out sprint until I felt safe again. My body just sensed that it was out of harm's way, and I turned back just to make sure. Now, I'm not certain that what I saw next was anything more than a trick of the brain. But just as I turned, I saw a rustling in the brush along the riverbank, and I saw a massive, wide hairy back disappear into the undergrowth on its way back towards the river.

Needless to say, I took off running again. I didn't spend any more summer days down by the river after that. I knew that something truly strange called that place home, and that I was lucky to have escaped it. *–Greg Draper*

Raggedy Man's Gonna Get Ya!

Between Sour Lake and Beaumont, at the end of a subdivision road, is a favorite parking place for teenagers. But in the mid-1980s, several carloads of kids were terrorized there by what became known as the Raggedy Man.

Witnesses reported that the Raggedy Man would come right up to the windshields of parkers and peer in curiously. He was described as being much taller and of a heavier build than an average man. His long hair, scraggly beard, and a not-quite-human expression were what gave him his name. There were no confirmed reports that the Raggedy Man was naked, but it's not clear that anyone ever hung around long enough to find out one way or another.

Legend of the Converse Werewolf

I have lived all of my life (except for four years away at college in Oregon) in Bexar County. And we have one doozy of a legend around here! Let me tell you what I have heard about the Converse Werewolf.

This is old-time ranching country. And part of being a rancher, especially back then, was being manly. One rancher wanted his son to go out and be a man, so he sent the 15-year-old out into the wilderness by himself and told him to bring home a deer for the family to eat. The boy went out and, days later, still hadn't returned. The rancher summoned all of his neighbors, and they went on a search party.

The rancher heard a noise off in the woods. He went running in that direction, thinking he had found his son—and he was right—but he got more than he bargained for.

What he saw was an eight-foot-tall creature that looked like a direct cross between a wolf and a gorilla. And it was eating his 15-year-old boy. The rancher shot at the beast, and it took off into the woods, but it was too late—the kid had been eaten.

The rancher plunged into a depression and went off the deep end. He stopped talking to people, stopped eating, and died shortly after seeing that gruesome sight.—*Big Chuck Hawlee*

Chester and the Swamp Thing

When Chester Moore, Jr., of Orange is asked, "Do you believe in Bigfoot?," his response is to the point: "Believing is for religion. Examining facts is what we should be doing."

Chester is a widely respected outdoors journalist and wildlife expert, a recognized authority on animal tracks, and a much-sought-after hunting guide. He has begun investigating the facts of Bigfoot sightings and has made plaster casts of unusual tracks found in the woods in Newton and Orange counties.

He has concluded that the tracks are not from any animal known to be native to the region. In his opinion, they "are from some undiscovered ape or large primate animal." And in his straightforward manner, he declares, "Whether you call it a Bigfoot or not and no matter what you believe, something has to be making these tracks."

Chester conducted a follow-up investigation of a recent sighting in a swamp near Orange after a reader of his column for the *Orange Leader* and *Port Arthur News* called him with interesting information. The reader said he had seen something odd in a swamp near the Sabine River, where he had gone bass fishing not long before. He was standing in a channel cut into the swamp years ago by loggers. Suddenly he was confronted by something big, hairy, and black, swimming noisily across the cut. The man assumed it was a wild hog. Feral hogs—or razorbacks, as they are called throughout the South—are abundant in the East Texas woods and river bottomlands. It was the only thing he could think of that would be that big, that black, and that hairy.

When the animal reached shore, though, the man was shocked to realize that the creature was not a hog. The thing stood upright, like a man, climbed hand over hand up the steep bank, and disappeared into the thick woods. And then there was the howl—an eerie, long,

because it gives them a natural early detection warning system if anyone is approaching them."

Chester quickly found some prints, but they were not well defined because of the surrounding forest litter and leaves. What aroused his curiosity, however, was the length of the stride. It measured close to five feet; the usual walking stride of an average adult man is less than three feet. "The only way a man's stride would be that long would be if he were running," Chester said. "And if anyone was running through this mud, the prints would show a sliding effect, which these clearly didn't."

Another set of tracks was found on the other side of the cut. The stride was roughly the same as that of the first set, but the tracks were much more distinct. At one point, the animal had stopped. There were two prints—a left foot and a right foot—next to each other. They were still fresh, made a few hours earlier. From the depth of the footprints and the length of the stride, Chester deduced that the animal in question weighed well over three hundred pounds and was probably between six and a half and seven feet tall.

He made casts of the footprints, which showed that the impressions were made by the ball of the foot, the arch, and the heel. The ground had been too muddy to make out the detail of the toes, but it was clearly visible where the animal had pushed off on its toes when it took a step. It was obvious that the footprints were made by bare feet. They were only about twelve inches long, smaller than typical Bigfoot prints, which average fifteen to eighteen inches.

However, larger tracks have been found in the woods of East Texas. Some measuring about fifteen inches were found along Slop Jar Slough in Hardin County in 1980. These were discovered by a couple of women who were picking mayhaws in a baygall thicket. Slop Jar Slough is where the wild man sighting was

drawn-out unearthly sound. The almost human wailing pierced the air and was so unimaginably loud that it left the startled fisherman knowing that this was no ordinary animal. This was an encounter with the unknown.

In the course of a preliminary investigation of the site, Chester discovered that there were others who had heard the howling. There were also reports of suspicious tracks along the muddy banks of the cut, and he wanted to examine them more closely.

"This palmetto flat is virtually identical to the habitat in Florida where the Myakka Ape, or Skunk Ape, has been seen and reportedly photographed," Chester said. "It's also typical of vast regions of bottomlands and swamps along the Gulf Coast from Texas through southern Louisiana and on into Florida. I think there's a good chance that the animals bed down among the palmettos,

reported by the *Kountze News* in August 1952. It's only a few miles from Bragg Road. In another sighting, a park ranger saw some tracks along a slough off Village Creek of a creature that had a stride longer than that of a man. Both accounts fit the pattern of the prints from the Sabine River. It appeared that something that makes large humanlike footprints and a long stride likes walking the swamps barefoot.

Chester points out that if all the prints were fifteen to eighteen inches long, that would be suspicious in itself. "If Bigfoot is a real breeding animal that lives in these woods, it has to grow to those optimum sizes. We should expect to find some prints that are smaller. A range of sizes argues for the reality of the animals, not against it."

There has been research associating these mystery hominid sightings with ghost lights and with energy fields, suggesting that the creatures may somehow be phantomlike and that this would account for their puzzling elusiveness. But from Chester's research, which includes not only casts of footprints but also hair and scat samples and carcasses killed in ways no recorded animal is known to kill its prey, it is obvious that the creatures are solid flesh and blood. What Chester may have found is evidence of the day-to-day struggle for survival of an as yet unknown primate.

Is Bigfoot Flesh or Phantom?

Given all this evidence gathered by Chester Moore and the Texas Bigfoot Research Center, the question is not whether Bigfoot is real. The question is, Why can't we catch one?

During a radio interview, well-known paranormal investigator and journalist Linda Moulton Howe told of speaking to people in the Pacific Northwest who claimed to have seen Bigfoot literally vanish right before their eyes. Over the years, she had collected a number of such stories, enough to make her suspect that the sightings had a paranormal quality to them.

However, many serious Bigfoot investigators who conduct actual fieldwork are reluctant to admit that the creatures may have a paranormal aspect. For such researchers, there is plenty of evidence that the animals are just undiscovered flesh-and-blood apes. They see nothing phantomlike about them and have no reason to think that the apes may be shape-shifters or denizens from another dimension that sometimes cross over into this world. For those investigators, such theories diminish the legitimacy of their research and the credibility of the physical evidence that they have so painstakingly gathered. In their opinion, Bigfoot's elusiveness comes from the fact that the creature is intelligent and highly skilled at camouflaging itself within its natural environment.

If you've ever been to a place like the Big Thicket, where visibility is no more than a few feet in any direction even under the best of conditions, it is self-evident how such a creature could make itself scarce in a heartbeat.

But do these considerations alone account for the

creature's elusiveness? Are we forced to either accept them or turn to paranormal theories? There are some researchers who think the issue is more complex than that. Their view is that Bigfoot is not phantomlike, that it is a physically real animal with weird powers or abilities. (This, incidentally, was the view held by Native Americans about the odd ape-man they knew. With this perspective, the physical evidence gathered by the flesh-and-blood believers need not be mutually exclusive with the observations of paranormal aspects. In other words, Bigfoot is real, but Bigfoot is also weird.)

Judging from what we have heard about the link between the sightings of the wild man and mysterious light-producing energies, there may indeed be unknown forces at play. Could there be a race of beings who have a profound knowledge of subtle energies and their relationship to consciousness and perception? Could these beings use this knowledge in some form of mind control or hypnosis to keep themselves hidden from the view of mankind or to alter the forms they present for our view?

None of this sounds as unbelievable or unlikely to us as it might to you, because in our years of pursuing the elusive hairy beasts, we have come across a strange phenomenon that may be an indication that Bigfoot is using weird, hypnotic powers. It's called the eerie silence.

Eerie Silence Phenomenon

Our first encounter of this bizarre phenomenon was a spur-of-the-moment trip one year to Bragg Road on the occasion of the spring equinox. Some ancient cultures attached great importance to the equinoxes and solstices. That year, the exact time of the equinox was two thirty-two a.m. We carefully timed our trip and arrived at Bragg Road a little after two a.m.

We had been there for about an hour when it suddenly dawned on us that something remarkable was happening. We didn't hear anything, and that was what was so weird.

We were in the midst of a vast swampland inhabited by untold thousands of insects, frogs, coyotes, and other nocturnal mammals, and not one of them was making the slightest noise. All around us was stone-dead silence.

We decided to see how close the eight-mile-long arrow-straight road aligns with magnetic north. We watched as the needle on the compass bobbed and then started spinning slowly. We stood there in amazement for several minutes, and the needle never stopped spinning. Obviously, we were being subjected to very unusual magnetic conditions for a compass to malfunction in this way.

Were these same conditions also affecting the insects and wildlife of the area, causing the utter silence we observed? As we realized our unusual circumstances, the creepiness of the situation was compounded by the spooky feeling that we were being watched. We could hardly get out of there fast enough. Little did we know at the time that it might have been the wild man watching us in that silence.

A caller on a radio talk show said he had been hunting in the woods of Jasper County, when he heard a howling sound he could not identify with any animal he knew. Then everything went completely silent. He decided to leave the woods, and all he could hear was the sounds of footsteps, muffled by the leaves on the ground, and the noise of occasional breaking of twigs as what seemed to be something very massive and heavy followed him. "I've hunted in those woods all my life," the caller said, "and I'm not afraid of anything. But I was scared. What spooked me the most was how quiet it was. The hair liter-

I could see something that had reddish brown hair all over it. It stood very tall, well over 8 feet. It had blackened skin along the facial areas that I could see.

ally stood up on the back of my neck. I will never hunt there again."

Intrigued, we began investigating the sightings reported on various Bigfoot Web sites and in other sources to see if they contained similarities. There were several that occurred in East Texas. Typical of those accounts is the following one posted on the Texas Birds Records Committee Web site of a sighting in Liberty County in the Trinity River swamp:

> I was riding my bike in the woods and going home on a trail, and I could feel something watching me or following me. I raced out of the woods to a better trail. I could hear in the bush that something was keeping pace with me. I cleared the woods and turned to look, and I could see something that had reddish brown hair all over it. It stood very tall, well over 8 feet. It had blackened skin along the facial areas that I could see. There were no forest noises, i.e., birds or wild game running around. That is what made me feel uncomfortable and why I began to leave most quickly.

This eerie silence, which affects witnesses as much as the sight of Bigfoot itself, may contain clues to the creature's elusiveness. The strange phenomenon may result from Bigfoot's mental manipulations of its energy biosphere, but it might be doing this for reasons other than hiding itself from humans. It could be that it projects this energy outward in a shotgun pattern to stun its prey and induce a state of dormancy in any life-forms that happen to be in the immediate vicinity, thereby causing the weird silence.

Obviously, much more research is required before any definite conclusions can be made about this baffling mystery, but if you ever find yourself in the woods and every-

thing suddenly goes utterly quiet, you might want to beat a hasty retreat: Bigfoot might be looking for a meal.

Invisible Man of Palmetto State Park

Many years back, my wife gave me a camera for Christmas. I took pictures everywhere, spending a lot of time photographing in Palmetto State Park near Austin.

One time, I had been out roaming around, and on my way back to my truck, I felt like someone was following me. I turned around—not a person in sight. I quickened my pace, but things only got worse. Soon I could hear footsteps behind me and off to the side. "Just make it back to the car," I kept telling myself, "and everything will be fine."

No one else was around, unfortunately. I was completely spooked and broke out into a full run. I tripped at one point and landed on my face, then rolled over, sat up, and looked back down the trail. I couldn't believe what I saw. Or more accurately, I couldn't believe what I didn't see!

I saw the tall grass off to the side of the trail getting flattened and parting, as if someone was pushing their way through it. But there was no one there. I jumped up and broke out into a full sprint until I was inside my car. I quickly took off, without even catching my breath, and felt something hit the car from behind as I sped off.

I thought for a long time that I had gone completely insane. But apparently, there are many stories of an invisible man who lives in the park. It made me feel better, even a bit proud. I am one of the few who has encountered it firsthand. I guess I don't need to tell you this, but I did not get a shot of it with my new camera.—*Anonymous*

Hairy Man Road

Yes, there is a road named Hairy Man Road, and it's located in the town of Round Rock. The legend goes that a young boy in the 1800s became separated from a settlers' caravan during a dark and stormy night while the group was trying to escape the rising waters of a nearby creek. The boy managed to survive on his own, but the separation from his parents and the threat of death by drowning traumatized him, and he became a hermit. He avoided contact with people and terrorized anyone

who dared enter his domain—the wooded area along what became known as Brushy Creek.

He frightened stagecoaches and solitary riders alike, and his legend grew in the area until one day the horses leading a speeding stagecoach trampled him to death while he attempted his infamous intimidation. The legend did not stop there. To this day, frightened travelers of the road swear that they have seen a large, very hairy man lurking in the bushes along the road. Teenagers use the road for thrill seeking, the young men hoping that stopping in the eerie woods will encourage their dates to seek safety in their arms.

Since 1994, an annual festival has been held in the Cat Hollow subdivision in honor of the Hairy Man. Food, music, games, and other activities are held in the park, and the grand finale is the Hairiest Man Contest. Not just head hair is judged. The hairier the back and chest, the better. This year's contest winner won a trip to Cozumel.

Sadly, Hairy Man Road is not what it used to be. Rapid population growth in the area has prompted the city to start reconstruction of the road in order to widen it and facilitate better drainage. I don't know if sightings will continue after the new road is finished, but I will remember the eerie feeling I'd got while driving down the twisting, densely canopied road.
—*Tim Stevens*

Goat Man of White Rock Lake

Located in the northeast quadrant of Dallas is the beautiful suburban area of White Rock Lake. The northern part of the lake is now a state park, while the southern area has been developed into waterfront estates. Recognized not only for its largemouth bass and white crappie fishing, the lake is also known to have a creature stalking its shores.

Stories abound from people who were picnicking at the lake during the dusk hours and saw a creature—half man, half goat—appearing out of the woods and throwing trash and even tires at the visitors in attempts to drive them away.

The goat man is described as a very large creature, about seven feet tall, with the horns and hooves of a goat but standing erect. The body and legs are those of a man, and the face is humanlike. His skin has a jaundiced appearance, almost greenish, and he has long, gnarled, fingers with grotesque fingernails.

Maybe this poor abomination of nature is trying to drive people away from his feeding grounds of local fish and game. He may be migrating farther from his White Rock Lake home as development advances in the area's natural habitat, as is the case for many of Texas's wild creatures.

Lake Worth Monster

In the wee hours of July 10, 1969, Mr. and Mrs. John Reichart and two other couples showed up at the Fort Worth police station. They were so plainly terrified that, as unlikely as their story sounded, the officers had no problem believing the six had seen something well out of the ordinary. As their story went, they had been parked along the edge of Lake Worth around midnight when a huge beast leaped out of nowhere and landed on the Reicharts' car. It was, they related, covered

with both fur and scales and looked like a cross between a goat and a man.

Four police units raced to the scene, only to find nothing. However, there was an eighteen-inch scratch running alongside the witnesses' car. They all swore the scratch had not been there before and were sure it was a scratch from the monster's claws. In the preceding couple of months, other reports of a monster had been received but were attributed to

pranks. The officers assumed that the Reicharts had been similarly victimized, but the frightening, aggressive nature of the attack made them take the incident more seriously.

Almost exactly twenty-four hours after the incident, Jack Harris, driving on the road to the Lake Worth Nature Center, said he spotted the creature crossing in front of him. It ran up and down a hill and was soon being watched by thirty to forty people, who had come to the area hoping to catch a glimpse of the monster after the *Fort Worth Star-Telegram* had run a front-page story:

FISHY MAN-GOAT TERRIFIES COUPLES PARKED AT LAKE WORTH

Within moments, police from the sheriff's office were on the scene as well, observing the fantastic sight. But when it seemed as though some of the spectators were going to approach the creature, it threw a car wheel at them and escaped into the thicket once again.

In the weeks ahead, parties of armed searchers made nightly forays into the woods and fields near the lake. Some saw the creature and thought it resembled a "big white ape." It left tracks reportedly eight inches wide at the toes and sixteen inches long. On one occasion, when men fired on it, they followed a trail of blood to the water's edge. Three people heard its cry and smelled the foul odor that was associated with it. They also came across several sheep half eaten, with broken necks that, they felt, were the handiwork of the monster.

The last sighting came on November 7, 1969, from Charles Buchanan. He said he had been sleeping in his sleeping bag in the back of his pickup truck when he was attacked by the monster. Buchanan shoved a bag of chicken at the creature. The beast stuffed it into its mouth, jumped into the lake and swam towards Greer Island.—*John V. Crawford, SubversiveElement.com*

Bad-Tempered Goat Man

The Lake Worth monster is an old legend from back in the late 1960s here in Fort Worth. It's basically a Bigfoot-style creature. It lived (or was seen) on Greer Island at Lake Worth, and there are supposedly 70–90 reports of people meeting it. It supposedly had a rather bad temper and was known for throwing tires and other objects at people who disturbed it. The most complete description I have found is that of a short humanoid with a long neck, with the head of a dog or a goat and a horn in the middle of its head.—*Robert Jensen*

Blood-Sucking Chupacabra

The goat man had better be careful about just where he shows himself, because another odd creature, the goat-sucking chupacabra, has really been getting around the state lately!

Chupacabra is Spanish for "goat sucker." These creatures were first seen in Puerto Rico, and sightings spread from there to Mexico and parts of Latin America. Unlike Bigfoot sightings, which have been reported for more than a hundred years, chupacabra sightings go back only as far as the 1950s.

Because of this and because the sightings were at first limited to Latin American countries, it was assumed by many that the chupacabra was no more than a superstitious regional legend that spread northward to Texas.

But superstition does not explain the reports of thousands of slaughtered livestock, particularly goats, farm animals, and chickens, that have been found with peculiar puncture wounds and their bodies drained of blood. Nor does it explain the repeated sightings of an oddly shaped beast.

According to eyewitness accounts, the chupacabra is about four feet tall and weighs up to about seventy pounds, with gray skin and spikes or perhaps hair running down its spine, short arms with claws, and rear legs like those of a kangaroo.

Chupacabra Shot Dead

July and October of 2004 showed a rash of chupacabra sightings in Texas. An Elmendorf rancher reported shooting one of the creatures and notified authorities of the possibly diseased animal that was killing his livestock. Pictures were taken of the creature, and samples of tissue and blood were taken for analysis.

A Lufkin resident shot and killed a similar creature in October. The resident was alerted to trouble by the family dogs barking and whining in the yard. The dogs indicated that the creature was under the house. After being shot, it was pulled out with a rope. A local veterinarian could not identify what type of animal it was.

Pictures of the dead critter show an emaciated animal with bluish gray skin. It looked similar to a starving greyhound with a serious case of mange. You would say that it's a dog, but it did not have the angular skull like one. The back legs were longer than the front, like a kangaroo's. It had a sloping forehead not unlike a deer's. When they picked up the head by the ear to photograph it better, the ear crumbled in their hands. The body looked like it had been dead for over a month, but it had only been a matter of hours. Its weight was 15 to 20 lb.

Whatever this creature was, it had never been seen before. It has totally baffled many animal experts.—*Tim Stevens*

Austin's Bat Attacks

When Austin approved plans to renovate Congress Avenue's bridge over Town Lake in 1980, the city had no idea what it was in for. Having incorporated 16-inch-deep expansion joints into the bridge's new design, its engineers had unknowingly drawn up blueprints for the perfect bat flat.

It turned out that the expansion joints—narrow gaps that ran the length of the bridge's underside—were an ideal roost for Mexican free-tailed bats. Consequently, hundreds of thousands of the little flying squatters soon were calling the bridge home.

Right off the bat, residents reacted with fear. They voiced vehement concerns over rabies. Many were horrified at the thought of all that guano contaminating the water below. Others were worried about the detrimental effects on the bridge itself, concerned that bat excrement would corrode its materials and collapse it into the lake.

Fortunately, before things went too far, an organization called Bat Conservation International stepped in and went to bat for its furry friends. The group swooped down to quash the city's misguided concerns and educate its citizens about the creatures'

benefits. BCI assured the public that the transmission of rabies from bats is exceptionally rare. Besides, the bridge colony alone can consume 10,000 to 30,000 pounds of insects nightly, including those pesky mosquitoes. Not to mention that bats are instrumental in the pollination of the agave plant, which begets tequila, which begets margaritas, which beget memorable nights on Sixth Street. (OK, so the Mexican free-tailed bats may not be responsible exactly, but you've got to hit Austin where it counts.)

Thanks to BCI's efforts, Austin's attitude toward its winged invaders turned a complete one eighty. In just a few years, the capital city was fully embracing the bats, demonstrating its affection the best way Americans know how: commercial exploitation. It now advertises what has become the largest documented urban bat colony in the world as a featured tourist attraction, which was estimated in 1999 to have a positive fiscal impact worth up to $8 million.

Today, it's a summer tradition to visit the bridge and witness the swirling dark clouds emerging into the sky. Locals and out-of-towners alike arrive nightly to cheer on the bridge's stunning nocturnal emission, which they can now do from a specially maintained bat-observation area.

Visitors can also attend the annual Freetail-Free-for-All celebration, sponsored by the same newspaper that once helped fuel the city's bat rabies fears. And let's not forget the nautical, bat-watching booze cruises, with honeymoon packages available.

In 1995, the Texas legislature designated the Mexican free-tailed bat the state mammal. The following year, Austin established a minor-league hockey team and named it the Austin Ice Bats, and 1998 saw the raising of a bat-venerating sculpture sponsored by several local businesses. That same year the United States Postal Service chose the Congress Avenue Bridge as the site to

announce its commemorative American Bats stamp series.

Austin, which previously despised its bats, has now crowned itself the Bat Capital of America. Once mercilessly unwelcoming, the city has gone—say it together now—completely batty.—*Wesley Treat*

Bat Watching at the Bridge

A few years ago my wife and I went to Austin to visit a couple of friends who had moved there from New Jersey. They were showing us around town—you know, all the usual touristy sites, cowboy bars, gun shops, the best Mexican food joints, etc. Then one night, they took us to the Congress Avenue Bridge to witness the great bat exodus.

It was a mild evening, and we arrived at the bridge just before sundown. We staked out a good viewing standpoint on a grassy embankment adjacent to the bridge. The bats are apparently very punctual and come out each night at almost exactly the same time. We must have gotten there a few minutes early, because it was not very crowded where we stood. Within a few minutes, though, more and more spectators began arriving. Some spread out blankets on the grass; others poured glasses of wine.

As soon as the sun dropped to a certain point on the western horizon, we started to see the first shadowy flashes of the speedy little bats flutter by us. One thing that many of the assembled bat watchers had apparently not anticipated was the fact that the furry little winged critters don't just fly out from under the bridge and then away into the night; they emerge from the structure and then fly everywhere! By this, I mean that they were in such close proximity to the crowd that you could almost reach your hand out in front of your face and snatch one right out of the night air. As this started to dawn on people around us, some began crouching down in recoil, others pulled blankets over their heads, and one girl behind me put her hands over her hair and began shrieking in terror.

Of course, none of this was really necessary, as the little featherless flutter-bys knew exactly where they were going and have no interest at all in getting tangled up in some sorority sister's coif.

After just a few moments, we could clearly see the millions of bats forming en masse over the water like an enormous black cloud. Then the cloud became a river, which began to flow away from us. It moved toward the horizon like a single living animal—a thick undulating serpent that slithered away into the gathering gloom of twilight. The spectacle was mind-boggling, millions of tiny furry flying creatures moving as if with one brain. The long dark column seemed to stretch as far as the eye could see. I wondered where they were all headed that night and imagined all the insects that would not live to see the dawn because of them.

Before long, the sky had darkened to the point where we could no longer see the bats. The aerial display only lasted a matter of minutes, and then they were gone off into the night. One thing was for sure, though—they would all be right back at the Congress Avenue Bridge by morning and would be ready to fly at show time the following night.—*Mark Moran*

CAUTION

You May Wish to Stand Back During Bat Flight, to Avoid Droppings

Local Heroes and Villains

Colorful characters and local loonies—every town across America has at least one. They might be famous, or even infamous, for what they have done. They might be a historically significant figure or just someone who marches to the beat of a different drummer. There are those who have garnered national, even international, renown and those whom people outside their own hometowns will probably never hear about. There are even some members of the animal world who have risen to local hero status in their communities!

The Lone Star inhabitants featured in this chapter have done something unique to set themselves apart from the crowd. For better or worse, they went their own way and played by their own rules, usually in outsize Texas fashion. They have helped make each of our towns and cities a more interesting place to call home. In fact, sometimes they made them a little too interesting.

Charles Whitman's Tower of Terror

On the first day of August 1966, a twenty-five-year-old college student stepped onto the observation deck of the University of Texas Tower and took it upon himself to selectively determine the fates of an unlucky portion of Austin's populace. As he fired his rifle indiscriminately at the pedestrians below, Charles Whitman held the university campus and surrounding area in a state of helpless panic for more than ninety minutes.

Though he would be remembered for the tower killings, Whitman's homicidal spree had actually begun hours earlier at the apartment of his mother, Margaret. Whitman had paid her a late visit the night before on the pretense that he wanted to study there while his wife rested at home. Sometime around midnight, Whitman strangled his mother and stabbed her in the chest. He then laid her body in bed and left a note confessing what he had done.

> I have just taken my mother's life. I am very upset over having done it. However I feel that if there is a heaven, she is definitely there now, and if there is no life after, I have relieved her of her suffering here on earth.

Whitman next returned home to his wife, Kathleen, who was asleep in bed. As with his mother, he stabbed her in the chest with a large hunting knife. She presumably never knew what happened. Then Charles turned his attention to a letter he had typed the previous evening, in which he attempted to explain the murders he was planning.

> It was after much thought that I decided to kill my wife, Kathy. . . . I cannot rationally pinpoint any specific reason for doing this. . . . At this time, though, the prominent reason in my mind is that I truly do not consider this world worth living in. . . . I intend to kill her as painlessly as possible. Similar reasons provoked me to take my mother's life also. I don't think the poor woman has ever enjoyed life as she is entitled to.

After killing his wife, Whitman scribbled an addendum to the letter, which began "3:00 A.M. Both Dead." In it, he asked that the money from his life insurance policy be used to pay off the bad checks he was planning to write. Anything that remained was to be donated to a mental health institution in hopes that research would prevent further tragedies like his. Additionally, he left requests that his dog be given to his in-laws and that the film left in his cameras be developed.

Whitman then set about packing a footlocker with supplies. Among the items were food, water, a radio, gasoline, toilet paper, a pipe wrench, and a notebook. He included two rifles and three handguns, plus a shotgun and another rifle he bought later that morning. He also, strangely, packed deodorant.

At around eleven thirty a.m., Whitman drove his footlocker to campus and wheeled it into a tower elevator. When he reached the twenty-seventh floor, he disembarked and climbed the stairs that led to the observation level. There, he bludgeoned the receptionist, stuffed her behind a couch, and shot her in the head. Phase two had begun.

Minutes later, a family of six arrived in the elevator and started up the stairway. Whitman fired his shotgun into the stairwell, killing two and wounding two others. The remaining pair escaped and ran for help.

Shortly before the tower's twelve-foot clocks struck noon, Whitman assumed his position on the observation deck outside, unpacked his weapons, and took aim. His first shot from the tower struck the abdomen of a pregnant eighteen-year-old. The girl would survive, but the bullet pierced the skull of her unborn child, killing it instantly.

Whitman proceeded to shoot several more people on campus before opening fire on adjacent Guadalupe Street. His

aim was extraordinary. From more than two hundred feet in the air, he shot a police officer through a space in a stone railing just inches wide. He also struck a boy riding by on a bicycle, as well as a man outside a barbershop some fifteen hundred feet away.

Word spread of what was happening, and pedestrians took cover. For blocks, nearly everyone who was outside crouched behind columns and parked cars. In true Texas style, some raced for their firearms and began shooting back. Unhindered, Whitman continued his attack, shooting through the tower's rainspouts.

Miraculously avoiding the sniper's barrage of bullets, several police officers dashed across open ground and into the tower. A little over an hour after the shooting had begun, three officers and a deputized citizen made their way onto the narrow observation deck. They moved out along the periphery, doing their best to avoid the friendly fire still coming from all sides.

Whitman became aware of the officers' presence and stationed himself in the far corner, where he waited for them to enter his sights. Unfortunately for him, he chose the wrong direction to aim his weapon; the two officers who reached him first approached from the opposite side. Before Whitman could swing his gun around, the

officers opened fire. Two shotgun blasts to the head and another to the chest, and Charles was dead. The tower clocks read 1:24.

In all, Charles Whitman wounded thirty-one people and killed fifteen that day. A sixteenth victim died a week later. In 2001, one of the first people Whitman had shot died of kidney failure; he had been born with only one, which was damaged by the sniper's bullet. The death was ruled a homicide, bringing the total to seventeen.

In one of the notes Whitman had written at home, he requested that his body undergo examination to find out what might be wrong with him.

After my death I wish that an autopsy would be performed on me to see if there is any visible physical disorder. I have had some tremendous headaches in the past.

When medical examiners fulfilled his request, they did indeed discover a small tumor in Whitman's brain. Experts continue to debate whether or not it could have had anything to do with his behavior. Were Whitman's murderous final acts the result of a physically damaged brain or an emotionally damaged psyche? Unfortunately, we probably will never know.

Charles Whitman's home

Old Rip

At the center of Eastland's town square, locked away behind two layers of glass, a Texas legend lies. Once famous around the country, hailed by fans and even a U.S. president, he now rests in near obscurity. His name is Old Rip, and although you may never have heard his name, you're almost certainly familiar with his story—the basics of it, anyway.

Remember this cartoon from Warner Brothers? A demolition worker pries open an old cornerstone, only to find a lonesome frog within. Suddenly, the frog bounds to life and begins to sing snappy jazz numbers. Thrilled by his discovery, the man attempts to capitalize on the frog's amazing abilities, only to have the creature go lifeless at every crucial moment.

The tale of the resurrected frog has become one of Warner Brothers' most popular cartoons. What most people don't know, however, is that the story is based on a real, live event that took place in Texas in 1928.

As Eastland was tearing down its decaying courthouse in preparation for a more modern replacement, scores of residents waited excitedly to find out if a certain local tale was true. Ernest Wood, who was county clerk when the old courthouse was constructed, was said to have placed a live horned lizard inside the building's cornerstone. It was a long-held belief that horned lizards could endure extended periods of isolation without food, water, or air, and Wood had evidently decided to test the theory.

That was in 1897, thirty-one years before. Had the famous frog survived?

As many as two thousand curious Texans crowded together on a cold February day to witness the opening of the cornerstone. As they looked on in suspense, the block was cleared and its covering removed. Officials pulled from the cavity a small collection of items that had been entombed there: newspapers, a Bible, then something that was described as looking like a piece of tree bark. It was the horny toad!

As County Judge Ed Pritchard held the desiccated creature aloft, the crowd was amazed to see it twitch, then wriggle to life. The little guy was alive!

The miracle snoozer became an instant sensation. He was dubbed Rip Van Winkle, a name quickly shortened to Old Rip, and travelers came from miles away to get a look at him. He went on tour, visiting Dallas, New York, St. Louis, and even Washington, D.C., for a meeting with President Calvin Coolidge. No heavier than a couple of ounces, the remarkable toad hefted a lot of weight. But sadly, after three decades encased in stone, Old Rip didn't have much life left in him. Less than a year after his emergence, he contracted pneumonia and died. He had been living on borrowed time.

Unwilling to give up their main attraction, though, Eastland had his body preserved and placed in a diminutive casket. Both Rip and his former residence were put on display at the Eastland County Courthouse, where you'll find them today. Warner Brothers' version may continue to enjoy fame as the mascot of The WB network, but Eastland is where you'll find the real deal.

Toad Worship

Here in Eastland, we still celebrate the memory of Old Rip. Chief among those who honor him is Bette Armstrong, who is also known as the Toad Lady.

Armstrong is a relative newcomer to Eastland, having moved there with her husband in 1993. But she quickly became obsessed with the story of Old Rip. Out of her store, Bette's Bits, she sells wooden and stuffed horny toads. But it doesn't end there. Each year, Eastland holds a parade in which Armstrong appears dressed head to toe in her own horny toad outfit. Bette has come to be known around town as much as the old toad she honors.

—Doris T.

ILOVETOADS

RIBBIT 1

Dan Blocker: A Man Called Hoss

"Really, this is what we're known for, the home of Dan Blocker. Even though he wasn't born here."

That may be the most extensive oral history you'll get on the subject should you decide to drop in at the little museum in the town of O'Donnell. If you're stopping here, though, you probably know as much. The fact that TV's Hoss Cartwright grew up here is what gives anyone from out of town a reason to pull through this way.

So it's a little odd that all the Dan Blocker memorabilia is kept in the museum's back room. To be fair, they did build a nice Western-style display area for it, though it quickly begins to feel like a barrier between the Blocker stuff and your grubby little hands.

If you can see well enough through the windows, it's possible to learn a few things about the big man from the little screen. Born in DeKalb, he was reportedly the largest baby ever born in Bowie County, at a whopping fourteen pounds. At age eleven, he wore a size XL shirt and pants with a forty-two-inch waist, as illustrated by one of his boyhood outfits, apparently stuffed with a pillow for a measure of realism.

**Age: 11
Shirt: XL
Waist: 42**

Blocker's family ran a grocery store just across the street from where the O'Donnell Museum now stands. Supposedly, that's where you would find young Danny when he wasn't at school. The storefront is boarded up now, but it still displays the Blocker name. A large Hoss-style hat has been painted on the building's face.

Next door, in Heritage Plaza, you'll find a bust dedicated to the man who made O'Donnell famous. Always with his hat, Blocker endures as Bonanza's most beloved cowboy, forever typecast in bronze.

The plaque below his head reads

THANKS TO FILM, HOSS CARTWRIGHT
WILL LIVE; BUT ALL TOO SELDOM
DOES THE WORLD GET TO KEEP
A DAN BLOCKER.

San Antonio's Prince of Thrones

Barney Smith is on the very rim of the art world. Few men have dared venture into the realm he has chosen, and none has done so with such zeal. He paints, he engraves, he sculpts, but he always works with the same medium: toilet seats.

Eyeglasses, cosmetology supplies, sports memorabilia, cartoon characters—you name it, he's put it on a toilet seat. He has seats sporting license plates for every state in the union. He made a seat honoring wooden nickels. Another is dedicated to the Global Positioning System. Yet another stands as a tribute to railroad crossings. There's even a seat commemorating his wife's gallstone surgery (sans the actual gallstone, which his wife has kept hidden from him). And the ideas just keep coming. One of his latest features a piece of Saddam Hussein's own toilet, recovered from an underground bunker in the Green Zone.

The whole thing started somewhere around 1970,

after Smith returned from a hunting trip with his father. Both came home with bucks, and both were eager to display the horns. Smith's dad mounted his to traditional wooden shields, but Barney, a master plumber, got the idea to affix his horns to a spare toilet lid. Flush with pride over his inspiration, he realized he had uncovered his new pastime.

Today, Smith has decorated more than seven hundred rings and lids, all on display in the garage adjacent to his San Antonio home. And he can tell you a story about each and every one. He will, too, if you've got the time. Every visitor is more than welcome to a uniquely tangential tour of his creations, which will cover not only the toilet covers, but any variety of topics. It's entirely possible for a person to learn about cosmetic dentistry, the D.A.R.E. program, and Japanese currency all in the same visit.

Considering the enthusiasm Smith displays, it's hard to believe that for many years he kept a lid on his hobby. No one was privy to the unusual gallery until 1992, when a man inquired about some of Smith's oil paintings, which were on display at a yard sale. Smith invited him inside to see more, but once the man got a look at the toilet seats, Smith recalls, "He wasn't interested in my oils anymore!" The collection has been open to the public ever since.

Of course, everyone has to ask him what his own toilet seat looks like. He insists it's undecorated. Besides, he prefers to work with molded wood; for personal use, he likes plastic.

Flying into the History Books—Backward

Texans have always had an independent spirit. As anyone who is even slightly familiar with American history knows, Texas was, for a time, its own sovereign nation. This individuality still permeates the character of most Texans. The idea of the federal government telling a Texan what to do doesn't usually sit well.

One Texan bucked the orders of the federal government in a truly legendary way. He became a folk hero for his actions, which, to a degree, are still shrouded in mystery. His name was Douglas Corrigan, but he was known better to the world as Wrong Way. In 1938, he either ignored an edict from the authorities intentionally or made one of the biggest blunders in history. The Galveston native flew from New York to Dublin, Ireland, in one of the earliest transoceanic flights in history. The problem was, he was supposed to be heading to California.

Corrigan became obsessed with flying after experiencing his first plane ride as a teenager. He quickly began making his own flights and became part of a core group of dedicated pilots in the early days of aviation. He worked in any capacity he could find in the industry, and in fact, he helped build the *Spirit of St. Louis*, the plane that Charles Lindbergh used to make the world's first-ever flight across the Atlantic Ocean. Inspired by Lindbergh, Corrigan quickly pledged that he, a man of Irish descent, would be the first to fly nonstop from America to Ireland.

There were a number of obstacles in Corrigan's way. First off, he didn't have a plane. Second, he didn't have the money to buy one. When he did finally manage to buy an aircraft, a new set of problems ensued. It was an old, ramshackle machine that aviation officials deemed far too dangerous to fly over an ocean. Corrigan spent most of his time barnstorming the nation, landing in small towns, and charging people for rides. Eventually, he was granted permission to fly from Long Beach, California, to New York nonstop and then return. It was a long trip, but at least there'd be terra firma under him if he was forced to land.

Corrigan barely made it to New York. His main fuel tank sprang a leak, and he had only four gallons of fuel left when he landed. Instead of fixing the leaky tank for the journey back to California, he simply outfitted his plane with more tanks. The plane was so weighed down by the extra fuel that it could barely struggle off the ground when Corrigan set out on his return trip. When it did lift off, something very curious happened.

It was a foggy day. To burn off some of the excess fuel, Corrigan flew east, out over the Atlantic, and was then supposed to turn around and head back to California. But what happened over the Atlantic is not clear. The only thing certain is that twenty-eight hours after takeoff, Corrigan landed not in Long Beach, California, but in Dublin, Ireland. He was sent to the American embassy—he had no passport, no permission to land, and no good explanation for what he was doing on the Emerald Isle. According to Corrigan, he took off into the fog and began heading in what he thought was the correct direction. His compass was from World War I, though, and didn't function properly. He wound up heading in the wrong direction with a leaking fuel tank, and by the time he realized something was wrong, it was too late to turn back.

Speculation has always held that Corrigan knew exactly what he was doing when he headed for Europe. His story is considered a ruse to get him out of the considerable international trouble he could face for violating orders from the U.S. government as well as for entering a foreign nation without permission or documentation.

Corrigan and his plane were sent back to the United States on an ocean liner. When the boat entered New York Harbor, cheering spectators lined the shore, fireboats shot plumes of water into the sky, and a ticker tape parade was arranged for him down Broadway. Going the wrong way had made him a national folk hero. Corrigan's daring and defiant exploits had lifted the spirits of a Depression-weary nation. The *New York Post* printed a front-page headline that read HAIL TO WRONG WAY CORRIGAN!—printed backward. Before long, the term Wrong Way Corrigan had entered the public vernacular and became synonymous with any overtly befuddled act.

After his famous flight, Corrigan led a fairly simple life, living on an orange grove in Santa Ana, California. He never confessed that he had planned to fly to Ireland all along. Until his dying day, on December 9, 1995, he maintained that his transatlantic flight was the result of a navigational error.–*Chris Gethard*

Ultimate Avenger

Of all the odd personalities to be found in Texas history, Jack Ruby remains one of the most curious. What made this seedy Dallas strip-joint owner with ties to the underworld throw his own life away to avenge the assassination of John F. Kennedy by murdering the killer? In the nearly forty years since his death, Ruby's name has become synonymous with, and inextricably linked to, countless conspiracy theories. We asked *Weird Texas*'s Dallas correspondent, Josh Alan Friedman, to do a little digging and see if he could gain some insight into just what kind of man this mystery wrapped in a riddle inside an enigma really was.

Jack Ruby: Hero or Villain?

By Josh Alan Friedman

He is frozen in our consciousness as the paunchy, black-suited figure who gunned down Lee Harvey Oswald on national TV two days after Kennedy's death. Jack Ruby believed he avenged his President's murder, saved Dallas's reputation in the eyes of the world, and spared the fair Jacqueline the horror of a murder trial.

Ruby remains a star player in the American mythology of the JFK assassination. He has figured in countless conspiracy theories and works of fiction and nonfiction. In 1990, Ruby's executor-attorney was asking $130,000 for the .38 Colt Cobra that killed Oswald, along with some mundane possessions, like an undershirt Ruby had bought at Sears. (Who the heck would want Jack Ruby's undershirt?)

An international glare came upon Ruby's dark little corner of Dallas life on November 25, 1963. "Anybody coulda killed Oswald, the way people's feelings was running at that time," says Dallas deputy sheriff Lynn Burk, who knew Ruby well and was present when Oswald was captured at the Texas Theater. "It didn't surprise me it was Jack. I'm surprised some policeman didn't kill Oswald first."

"He stuck by what he did," says Captain Ray Abner, who was Ruby's personal guard in jail. "He said he loved Kennedy and that he was glad he did it. But I believe Jack just intended to wound Oswald. Spend a couple years in prison, sell a book and movie rights. He was a small figure who came up from the Chicago underworld. He was a guy who wanted to be a big shot."

On Ruby's last day as a free citizen that November day in '63, he was a balding, fifty-two-year-old. He had oily, slicked-back black hair, a cleft in his chin, and five-o'clock jowl shadow, and he wore a tie stickpin and diamond pinkie rings.

His strip joint, a second-rate club called the Carousel, was located one flight up on Commerce Street, between a parking garage and a short-order restaurant. Jack Ruby's stage was the size of a boxing ring, with a five-piece bump-and-grind orchestra but no dancing. The bar was boomerang-shaped, finished in gold-plated plastic and gaudy gold mesh drapes. Overhead hung a gold-framed painting of a stallion, which Ruby believed had "real class." Ruby was obsessed with class.

Terré Tale, a Dallas strip queen of the '60s, says she met Ruby when she innocently answered a newspaper ad for a cocktail waitress at the Carousel: "They sat me down next to a guy with more arms than an octopus. I didn't even know the Carousel had strippers. I'd never seen a strip. But Jack Ruby was nice to me. He told me he could make me a star, put me in an apartment, send me to the beauty parlor every day."

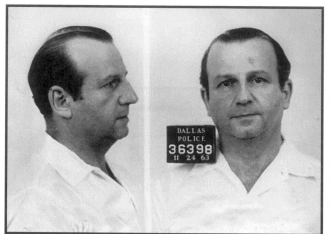

Tale refused Ruby's offer, but a few years later, she was headlining at the Colony Club, two doors down from Ruby at 1322 Commerce. Abe Weinstein's Colony Club was Dallas's most reputable burlesque house from 1939 to 1973. Ruby envied this deco cabaret, which seemed to possess the elusive class he so craved.

"My club was a nightclub," says retired owner Weinstein. "His was just a joint. I had big names, he had nobody."

Ruby, whose God-given name was Rubenstein, was a pain in the neck to Weinstein, bottom-feeding off the Colony's action for three years. "My relationship with Jack was bad," says Weinstein. "He threatened to kill me one week before he killed Oswald. He tried to hire away my waitresses and employees. Here's my opinion: Jack Ruby killed Oswald because he wanted to be world famous. If he'd have killed Oswald before the police got Oswald, he would have been a hero. But it was no great thing to get him in the police station."

According to Weinstein, Ruby had a Dr. Jekyll and Mr. Hyde personality. "If you went into his club and he'd never seen you before and you said, 'Jack, I'm hungry, I don't have a place to sleep,' he would feed you and give you a place to sleep. But if he didn't like you, he'd stab you in the back."

But there are those who saw more good in Jack Ruby than bad. Joe Johnson worked for him for six years, starting in 1957. Johnson led a five-piece R&B group. His trademark was belting out sax solos as he walked along the bar top. "I was part of a family," Johnson says. "Ruby was the best boss I had in Dallas. After he shot Oswald, the FBI followed me everywhere I'd play. I got six pages in the Warren Report."

And certain Ruby girls showed great devotion for their boss. Little Lynn liked Ruby enough to show up at the jail crying after he was imprisoned. The nineteen-year-old, blue-eyed stripper carried a Beretta pistol in her scarf to give him. Skilled more in the art of revealing than concealing, Little Lynn turned out to be a poor smuggler. The gun was quickly detected, and she was arrested at the entrance.

Shari Angel, a former Carousel headliner, tried to raise money for a medal or a monument for Jack. "He was a wonderful man," she told the *Dallas Times Herald* in 1986.

A little-known literary gem, *Jack Ruby's Girls*, published in 1970 by Genesis Press in Atlanta, gives an insider's peep into Ruby and his club. IN LOVING MEMORY OF JACK RUBY reads the dedication by Diana Hunter and Alice Anderson. Profiled within was the love-hate relationship of half a dozen Ruby strippers.

"Jack Ruby's Carousel Club was in the heart of a city that never took the Carousel to its heart," wrote the authors. Anyone who reads on will understand why. "Dumping" champagne was a Carousel ritual. Girls accidentally spilled bottles of the rotgut, marked up to $17.50 from the $1.60 wholesale price. Ruby beer went for sixty cents a glass, and it wasn't fit to drink. The girls were told to waste as much as possible while sitting with the suckers in the booths. But Ruby didn't allow hooking, claimed the authors; only the false promise of sex so that the girls could hustle champagne.

Before the Kennedy assassination, Dallas had a small-town camaraderie that may seem odd today. Ruby was friendly with many people in law enforcement and often brought sandwiches up to police headquarters. Free drinks went to the servicemen, even reporters, with whom Ruby tried to ingratiate himself. That's why he didn't seem out of place in the basement where Oswald was shot.

Today, most of the strippers who worked for Ruby have evaporated from Dallas. "I didn't live forty-seven years by talking about it," spat the ex-husband of a Ruby stripper, who hung up on me when I called to interview him. One former Ruby associate, when asked for the whereabouts of the girls, put it this way: "I would figure most became prostitutes or addicts or died. A stripper's career is ten years, and the few who survive afterward must be quite strong and pull their lives together."

Ruby's girls were not that strong. Suicides became part of the conspiracy lore. Baby LeGrand, whom Ruby wired money to minutes before killing Oswald, was found

hung by her toreador pants in an Oklahoma City holding cell in 1965. She had been arrested on prostitution charges, and her death was ruled a suicide. Tuesday Nite was another suicide.

Not many people came to visit Ruby in jail, according to Ray Abner, who was assigned to guard his cell for more than a year following his arrest. "None of the girls came to see him," Abner says. Just his lawyers, his sister Eva, and his brother Earl. "I couldn't help but overhear his conversations, so I'm pretty sure he wasn't involved in any conspiracy."

Ruby was riding high during the months after he shot Oswald. He doted on his daily shipment of fan mail, over fifty letters a day congratulating him, calling him a hero. "But after a while," Abner remembers, "the fan mail dropped off, and he got depressed."

Ruby was convicted, and he died of cancer in January 1967 while awaiting a retrial. In the meantime, those who made their living in his champagne hustle world had to go elsewhere for work. *Jack Ruby's Girls* documents the pilgrimage of two strippers after the Carousel closed: Lacy and Sue Ann applied for jobs at Madame DeLuce's upscale whorehouse in the Turtle Creek area of Dallas. But DeLuce believed Ruby "ruined" potential prostitutes—all tease, no sex is what Ruby taught them. He didn't allow that type of hanky-panky in the Carousel. "This is a *#%#@!* high-class place," he would remind any Tom, Dick, or Harry, as he kicked them down the stairs.

A Vote for the Man in the Ladies' Lingerie

I wanted to let you know about one of our local note-worthy inhabitants here in Austin. He's a homeless cross-dresser and sometime mayoral candidate.

Austin, perhaps more than any other city in Texas, knows how to have a good time. From the bars and bands of Sixth Street to the relaxation of Barton Springs, this town appreciates living right. There's one Austin resident who goes above and beyond all others in his quest to live a uniquely enjoyable life: His name is Leslie Cochran.

Leslie was formerly very visible, living in a makeshift lean-to he constructed for himself on Sixth Street. His home stood out not just because of its location, but because of the numerous messages Leslie painted on its side, explaining his plight in life as well as accusing the Austin government and Police Department of various wrongdoings. After a number of years spent in this abode, Leslie was forced to move along by the Austin police. He is still often seen around town, just not at this permanent location.

Austin residents have come to embrace this eccentric character. This has been proven time and time again during the city's mayoral elections, in which Leslie usually runs. In the last election, he received over two thousand votes for mayor of one of the state's most prominent cities. Leslie Cochran is undoubtedly a local hero of the highest caliber.—*Kent W.*

Shorty, Celebrity Squirrel

It isn't your typical community that accepts homeless freeloaders into the neighborhood. After all, nobody wants a hirsute vagrant pestering people for morsels, especially around the city's historic downtown square. In Tyler, however, citizens not only tolerated their local mooch, they were downright fond of him. Shorty, as he came to be known, frequented the grounds of the Smith County Courthouse, regularly begging folks for food and attention. The locals were happy to accommodate him. The town even went so far as to install a special pedestrian crossing and to lower the speed limit along Broadway for his safety.

It just goes to show how far being cute and charming can get you. After all, Shorty's fat, furry cheeks were probably pretty tough to say no to. Not to mention his bushy little tail. For fifteen years, Shorty called the square home. When he finally passed away, in 1963, Tyler decided that's where he should be buried too. Residents organized a funeral for the little guy and laid him to rest in a park across from the courthouse. A marker was erected bearing his image.

Not everyone had so much respect for Tyler's mascot, though. Twice, hooligans made off with Shorty's grave marker. The police located the missing marker the first time but weren't so lucky the second. Though the city eventually replaced the headstone, it's a surprise they did, since most residents seem to have forgotten about Shorty, anyway. There's no mention of him in any of Tyler's online visitor information, and both the city staff and local historians don't have much more than a vague recollection of his story. Despite having been memorialized right in the center of town, Shorty seems to have passed into obscurity. It just makes you wonder how many other fuzzy little mascots are out there—their stories forgotten, their tiny caskets overlooked.

I swear Pop, I have no idea how this gigantic monument to a long-dead squirrel got in my room.

Ron Sitton: Quintessential Texan

Red bandanna around his neck and toothpick between his teeth, Stetson-crowned and mustachioed, Ron Sitton is the image of the Lone Star State distilled down to its iconic elements. He is a rare surviving member of a species that has mostly devolved into a line dance of starched blue jeans and loud-striped shirts.

Along with his beefy companion, a longhorn steer named Shiloh, Sitton can be found most of the week at the historic Fort Worth Stockyards, once a working center of cattle trade, now a family-oriented tourist stop. He's there to chat with the visitors, kidding them with a friendly wisecrack in his soft-spoken Texas drawl. He keeps a Polaroid camera in Shiloh's saddlebag and sells photos to anyone daring enough to mount the massive bovine creature. Of course, Shiloh is as tame as can be. On cue, he'll turn his head and pose for the camera.

Sitton is no dressed-up "streetmosphere" cowboy, though. He's the real deal. At his ranch, he breaks and trains two-thousand-pound Texas longhorns. He likes to call himself the cow whisperer. His favorite pastime, though, is meeting people and making them laugh. That's why he comes out to the stockyards.

"You know what people want?" he asks. "Just to laugh and have a good time, forget all their worries. A lot of people have complexed their lives. If you take a few seconds or a couple of minutes to break 'em up, put all that behind 'em, then you're doing good. You're doing good with society."

That philosophy has made him a pretty popular guy in these parts. When he's not at the stockyards, he's out by request at parties and conventions. His charismatic persona has led to campaigns for Schepps Milk, Justin Boots, Kellogg's, and Ford. He's been on MTV, shot promos for *COPS* and *American Chopper*, and taken part in shoots for *Penthouse*. He's worked with George Strait, Governor Rick Perry, Vanna White, and Madonna. He did some work for Bill Clinton, too, though he declines to say exactly what it was.

In usual cowboy fashion, Sitton speaks humbly of his adventures. He loves to tell the stories but takes his fame in stride, just as he did one action-packed summer day in 2004. As he tells it, Sitton and another of his companions, a longhorn named Buckwheat, were out doing their usual hobnobbing at the stockyards. "All of a sudden," Sitton recalls, "this lady come flying around the corner over here on a horse and said, 'Somebody's breaking in a car! Somebody's breaking in a car!'" So Sitton climbed onto Buckwheat's saddle and giddy-apped down the street to check it out.

The would-be car thief got more than he bargained for. Before he knew it, the place was swarming with police, helicopters, and news reporters. Not the typical response for an attempted vehicle break-in, but when dispatch announces a man on a longhorn steer is chasing down a burglar, you can bet everyone with a scanner is going to want a peek.

The bandit tried to make a break for it, but he wasn't going to get past Buckwheat. Besides, the man in the white hat always prevails. Sitton grins and says, "We caught him!"

The Digitized Man

It was twenty-three minutes past midnight on August 5, 1993, as death-row inmate Joseph Paul Jernigan lay strapped in the execution chamber at Huntsville. Having donated his corporeal self for research, he knew that the body he had used, and misused, for the last thirty-nine years would in just eight minutes belong to science.

Jernigan had been sentenced to death more than a decade before as a result of a brutal murder in Dawson. While trying to make off with a seventy-five-year-old man's microwave oven, he and his accomplice were taken by surprise when the appliance's rightful owner unexpectedly returned home. Fearing the elderly man would be able to identify them, Jernigan attacked him, beating him repeatedly in the head with an ashtray, then stabbing him and firing a shotgun into his chest.

Years later, he would make an effort at redemption by willing himself to science. But as he anticipated the first of his injections and the unending sleep it would bring, he was entirely unaware what his gift to science would lead to. Unbeknownst to Jernigan, researchers were at that moment awaiting his corpse, making preparations to undertake a unique endeavor.

After Jernigan's execution, his body was prepared, air freighted (postage: $201.88), and unpacked in a lab in Colorado. In just eight hours, Jernigan had become the property of the Center for Human Simulation, an organization whose goal it was to digitize an entire cadaver into a versatile, medically accurate, three-dimensional model of gross human anatomy. Joseph Paul Jernigan was destined to become the new definition of man.

The transformation, however, wouldn't be pretty. Following preparatory scans, Jernigan was cleaved into large sections— cut across the chest, thighs, and calves— and set in blocks of blue gelatin like chunks of banana in a Jell-O mold. He was then deep-frozen and, one block at a time, mounted onto a device called the cryomacrotome, a movable table equipped with a fourteen-inch saw blade.

Section by section, the individual Jernigan-cicles were sliced away in increments thinner than a piece of prewrapped cheese. Each slice was photographed and subjected to CT and MRI scans. Jernigan was becoming something like the reverse of Frankenstein's monster.

Once he had been shaved entirely away—a process that took nine months to complete—he was reconstituted into fifteen gigabytes of data and made available on the Internet. There, the former convict from Waco was reincarnated as the Visible Human, an interactive model that could be explored inside and out by anyone with a Web browser. He lives on via computers all over the world, with everyday Joes enjoying fly-throughs of his bones, his brain, his colon.

He has also become the basis for a variety of medical applications and instructional tools that present a level of detail not previously achieved, making it possible to demonstrate cutting-edge procedures without risk to living patients. Jernigan is a whole body ripe for experimentation. That is, with a couple of exceptions. He's missing his appendix. And a testicle.

If you haven't seen him yet, here are a couple of links that give a sample of the scientists' handiwork: www.nlm.nih.gov/research/visible/visible_human.html and www.uchsc.edu/sm/chs.

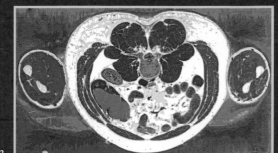

abdomen

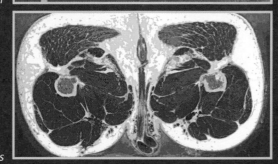

thighs

head

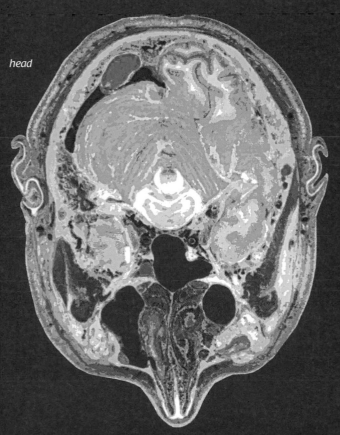

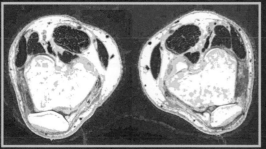

knees

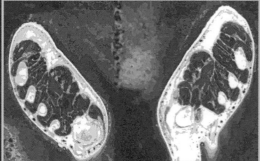

feet

The Texas Poultry King

In the town of Pittsburg, a giant hat—bolted to an equally gigantic cranium—casts its shadow across U.S. 271. The hat is a tall black number ornamented with a smart, sassy buckle like those worn by the men who landed at Plymouth Rock, a distinctive visual that might lead the unsuspecting to assume the display to be some strange tribute to Thanksgiving.

The look, however, is not accidental. The enormous head belongs to Bonnie "Bo" Pilgrim. It, and the oversize hat it wears, is the trademark image with which the Texas chicken king has marketed his line of Pilgrim's Pride poultry products for years. It's a look that became so well connected with Bo's chickens, in fact, that he made it the company's logo.

Bo also stars in the company's television ads, rising to the rare status of food-industry celeb, much like Colonel Sanders and Dave Thomas (for both of

whom, incidentally, Bo acted as a supplier). Sporting a black suit and his colonial-style hat, the bespectacled pitchman has for years been remembered for his deadpan "I won't sell a fat, yella chicken," delivered while cradling his feathered friend Henrietta. Well into his seventies, Bo still hawks his fowl in commercials notorious for their almost-used-car-sales goofiness, manning the chuck wagon for a group of diet-conscious cowboys or formation skydiving with hens in tiny parachutes.

Although his company, which began as a simple feed store in the 1940s, now brings in more than $5 billion in net sales annually, Bo Pilgrim continues to make his home in rural Pittsburg, near company headquarters. Nestled among the other residents' humble dwellings, the chicken mogul's eight-bedroom, nine-bathroom,

Louis XV–style mansion sticks out like the thirty-seven-foot-tall noggin at the other end of town. The locals refer to the twenty-thousand-square-foot manor, which is secured by gates adorned with the Bo-head logo, as Cluckingham Palace.

The Pilgrim presence is just as obvious across the rest of town too. In addition to Bo's mansion and giant bust, there are also the Pilgrim's Pride Distribution Center, Pilgrim's Feed Mill, Pilgrim's Pride Farm Supply, and yes, even Pilgrim Bank. Pittsburg is often spoken of as "Bo's town." But there are no obvious complaints of autocracy here; the poultry potentate appears to be rather generous with the community, supporting local events, donating park facilities, and personally teaching Sunday school. It's like living in Pottersville, but with a kinder, gentler Mr. Potter; A Wonderful Life after all.

Sporting a black suit and his colonial-style hat, the bespectacled pitchman has for years been remembered for his deadpan "I won't sell a fat, yella chicken," delivered while cradling his feathered friend Henrietta.

Bo hasn't remained above reproach, however. He received nationwide and mostly critical press in 1989 for his farcically bold performance in the state's capitol, which was momentarily dubbed Cackle-gate. As the Texas legislature was preparing to vote on a workers'-compensation bill, of which Bo was in favor, the chicken tycoon walked onto the senate floor and began to openly hand out $10,000 checks. Though some legislators turned him down, many accepted, returning the checks only after the news media got hold of the story. In the end, Bo's exploit fueled a heated ethics debate that led to

a reform in campaign-contribution laws.

Bo later admitted that he learned a valuable lesson from the ordeal, which he was able to sum up in three words: "automatic fund transfer." Really, though, when you consider it, the issue shouldn't have been such a big deal. To a man who unashamedly confesses to be worth several hundred million dollars, a stack of ten-grand checks is chicken feed.

Personalized Properties

Oh, Give Me a Home on the Strange!

t is said that a man's home is his castle, but in Texas, that statement is only partially true. Yes, some of the state's residents actually do live in castles, but there are others who live encased in beer cans, in vampire houses, or in oddly shaped constructions of their own design. Their homes may not be up for any decorating awards, but they are clear expressions of their creators' individuality.

These unique home owners may be artists whose work cannot be confined to studios or galleries and spills over into the immediate surroundings. But more often, they are folks with little or no connection to the mainstream art world. They are self-taught and self-styled, inspired by their own very personal fantasies.

Looking at some of these properties, we can only wonder what might have been in the mind of the owners. But perhaps it's better not to know. Suffice it to say that these folks followed their unique vision and created their own, slightly off-center environment in which to spend their lives.

Alamo House

For a confrontation in which the home team took such a nasty whomping, the battle of the Alamo seems to be a source of never-ending pride. This "Shrine of Texas Liberty," the site of the most famous, if not the most successful, battle for Texas independence, endures as a cherished state icon. In fact, the Alamo is so closely associated with Texas that you can't travel anywhere in the state without being reminded of it. The name appears on labels for beer, cologne, hotels, steak sauce—you name it. There's even an Alamo car rental.

So naturally, with so much Alamo enthusiasm going around, Texans wouldn't be satisfied with just one. At present count, there are no fewer than four Alamos scattered across the state. In addition to the original one in San Antonio, there are Alamos in Brackettville and outside Dripping Springs—the first the location for the John Wayne film *The Alamo* and now a kind of theme park, the latter a movie set for the more recent cinematic release. That particular Alamo is presently available for weddings and school field trips.

Possibly the best testament to Alamo pride, however, is the replica in Holiday Lakes, just northwest of Angleton. An unmistakable likeness of the San Antonio mission, it's a custom-built private home.

The building was constructed in 1989 by Ken Freeman, a brick mason who came up with the idea while killing time with some hunting buddies. Supposedly, his friends challenged his ability to carry out the harebrained scheme, so he committed himself to proving them wrong. The result was an eighteen-hundred-square-foot three-bedroom, two-bath house, with a barracks to boot.

The current residents, who moved in sometime in 2003, say the fact that the house resembles the Alamo didn't have a lot of impact on their purchase, but it's still pretty cool. The place needs a little work, they say, but they currently have no plans to change its appearance.

Of course, the original didn't have so many NO TRESPASSING signs on the lawn, though it may have helped if it did.

Little Graceland

There came a point when Simon Vega's wife got tired of having strange people constantly in her Los Fresnos house. The people were there by invitation from her husband to look at his Elvis Presley memorabilia, but that didn't help Mrs. Vega's mood. So Simon did what any true Elvis fan would do: He added a second story to his garage, moved everything up there, and created a two-room museum that he called Little Graceland.

Naturally, as these things go, Little Graceland has since extended beyond the garage and invaded the rest of the property. Vega built a gate across his driveway that looks very much like the one at the original Graceland, as well as a duplicate of the familiar stone wall that visitors have covered with signatures.

Vega is no ordinary Elvis fan (if there is such a thing). He actually knew the King. He served with him in the army in Germany, an association that obviously left a big impression on him.

The house in which Elvis was born, in Tupelo, Mississippi, is a landmark attraction. But Simon has his own model, built to scale. About the size of a small playhouse, it is an exact replica, complete with a copy of the original historical marker.

Upstairs in the museum, visitors can see the usual Elvis memorabilia — records, T-shirts, collectors' plates — plus some less common items, like the Good Conduct Medal that Elvis earned in the army. Elvis gave it to Vega personally when they were both stationed in Germany.

In January and August, Vega hosts a festival around the dates of the King's birth and death. The first festival was held about ten years ago, attended by about twenty people. Now the event has grown to nearly one thousand fans, who make the drive to southern Texas to enjoy food, music, and, of course, Elvis impersonators.

As Vega said to a local newspaper, "Elvis told me once he wanted to make people happy and that's why he performed. I'm trying to do the same thing, keeping people happy in his name."

Munster Mansion

Martha Stewart living it's not. Okay, she might approve of the antiques, but the gargoyles and the electric chair probably wouldn't appeal to her sensibilities. Then again, the secret dungeon might. Who knows?

These accommodations, located in suburban Waxahachie, aren't for the *House Beautiful* crowd anyway. They're all part of a theme cooked up by Charles and Sandra McKee, a fairly normal couple who've chosen to live in an admittedly abnormal residence. They've spent several years now reconstructing as accurately as possible the Victorian-style mansion from the 1960s sitcom *The Munsters*.

They'll admit that making a fictional dwelling a reality is a bit unusual, but their results are impressive. Except for a few things here and there, the McKees have hit the mark—1313 Mockingbird Lane has left TV Land and materialized deep in the heart of Texas.

Just inside the front doors is the mansion's ascending signature oak staircase, at the bottom

of which, as rerun watchers may recall, Lily kisses the family good-bye every morning. Not only has the staircase been designed with the proper number of steps, but its center part raises up to reveal the McKees' fire-breathing house pet.

Next to the stairs, you'll find the Munsters' coffin-shaped phone booth, something Sandra at first felt was too creepy to have in her home, though she eventually relented to have it included for the sake of accuracy.

The living room, as of yet, houses no obnoxious raven, but it does boast an organ, a handmade replica of Grandpa's electric chair, and drapes that were custom-made to match those on the original set. The McKees even included the trapdoor that leads down into Grandpa's laboratory, which is actually a storm shelter, a facility more practical for Texas.

The second floor comprises the Munsters' bedrooms, arranged as they would have been on TV: one for Herman and Lily, one for Grandpa, one for the beautiful Marilyn, and one for young Eddie, which features a bookcase behind which is a secret passageway just for kicks.

With a bit of dusting—the vacuum set on BLOW instead

It's no surprise; the McKees spent hours poring over photos and videotapes to nail down the details. Yet because a sufficient portion of the floor plan was kept offscreen, they were able to incorporate some personal space as well.

of SUCK—you'd think the Munsters actually live here. It's no surprise, since the McKees spent hours poring over photos and videotapes to nail down the details. Yet because a sufficient portion of the floor plan was kept offscreen, they were able to incorporate some personal space as well. Most importantly, as Sandra pointed out, "they never showed the bathrooms. So we were lucky on that one."

It's certainly not your typical do-it-yourselfer, which is why the Munster Mansion has attracted unremitting attention. After all, a re-creation of a Gothic sitcom house sticks out in suburban Texas like Herman's forehead. However, save for a neighbor who called the house an eyesore on a local radio show and a group of churchgoers who spread rumors about the building's housing a cult, the attention has been positive—so positive, in fact, that the McKees have played host to three of the original Munsters cast members and have been able to organize a growing Halloween charity event. Weird stuff can pay off if you play your coffins right.

Ira Poole's Lawn of Liberty

In 1987, Austin citizen Ira Poole held a press conference in his front yard on East Martin Luther King Jr. Boulevard for the dedication of a new monument. In a town where residents sculpt giant blue genies and spray-paint their lawns with polka dots, a bit of yard art wasn't unusual.

Unlike most others, though, Ira's display had purpose. A man proud of his country, he had assembled a commemorative to the bicentennial of the U.S. Constitution. As he wrote in his press release, he wanted to honor "the most famous document ever written in the history of the United States." He unveiled the monument on the Fourth of July, a tribute to all the symbols of the United States, he explained.

Cast in concrete is the continental U.S., bounded by rock beds marking the Pacific and Atlantic oceans. Towering above is a model of the Statue of Liberty that Ira had picked up at an antiques shop, and behind that flies Old Glory. A waterfall beneath Lady Liberty stands in for Niagara Falls.

At the edges of the display are a braided hibiscus and a smallish boulder. "This represents Hawaii out in the Pacific," Ira says of the tree. "The big rock is Alaska." There's also a slab in the shape of Mexico, sporting a tiny bullfighter.

Planted at the other end of the yard is a nine-hundred-pound sphinx, sculpted to scale, an unrelated item Ira had made in the 1970s. Molded from a model he and his students had built when he taught fifth grade, it rests on a foundation shaped like Texas.

Originally, Ira wanted to construct his tribute to the Constitution as a class project. "I was going to do it just like I did working with the kids making that sphinx. I was just being patriotic and teaching the children." The school staff, strangely, couldn't see it that way and said no. "They didn't want me to do it there. They thought I had some kind of political ambition."

He unveiled the monument on the Fourth of July, a tribute to all the symbols of the United States.

So Ira figured that "if they don't want it, I'll just put it in my yard." And so he did. It's there now, a reminder to any passerby of one man's love for his country.

A Cathedral of Junk

If you are in Austin, don't miss Vince Hannemann's tower of refuse out on Lareina Drive. It's a truly amazing amalgamation of other people's castoffs. Cruising its corridors, you feel as if you're drifting through a record of your life chronicled in the form of everything you've ever discarded. To your left is the plastic rocking horse you got for your sixth Christmas, and to your right is the coffeemaker from your college dorm. High above hangs the hideous lamp you thought looked cool over your wet bar and the crutches you earned hanging it.

Hours could be wasted discovering the memory-provoking items inside this veritable Cathedral of Junk as you inspect its various nooks and the obscure castoffs therein. A careful search uncovers works within the work — smaller junk-based sculptures growing out of the larger structure's walls. If you could tear away its layers, the cathedral would yield more surprises, revealing its hidden secrets to you much the way the all-knowing Trash Heap did to her friends on Fraggle Rock.

Vince estimates that the assemblage weighs about sixty tons and consists of stuff previously deemed no longer useful: mailboxes, street signs, old typewriters, and on and on. There are over seven hundred bicycles, as well as half a dozen motorcycles and some fifteen weed eaters. Vince once inventoried the cathedral and compiled a list of its components so he could print them on T-shirts. He says it takes about twenty minutes just to read it.

Though he was once referred to as a "mini Christo," and accused of looking for publicity rather than trying to create real art, Vince confesses that neither really applies. To him, it's just something to do. He equates it to a child's fort or a clubhouse. "It's like, why build a sandcastle? It's just to have fun. It was kind of my version of escaping. Make my own little private world, you know? The way I want it. Playing is the main reason why."

Vince has been playing with his cathedral since he moved into his house in 1989. Around 2000, however, recess nearly came to an end when Vince made a brief decision to scrap the whole project. Owing to what he calls "a little mental craziness," he began tearing his creation apart and selling its parts for scrap. "I just wanted to move out of here and get away."

He continues with a smirk, "Obviously, that didn't work. It was impossible. I hurt myself trying to take it down. The back tower was three stories tall." Vince dismantled the first two stories and called it quits. "It's just too solid," he said, laughing.

He's since returned to his senses—or left them again, however you see it—and is currently rebuilding.

Beer Can House

To say John Milkovisch merely enjoyed a cold one is like saying Houston roads occasionally experience a little congestion. The man simply loved his brew. Consuming a six-pack a day, he believed it was the cure to whatever ailed him.

But he also believed in never throwing anything away. At a rate of roughly 2,200 beers a year, that sort of thinking quickly generates an overwhelming stockpile of empties. And there was only so much room in the garage of his Houston home. Eventually, something had to be done.

Since Milkovisch couldn't bring himself to throw the cans away, recycling was his only option. Now, to most people, that would mean dumping the cans at the local sorting facility and collecting a few quarters. But Milkovisch had a better idea.

By 1968, he had already begun to demonstrate a knack for distinctive home improvement. He was paving over both his front and back lawns with concrete—he said he was tired of mowing—embedding rocks, bits of metal, and other items in the concrete. He created mosaics in the pavement and erected woodwork inlaid with marbles.

Then the cans came into play. Milkovisch cut off the ends and flattened the cylinders to form sheets, then connected the sheets to form panels and fastened them to the outside of his house. He joined the tops and bottoms of the cans into chains and hung them from the eaves. He even saved the pull tabs, linking them to create glistening curtains of beverage-container nostalgia.

From the looks of it, Milkovisch didn't appear to favor one brand of beer over another. Reportedly, he would buy whatever was on sale, which explains the assortment of labels adorning the house: Jax, Texas Pride, Pearl Light, Falstaff. Some of those you can't even buy anymore.

The additions continued until Milkovisch's death in 1988, though his son, Ronnie, briefly carried on his father's work. Today, the house is pretty much the way John Milkovisch left it, though the labels are fading and the occasional aluminum chain comes free.

After his wife, Mary, passed away in 2002, the house was acquired by the Orange Show Center for Visionary Art, a Houston organization dedicated to preserving folk-art projects. At present, the Beer Can House, which is at 222 Malone Street, is closed to visitors, but plans are in the works to restore the site and open it as a museum. In the meantime, the exterior is well worth seeing.

Mysterious Kettle House

You probably wouldn't consider steel to be the best building material for a salty environment, but the composition of the Mysterious Kettle House on Galveston's shores is just one of its puzzling traits. Consider, for example, that it's also the only structure in sight that isn't on stilts, another unusual design choice for a building so close to the water. Nevertheless, the Kettle has existed for some fifty years.

Supposedly it was erected by a gentleman who used to build storage tanks for oil companies, though his exact identity is unknown. The neighbors, some of whom were residents when the Kettle went up, have seen the man but know little about him.

One local says the structure, which he refers to as the Tank, was originally built to serve as a convenience store, though it never opened. It just sits empty. On occasion, someone will show up, do a little work, then disappear for years. There have been reports of strange figures arriving in the wee hours of the morning, performing some arcane maneuver with a winch, then vanishing. No one would be seen again for months.

Activity at the site, though still intermittent, appears to have increased in recent years. About the turn of the century, the owner (or owners—nobody's sure) removed the Kettle's rusting top and added a wooden roof. Since then, the windows have been replaced, air-conditioning has been installed, and a mailbox has materialized near the road. Still, no one lives there.

Rumor has it that the city was displeased with the deteriorating hulk and that the improvements were simply to keep the Kettle from being torn down. But who is so intent on keeping the structure intact?

Until it spins off its foundation and ascends into the sky, we may never know.

Steel House

When a house like this reaches so far beyond any equivalent, it makes for a difficult explanation. You can stare at it as you would at a cloud and see it constantly change shape, transforming from some kind of splashdown from space into a Tim Burtonesque toy factory. It even changes color as clouds pass above it on Canyon View Drive in Lubbock, shifting from a muted brown to a bright, saturated orange. But it won't remain the same long enough to classify. "Organic machine," to paraphrase its creator, is probably as close as you can get.

The neighborhood kids, of course, have an easier time with it. They just call it the Jetsons House. And it really could be the home of some futuristic people who rocket to the moon just for fun.

Robert Bruno, the soft-spoken sculptor-welder-designer who fathered the creation, says he didn't start the whole thing to become a home owner; he just enjoys sculpting. He admits that the Lubbock area isn't a place that offers a lot of distractions, so when he moved there to teach architecture at Texas Tech, he knew he would need a project that would keep him busy.

And keep him busy it has. The first pieces went up in 1974, and he's still working on it. Why thirty years? That's a question Robert gets asked fairly often. "That's how long it takes me to do it," he'll reply casually. He didn't plan for the work to last this long, but the house became more complex than he had originally envisioned.

Anyone who gets a close look will understand. The entire shell is a patchwork of quarter-inch-thick steel puzzle pieces, cut as needed and individually welded. Arcs and trapezoids

interconnect and lead in different directions to form arches and windowsills. The interior is even more intricate, with its multifaceted columns, platforms, and stairways. Technically the building is three stories, though that's hard to define with the way the living space continually drifts in three dimensions. There's definitely something alien about it. Yet it fits in naturally with the surrounding rough Texas terrain.

The indigenous characteristic can be accounted for. Robert, an artist and intellectual who loves to speak of intent and use words like "substantive," admits that if there was one outside influence on the project, it would be the harsh outdoor environment he has worked in for

three decades. As for the extraterrestrial aspect, well, ask him where he's from, and he'll joke, "Another planet?" (Turns out that he had lived in California previously, but that really ends up being the same answer.)

In 2004, Robert reached a stage that enabled him to sell his "cardboard house," his term for the flimsy Sheetrock dwellings of other mortals, and to finally take up residence in his more distinctive accommodations. Though he doesn't mind people taking quiet snapshots from the outside, moving in means he's had to put an end to visitor tours. He's now working on the interior, with its stained glass and wooden accents. With any luck, the drapes will be up by 2014.

A Concrete Menagerie

Sometimes retirement is roadside tourism's best friend. It not only allows for extended meandering to the less-crowded areas of the map but is often responsible for yielding some of the most unusual attractions.

Audrey the dinosaur is one result. She's a fifty-foot-long, seventeen-foot-high apatosaur overlooking U.S. 60/83 in an upper corner of the Panhandle. Audrey—or Aud, as her owner calls her—watches over traffic into and out of the town of Canadian, acting as the town's unofficial greeter.

Gene Cockrell, the dino's friendly creator, says he put her there for the kids. When he was young, there was an old cedar tree near that spot that, he says, looked like a bear, which he always kept an eye out for when going to town. He built Aud in its place so that a new generation would have something to look for. "And they do," he says with a smile. "They look for it!"

Anyone who stops in Canadian and asks about Audrey will discover, however, that she isn't Gene's only creation. Several years of retirement have produced a virtual zoo in his front yard. He started out making arrowheads, but having tired of that, he began fabricating concrete statues.

He has about thirty pieces scattered around his place, including a spaceship, Indians, a satyr, cacti, and more dinosaurs. There are two statues of Jesus—one standing, one nailed to a cross. A tree has grown up in front of the latter. The cross would be too hard to relocate, but Gene can't bring himself to cut down the tree.

Gene says his wife likes most of the figures he's created, though she can't say much about the two women he's sculpted. There's a cowgirl out front that started out in the nude, though she didn't stay that way for long. "My wife and another lady—they put clothes

on her real quick," he says. The other, a concrete girl, is dressed too and out back.

Gene's little theme park gets quite a few visitors. Naturally, a lot of them include children, who can't help but climb all over everything, sometimes breaking teeth in the process (the animals', not their own). Gene put up a warning sign, but the children usually ignore it. He doesn't mind so much, though. He says he just likes that people enjoy what he's made.

Still, he has a hard time believing how many people stop by. He's glad they like his work, but he doesn't consider himself to be an artist. If you tell him you drive around looking for attractions just like his, he might ask you, as he did one visitor, "You go all over the country looking at junk like this?"

Giant Ladybugs and Sunflowers Beloved of Motorcycle Gangs

Considering the fuss the art community has made in recent years over what they like to label as folk art, it seems that those actually responsible for it rarely understand what the big stink is all about.

"It's just a conversation piece" is how Earl Nunneley explains his contribution to the genre. To him, it's no big deal. "When I semiretired, I just didn't have enough to do."

Now in his late seventies, Earl has entertained himself the last decade or so by constructing eye-catching works on a plot of land in Saint Jo, near the Oklahoma border. Although he began the display simply as a way to keep busy, it eventually became such an attention grabber that he was compelled to move his fence back to accommodate parking. Apparently, the sights are especially popular with the motorcycle crowd, who stop there in groups as large as fifty at a time, their flashy Hogs lined up along the country road.

Situated on Earl's Running N Ranch, the works are mostly assembled from thirty-five-foot utility poles, which Earl treats like big boys' Popsicle sticks. Towering over the collection are a pair of enormous cacti and what has to be one of the world's largest weather vanes. Weighing three tons, it balances on a one-inch pin.

The most prominent piece, and the first one Earl created, consists of fourteen poles arranged in a fan. Embedded into five feet of limestone rock, the array of poles is aligned with the sun to make a single shadow

during the vernal and autumnal equinoxes. Why? As his brother Jerry explains it, "It's just one of them things. He just wanted to do it, and he done it."

At one time, Earl had giant sunflowers in his field assembled, in part, from satellite dishes. Unfortunately, a thunderstorm made quick work of those. "Lightning struck them and just put them into splinters," Earl laments. He has since replaced the superflowers with smaller versions made of rotary aircraft engines, which he paints different colors each year for a fresh look.

Earl also likes to annually rearrange his ladybugs—five Volkswagens adorned with spots and, when they're not being fixed up, usually appended with insect legs.

Earl says he has a new item on the drawing board, which he hopes to have up sometime soon. That's the most he's willing to divulge on the subject, though, because he likes to keep his ideas a secret until they're completed. All he'll say is, "It's a very nice one, another conversation piece."

Monument to the Perfect Food

"I say it is the most beautiful show on earth, the most colorful show on earth, and the most unique show on earth." Such are the words the late Jeff McKissack modestly used to describe his Orange Show, a highly unusual and perplexing tribute to what he believed to be the world's most perfect food.

Starting with a plant nursery, McKissack began constructing the attraction on Munger Street, across from his Houston home, in 1968. He gave a variety of reasons for starting the project, which included his continuing failure to build the perfect orange juicer, as well as the inspiration he had gained from a handshake he had once shared with the inventor Thomas Edison—who, incidentally, hailed from West Orange (New Jersey).

The result is a visual hurly-burly structure of mosaics, spoked wheels, and whirligigs. Signs proclaiming GO ORANGE, BE STRONG and BE SMART, DRINK FRESH ORANGE JUICE adorn the walls. Passages lead to multiple spaces and levels, partitioned by multicolored railings and connected by occasionally treacherous stairways. Though the assemblage takes up only three thousand square feet, it's easy to get disoriented.

A multitude of puzzling displays fills the Orange Show. A scarecrow, a butter churn, a steam engine, a mannequin in a bridal gown—no matter how off the subject it seemed, McKissack always found some way to link it back to oranges.

Facing the various display areas are nearly a hundred painted tractor seats, many of which occupy a mezzanine overlooking what's known as "the pond." This is where McKissack built a mock steamboat with which he planned a stage show. Battery-operated animals were to ride on the boat and put on some kind of performance. McKissack insisted that people wouldn't know if the animals were real or not, though it's difficult to tell whether he was being facetious or just a bit delusional.

When he finally opened the attraction in 1979, McKissack believed his orange-themed opus would draw four out of every five Americans, becoming more popular than Disneyland or the Grand Canyon. The crowds he was sure would come didn't materialize though, and the hopeful visionary passed away eight months later. Some

believe he died of a broken heart.

But he would be happy to know that the Orange Show was purchased soon thereafter and preserved almost exactly as he had built it. In addition, the effort spawned the Orange Show Center for Visionary Art, an organization that promotes and maintains similar projects throughout

Houston. The foundation has been so successful, in fact, that it has attracted more than half a million visitors to the Orange Show since its creator's death. Perhaps McKissack will get his message out after all.

Plastic Flower Man

If you want to find Cleveland Turner, ask almost anyone in Houston's Third Ward where you should go. Just tell them you're looking for the Flower Man.

"Oh, yeah! The Flower Man! Take a left down there. You'll see him!"

Cleveland is recognized throughout the neighborhood, pedaling around on his bicycle adorned with plastic flowers. He gets a "Hey, Flower Man!" just about everywhere he goes.

And his house is as well known as he is. Painted in vibrant colors and decorated with old toys, broken clocks, paintings—just about anything Cleveland finds—it's a fantastical incongruity in what is a mostly impoverished community. Surrounded by blocks of decaying buildings, it sticks out cheerfully in a neighborhood of sore thumbs.

"I find most of my stuff out in West University," he says. "That's out in the rich folks' neighborhood."

That's also where Cleveland works, tending the gardens of affluent residents, who are happy to let him sift through their junk. Every day, he'll cart something home to add to his display, which leads to a series of ever-changing arrangements. In a year's time, it's a totally different show.

Cleveland once lived in a smaller, corner, house a few blocks away. He didn't have much of a yard, so his collection spilled out onto the curb and into the street. He even had a display in a nearby lot, the centerpiece of which was a bright-red fiberglass cow that had been given to him at the end of a citywide public-art project. When he moved, the cow took to roosting up on Cleveland's roof. Home Depot helped him put it up there.

Amid his decorative junk, the Flower Man grows as many real blooms as he can find room for. "A house is not a house without flowers," his mother used to tell him. As a child, he would help her care for her flowers, which, Cleveland says, is how he learned to love them. "Anything that bloomed, I'd take care of it. I just really like flowers!" He even tended wildflowers in the days he was living on the streets.

You wouldn't know it by looking at him today, but for seventeen years, the Flower Man was homeless, hooked on Thunderbird wine, and eating out of Dumpsters. He was finally found close to death, lying in the weeds along Chenevert Street. After he spent several weeks in the hospital, clarity finally came to him, and he turned his life around.

Twenty years or so later, Cleveland is still dry and full of enthusiasm. Though he's entering his seventies, he doesn't look a day over fifty and radiates the energy of a man a third his age.

He'll cheerily welcome anyone into his house for a tour and a chat. He's always happy to tell his story and to explain some of his more prominent bits of junk, pausing occasionally to adjust an old doll or some Mardi Gras beads. And if you want to know about his decorating technique, he'll share that too. "Something that strikes my eyesight," he says. "If it looks good to me, it's going to look good to you. But if it don't look good to me, I'll take this here and move it down further. You just got to keep a-moving junk around till you get that— boom!—and say, 'Oh, there it is!' "

Roadside Oddities

As it turns out, there's one thing in Texas that isn't bigger after all. That's a Texan's capacity for restraint. It seems there's almost nothing Texans won't do to get people to turn in their direction. It's all part of that great big Texan personality thing. "Hey, over here! Look at me!"

This character trait is probably due in large part to the sheer scale of the state. What may turn a head anywhere else would merely recede in Texas into its vast expanses. It takes a particular effort just to remain on radar. Drawing any real attention requires something uniquely outrageous.

As a result, Texas is freckled with oddball expressions of individuality—attractions that are weird, sometimes perplexing, their owners seeking to divert motorists up their particular driveway. Whether a deliberately eye-catching *objet d'art* or the exploited remnants of a legend, these spectacles are perfect for breaking up those long, long drives on the state's 300,000 miles of roadway.

Anyone who has seen the film *Field of Dreams* probably remembers the scene when Kevin Costner is standing alone in the middle of a vast cornfield and hears a ghostly voice whispering, "If you build it, they will come." Well, apparently Costner's character is not the only one who has been hearing voices urging him to build things. Across the country we find strange and puzzling constructions erected by visionaries and dreamers. Why many were built and for whom is often a riddle, and may forever remain a mystery to all but their creators.

Eiffel Tower of Paris, Texas

Miss out on that trip to Paris while you were in college? Well, sew an American flag to your rucksack and strap it on your back, because you can take that trip after all—sort of. And there's no need for converting your dollars to those irksome euros. Heck, you won't even have to learn to say, "Où est la toilette?"

Just two hours northeast of Dallas, you'll discover the romantic city of Paris, where you and your amour can rendezvous beneath the majestic Eiffel Tower. Okay, so at only sixty-five feet, "majestic" might be overselling it. But for a short time, this attraction was the second-tallest Eiffel Tower in the world. It was bested when Paris, Tennessee, rebuilt its sixty-foot version with an added ten feet, and again when Las Vegas constructed a one-half-scale replica of the original Eiffel Tower shortly thereafter.

Rather than enter into a "which is the tallest" race, the people of Lamar County decided instead to make their landmark distinctly Texan. In 1998, a giant red cowboy hat was bolted to the top of the tower. It was a gimmick that has set Paris, Texas, apart from the others in a way that isn't likely to be duplicated.

Signs warn against climbing the tower, declaring it an "unsafe activity" in both English and Spanish, though, curiously, not in French. Climbing wouldn't do any good, anyway, since there's no observation deck. But if you find you can, swing by in midsummer. On the third Saturday of every July, the city holds a much scaled-down version of the Tour de France, which they call the Tour de Paris.

If that's still not enough for you, well, you're pretty much out of luck. French fever hasn't really caught on in the rest of the city, so there aren't that many options. If you look around, though, maybe you can find yourself a beret, a baguette, and a copy of *Gigi*.

Britten Leaning Water Tower

Before that big, showy cross moved in down the road—more about that later—the town of Groom's prime attraction was nothing but an old water tower. It wasn't exceptionally tall, it was never ablaze with blinding floodlights, and it didn't dole out measures of spiritual uplift. Yet travelers adored it all the same because it had a funny way about it: It listed a bit—you know, to the side.

Some thought it had been nearly toppled by an earthquake, while others, obviously more familiar with the Panhandle's geological track record, chalked it up to a passing tornado. The more imaginative placed blame on a clumsy aviator. Naturally, these were all just rumors and entirely unsubstantiated. If you had no shame, you might go for the cheap joke and say the rumors didn't hold water.

The real force responsible for the tower's tilt was far more powerful—and purely intentional. Yes, the lean was deliberate, a direct result of the most formidable influence known to man: American marketing. It worked like a charm too. Passing motorists pulled off the highway just to make sure they saw what they thought they saw. Next thing they knew, they were finding themselves in the parking lot of Ralph Britten's truck stop and restaurant, where the as-long-as-we're-here factor would take hold.

Originally, the tower was meant to serve as the restaurant's water supply. However, having found a simpler solution for water storage, Britten decided instead to have the tower serve as an attention getter. Using a bulldozer to lift the massive tank into place, Britten and his crew buried one side partway in the ground and set the whole thing at an eighty-degree angle, give or take a few degrees. According to Ralph's son Chris, who now owns his late father's slanted structure, the tower stands today as it did then: no anchors, no concrete, no guy wires. It's just balanced there, two of its legs completely off the ground. Thanks to his father's brainstorm, says Chris, the Leaning Tower Truck Stop was the talk of I 40. Truck drivers' CB radios echoed with gossip about the tower leaning farther and farther to the side, ready to collapse any day. People would come rushing in, yelling, "That tower's fixing to fall! That tower's fixing to fall!" Word spread, and curious travelers filled

the parking lot, while truckers lined up to take advantage of Ralph's diesel happy hour, when fuel was twenty cents cheaper by the gallon. Creative hype and a simple, off-kilter reservoir made the east end of Groom a hot spot of automotive activity.

It's just too bad there wasn't any water in the water tower. After five years or so of successful enterprise, an electrical fire closed the truck stop for good. Only the tower has survived.

Amazingly, Ralph Britten's gimmick still works. The Leaning Tower of Texas, as it's come to be called, continues to attract tourists and unsuspecting passersby off the highway, most of whom get a snapshot, posing in predictable fashion.

AUSTIN'S MOONLIGHT TOWERS

THIS IS ONE OF 31 ORIGINAL MOONLIGHT TOWERS INSTALLED IN AUSTIN IN 1895. SEVENTEEN REMAIN. EACH TOWER ILLUMINATED A CIRCLE OF 3000 FEET USING 6 CARBON ARC LAMPS (NOW MERCURY VAPOR). AUSTIN'S TOWER LIGHTS ARE THE SOLE SURVIVORS OF THIS ONCE-POPULAR, INGENIOUS LIGHTING SYSTEM. 1993

Moonlight Towers

They've endured tornadoes, wrecks, and city development. They were spurned, applauded, forgotten, eventually remembered, mended, revered, and, finally, forgotten again. A wider range of emotions has never been expressed over what are essentially streetlights. They are Austin's intermittently beloved Moonlight Towers, seventeen 165-foot spires of cast iron and wrought iron shining down on the city.

Though not much to look at today, they were once considered modern-day marvels. The bluish light they cast over the urban landscape was thought to be beautiful. Their unique radiance inspired O. Henry to call Austin the City of the Violet Crown.

You might not know it to look at them, but the towers are over a hundred years old. In the early 1890s, Austin made a deal with Detroit, to buy the towers for

$70,000 and some railroad tracks. Installed at thirty-one key points around the city, the lights were switched on, on May 6, 1895. Originally, they were topped with powerful carbon-arc lamps, a method of lighting that, incidentally, preceded Thomas Edison's incandescent bulb. The towers' manufacturer sold its system on the claim that anyone could read a watch by the light within a three-thousand-foot circle without squinting.

Subsequently, the Moonlight Towers had their detractors. Residents feared that the twenty-four-hour lighting would cause lawns to grow out of control. Farmers contended that their corn would become so tall that it would be impossible to harvest and that their hens would exhaust themselves producing eggs nonstop. Naturally, none of this came to pass, although some did report a few confused roosters cock-a-doodle-dooing at inconvenient hours of the night. The "artificial moonlight" of the carbon-arc lamps was maintained by one man, whose sole job was to trim the carbon filaments and to scale the towers each night to ignite them. The ascent was made easier by hand-operated elevators in the center of each truss, which still exist.

Eventually, the bright blue lamps were replaced with less appealing mercury-vapor bulbs, cutting back on maintenance. Additionally, switches were installed in each base, which were replaced during World War II with one central switch in preparation for air raids.

Only seventeen of the original thirty-one towers still remain. Some were damaged by weather, while others were removed in the name of progress. More than one tower fell victim to an unfortunate collision with a bus or some other wayward contraption. No injuries resulted from such incidents, but the towers haven't escaped human tragedy entirely. One unfortunate employee,

named Gilbert Searight, reportedly fell to his death from the tower at Guadalupe and West Ninth streets just weeks after its installation. *Ripley's Believe It or Not* told the story of eleven-year-old Jimmie Fowler, who fell from the top of the very same tower thirty-five years later, bouncing along the framework sixteen stories to the ground. He awoke from a coma nine days later, coming away with nothing more than 187 stitches.

In fact, the very existence of the Moonlight Towers may be a direct result of human casualty. A decade before they were erected, Austin was terrorized by a string of brutal murders. Eight people, almost all women, were discovered throughout the city with their bodies sliced open and their skulls split open. City leaders met to discuss ways of ending the killings, and the idea was put forth to floodlight the entire city. The arc-light towers were the solution.

By the mid-1980s, the Moonlight Towers had served their purpose and were all but obsolete. Having fallen into disrepair, they were becoming a hazard. Removing them was out of the question, since the steeples were an all-too-familiar part of Austin. So the city began a restoration plan that concluded with a celebration on the towers' one hundredth anniversary. The mayor proclaimed May 1995 to be Moonlight Tower Centennial Month.

However, a few years later, the enthusiasm for the structures turned to apathy. At any given time, about half of the towers' lights are burned out. Utility management says the lights simply aren't a priority. Yet once a year one still receives the spotlight. Every Christmas, the Moonlight Tower in Austin's Zilker Park is decorated with more than three thousand lights, transforming the tower into the celebrated holiday Zilker Tree. If the reports are true, however, the Zilker Park tower is just a replica.

Miraculous Monuments

Cross of Our Lord Jesus Christ

Stop for a nice long look, and you realize it's just an obelisk with arms. Unsuspecting motorists will often comment, "That is one big freakin' cross," but those in the know refer to it simply as "the cross." It towers over the west end of Groom, a small town with not much else to put in the travel brochures except its leaning water tower and a diner called Blessed Mary's.

The cross was built to inspire the Good Samaritan in us all, or at least those traveling Interstate 40, but its rampant gigantism has probably subverted its status to yet another wild roadside attraction. Erected along the "Mother Road"—Route 66—it joins the Wigwam Motel, the Blue Whale, and the Cadillac Ranch in America's prestigious collection of historic Route 66 kitsch.

The cross is 190 feet tall and 110 feet wide. The frame is covered in corrugated steel, the same stuff one would use to make a toolshed. It's like a place you'd keep your rakes—the really long ones. Of course, the big one isn't the only cross you'll see here. Encircling the base are impressive bronze statues depicting the thirteen stations of the cross. Several yards away is a depiction of a scene of Jesus and the two thieves hanging from crosses. The property's lights are also in the shape of crosses.

Sadly, most people miss these bonus features. Problem is, the cross is so enormous, it defeats attempts to draw travelers off the highway. After all, you really don't have to pull over to see it. But the Web site appears thankful for an almost 4 percent detour rate.

One thing the cross's builders won't tell you, though, is that their 1250-ton edifice isn't the tallest. The cross in Effingham, Illinois, beats it by an entire eight feet. Yet, surprisingly, billboards in Groom still invite you to see THE LARGEST CROSS IN THE WESTERN HEMISPHERE.

Stonehenge II

Still thinking of Europe? Well and good if you're looking for stories to impress the chicks, but if you just want to see the sights, you may as well save some time and hit the good old Texas highways. Care to see Big Ben? Hey, the University of Texas's clock tower is just as good, plus you can still see the bullet holes left by the men who brought down Charles Whitman.

Then again, maybe you're more interested in ancient ruins, like the mysterious Stonehenge. Well, we've got you covered there too. And this one isn't falling over.

Al Shepperd, a world traveler interested in ancient cultures, re-created the peculiar ring of stones at his home in Hunt in 1989. The idea came to him after a friend, Doug Hill, presented him with a large piece of limestone left over from a building project. Shepperd placed the stone upright in his field, then asked Hill to build an arch to direct attention to it. When the arch was completed, it reminded the two so much of England's monument that they decided to reconstruct the entire thing in metal and plaster. They dubbed the reproduction Stonehenge II.

A year and a half later, Shepperd visited Easter Island, and employed Hill to help him build two giant stone heads. After studying ancient Indian tribes in Alaska, Shepperd planned to add a totem pole to the collection. Unfortunately, he passed away before he and Hill got a chance to build that.

Thankfully, however, Stonehenge II and the companion heads have remained under the care of Shepperd's family and are still open to anyone who wants to stop by. Of course, this Stonehenge doesn't include any crystal-gripping, cloak-wearing geeks to make fun of, but a visit won't cost you £15 and, unlike the other one, you can actually get to touch it.

This Land Is Your Land

According to Russell "Rusty" Neef of the city of Pampa, his town rivals any town when it comes to its number of public parks. "Some of them are real nice; some aren't that great. But we do have them." In fact, Pampa has thirty-seven, which is an amazing one park for every five hundred inhabitants.

Naturally, that means there's a lot of open space to fill. So when the parks and recreation department decided to build a sculpture walk, they persuaded Rusty, the city's premier welder, to make a contribution.

He initially had the idea of putting together three simple musical notes, but what he ended up with was three full measures. His wife, a schoolteacher, convinced him to depict a whole tune, especially one that everybody would know. "This Land Is Your Land" seemed like a good choice, since even her youngest students knew how to sing it.

Plus, it was written by folk musician Woody Guthrie, who had called Pampa home back in the 1930s. It's where he had endured both the Great Depression and the Dust Bowl, two events that greatly influenced his music, though Rusty isn't sure Guthrie started writing the song there. Unfortunately, the tune had notes that went off the scale, making a sculptural depiction difficult. So Rusty solicited the help of the music instructor at his wife's school, who rearranged everything so he could mount it.

Still, Rusty did receive one complaint: "I was criticized by a lady here in town who thinks she's a great pianist. She chewed me out about putting the sharp sign in the wrong place. She said it was supposed to be above the scale." Unable to make the sign float, Rusty had to lower it so he could attach it.

When all was said and done, the sculpture measured 142 feet long and more than 10 feet high. It is, in all probability, the largest musical scale in the world. And it was built to last too. Rusty reinforced it to support the weight of all the people who, he knew, would try to climb it—though he would prefer they didn't—and he hermetically sealed every piece to prevent corrosion. Plus, he went ahead and coated it with $160-a-gallon paint, the kind used to protect offshore drilling rigs.

By Rusty's estimation, "This Land Is Your Land" should be sticking in the heads of passing motorists for at least the next century.

Cadillac Ranch

It stands unadvertised on the outskirts of a remote north Texas city and yet remains the most familiar roadside attraction in the state. If it weren't for the Alamo, it might be the most familiar attraction, period.

For more than thirty years, Cadillac Ranch has lured sightseers into a dusty Amarillo wheat field with the promise of offbeat nostalgia. Though it was dreamed up well after the Mother Road fell into obsolescence, this unique work of art captures perfectly the character of bygone Route 66 kitsch.

It's Americana within Americana. Not only is it the ultimate example of roadside playfulness, but it is a tribute to a distinctly American automotive motif: the tail fin. Aimed at the vast Panhandle sky, ten rear ends, built between 1949 and 1963, illustrate the rise and fall of the tail fin. Actually, they might each be just a pampered collector's item if the whole lot weren't situated halfway in the ground—a sight some classic-car enthusiasts find difficult to bear.

Most, however, look upon Cadillac Ranch with fondness. It's a Lone Star icon, embedded not only in the

landscape, but in the hearts of many who make the trek to see it in person. Some, who had first visited as children, have brought their own kids for a look. It's one of very few roadside attractions to maintain its allure across generations.

It seems that those who stop by can't resist leaving a little something of themselves behind. Decades' worth of aerosol scrawl covers every inch of the monument. If you could leaf through the strata of spray paint, you would see declarations of love, delirious observations, incomprehensible doodles, demented messages to the world, and countless names and initials. Certain layers mark significant moments, much like the rings seen in a tree: a wash of white on a major anniversary, original colors for a historical restoration, a coat of black upon the death of one of the work's creators.

The appeal of Cadillac Ranch is hard to pin down, but its charm and its ability to capture within its own skin the memories of those who come to see it have ensured it a place in Texas lore. Assuming the ever thickening layers of Krylon stay ahead of the rust, it should continue to beguile and bewilder for generations to come.

Eye of the World Museum

Check out the unusual museum located, oddly enough, at the Lone Star Steakhouse in Beaumont. The museum is actually a two-foot-wide passageway over which hangs a placard that reads simply MUSEUM.

Taking up the full length of a twenty-seven-foot-long display case, the Eye of the World is a remarkably detailed, hand-carved display of, well, almost everything. Created by "Poppa" John Gavrelos, a Greek immigrant and career restaurateur, the display includes the Parthenon, the Statue of Liberty, the Tower of Babel, and an assortment of other meticulously fashioned structures built to scale. It is Poppa's eye on the world that interested him.

The viewer will discover, scattered throughout, small wooden people and scenes of various sizes—a whittled, glass-enclosed Lilliput. Along the front edge reside even more characters—nine yards of tiny tableaux, comprising miniature scenes from the Bible depicting every story you've ever heard and probably some you haven't. At one end is little Noah building his ark; at the other, a teeny Jesus carries a Popsicle cross.

According to John Gavrelos—the artist's namesake and great-nephew—who now runs the steakhouse, Poppa Gavrelos worked on those scenes from 1923 to 1948, carving his models from whatever wood he had on hand, mostly plywood and vegetable crates. Pieces have gone on display recently at other museums, but before that, none of it had been touched for nearly forty years. Even today, it's just as it was when it was placed in the room in 1953, having been arranged exactly according to Gavrelos's specifications. "He wanted everything just right," said John. "He was very particular."

CHRIST BEFORE PILA[TE]

VISION OF PETER.

Forbidden Gardens

You would think Texas has enough eccentric millionaires. It shouldn't have to import any. Yet sometimes a little foreign competition is just what's needed to keep roadside weirdness at its best.

In 1996, a real-estate magnate from Hong Kong raised the bar a notch when he opened what remains one of the most wonderfully odd attractions to hit the state. Ira P. H. Poon, who reportedly felt a desire to educate the public about Chinese history and culture, spent millions of his own money to open the Forbidden Gardens, a sort of historical theme park in Katy, just west of Houston.

The centerpiece of the forty-acre park is an enormous one-twentieth-scale model of Beijing's Forbidden City, a restricted-access imperial complex consisting of several palaces, built in the fifteenth century. Ensuring as much accuracy as possible, Poon had the miniature palaces built using traditional materials and construction techniques. Composed of approximately two hundred amazingly detailed buildings and populated by between ten thousand and twenty thousand tiny, hand-painted royal figures and their servants, the exhibit is one of the world's most amazing miniaturizations.

Perhaps even more breathtaking is the expanse of diminutive soldiers representing the vast terra-cotta army of Emperor Qin (pronounced "Chin"). The original terra-cotta army, discovered in 1974 in China, was constructed to guard the tomb of the first emperor of unified China. It consists of some six thousand life-size statues buried in formation, now mostly excavated and on display as a tourist attraction. The army is re-created here at Forbidden Gardens in one-third scale.

Poon had originally planned to build the attraction in Seattle, where he lives, but decided that the rainy weather would be detrimental to the outdoor museum and instead located it in Texas. Unfortunately, he didn't reckon on the blazing sun and humid Gulf air, which has taken its own toll on the models. Consequently, he's had to spend time and money on almost continuous maintenance, which has delayed the miniature Great Wall and other additions that he's planned since the park's opening.

What's most surprising about Forbidden Gardens, though, is the fact that hardly anyone knows it exists, since advertising for the attraction is almost nonexistent. Reasons for that are not hard to come by, since Poon is rather reserved, shying away from any kind of publicity.

Perhaps one day, Poon's staff will outpace the weather, enabling him to complete his masterpiece so he can reveal it to a wider audience. Otherwise, it may just have to be unearthed over time, like Qin's clay cavalry.

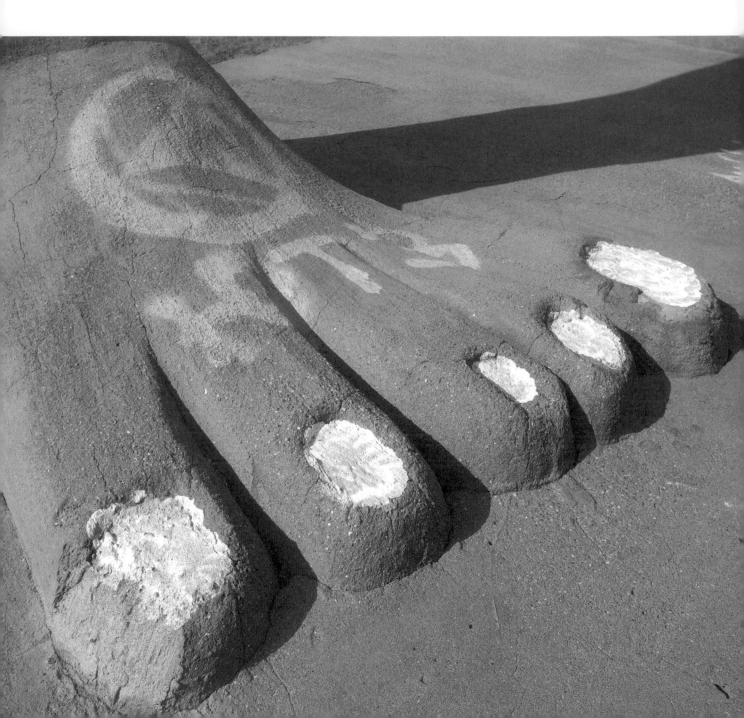

The Ozymandias Legs

There's no denying that most of Texas is flat. In some areas, the highest point is a Dairy Queen sign. So when something like a gigantic pair of legs breaks the clean edge of the horizon, people take notice.

From afar, they look like a couple of monstrous thorns protruding from Amarillo's side, which is exactly what a lot of people consider the work to be. It was commissioned by Stanley Marsh 3, a local helium king associated with Cadillac Ranch and a number of other local oddities he refers to collectively as "a legalized form of insanity."

This particular dose of madness is purported to be the ruins described in a nineteenth-century sonnet by the poet Percy Bysshe Shelley, the husband of the author of *Frankenstein*. The sonnet, titled "Ozymandias," tells of a pair of detached limbs in the desert, the remains of an ancient statue. Supposedly, those limbs are the same ones that now stand just off I-27.

The enormous gams, like everything else in rural Texas, are cordoned off by endless barbed wire, but visitors can read all about them on a nearby Texas historical marker. The marker cites Shelley's poem, describing "two vast and trunkless legs" and "near them . . . half sunk, a shattered visage."

A thoughtfully placed asterisk directs readers to a footnote explaining why no such shattered visage accompanies the stumps before them. The visage—or "face," as the plaque helpfully explains—was apparently damaged by students from Lubbock after they had lost to Amarillo in an unspecified competition. The face now resides, the footnote adds, in the Amarillo Museum of Natural History.

Of course, you have to realize that the man behind the whole thing is the same person who was described in a 1999 poll as being both a "subversive genius" and a "ridiculously foolish eccentric." It turns out that the historical marker is a sham—the big face doesn't exist, and Amarillo has never had a museum of natural history.

Quite simply, as Marsh has pointed out, Shelley's poem is about the futility of monuments. So he built a monument to it.

Alligator Park

Typically, the most use a Texan has for an alligator is to make a nice pair of boots. But way out west in El Paso, residents have a curious attachment to the natural aesthetic of an alligator just the way it's hatched.

In the early 1880s, as part of an effort to cast off its image as a dusty frontier town, El Paso made a concerted effort to expand and modernize. Newspapers were founded, public schools and transportation were established, and the downtown area was beautified. The latter venture included the creation of a park, which featured trees, a pond, and, of all things, live alligators. After all, if anything says "contemporary metropolis," it's large hissing reptiles.

San Jacinto Plaza, as it was named, quickly became the focal point of the downtown district, and its alligators were the main attraction. Visitors surrounded the pond daily to watch the reptiles, despite the fact that, as anyone who's been to a zoo can tell you, they don't move much. In fact, those who recall seeing the gators in later years have described them as being "torpid" and "sluggish," though their characteristic stagnation apparently didn't make them any less popular. Locals even started referring to San Jacinto Plaza as La Plaza de los Lagartos, or Alligator Plaza.

Reportedly, anywhere from three to seven of the big lizards lived in the park at various points in time. How they originally got there, however, has remained unclear. Some say that after the pond was installed, someone felt it looked a little empty and simply donated the money to chuck in some gators. Others believe the parks commissioner who built the square had alligators in mind all along. He is said to have kept them as babies in a barrel of water at a local saloon until the park was complete. But the most popular story seems to be the one about a Mexican rancher or a local miner who decided to give the alligators to the city after he received two babies in the mail as a joke.

Regardless of how they got there, the alligators were beloved members of the community for several decades. During cold spells, it's said, residents would wrap them up and take them to the local saloon to warm them. (Now there's a thought—imbibing locals and a saloon full of alligators. Forget our invitation to that party!) The alligators were included as part of public events as well. One was the focus of a weight-guessing game, the winner of which received a trip to Mexico—not much of a prize when you consider Mexico is about twelve blocks away.

Unfortunately, the animals also saw their share of abuse. They were sometimes kidnapped and left as a prank in an office or a swimming pool. One died from mishandling after outsiders picked him up and tossed him into the pond. After several other mishaps, the alligators were relocated to the El Paso Zoo in 1965 for their own protection. Officials returned them for two years in 1972, but after further trouble, it was "see ya later" as they were removed for good.

Today, people still refer to the site as Alligator Park, and it remains a busy area. Though the pond was removed long ago, the memory of its inhabitants has been preserved in the form of a statue. Rising out of the center of the park are four colorful gators, somehow both friendly and frightening at the same time. Sure they're just fiberglass, but the new versions aren't any less visually appealing than before, and really, they don't move any less.

Mills Street fronting San Jacinto Plaza,
El Paso, Texas

Pumping and Thumping in Luling

While traveling down Highway 183 in central Texas, the densely packed growth along the highway suddenly opens up, and you see the town of Luling. A little farther down the highway, it hits you—the smell of crude oil. One of the most significant oil reservoirs in the Southwest was discovered in Luling in 1922, and it created a boom in the community. Formerly just an area of agricultural and cattle shipping, the town now had another economic advantage: Not only did pump service, welding, and oil company businesses dot the road, but so did the oil pumps.

What do you do with nasty ole' oil pumps sitting around the center of town? Why you purdy them up Texas-style, of course! With over 180 pumps working in the small area, the residents banded together to make them a little more attractive, since they had to look at them all the time—everything from grasshoppers and football players to the Red Baron and Shamu decorate mechanical eyesores, which have now become a local attraction.

Luling is not just oil. It is also the Watermelon Capital of Texas. Visitors come from all over the state for the annual watermelon thumping contest. (You thump the melon to see how ripe it is.) They even have a water tower painted as a watermelon.

Speaking of water towers, many places in Texas paint their towers for their nomenclature. Poteet is the strawberry capital and has a strawberry-painted water tower. Also, local high schools will adorn their area's water tower with the mascot and name. A central Texas company that sandblasts and paints water towers has told me that he has to turn business away since his job lists are already filled for several years.—*Marlene Stevens*

Head Scratchers

Some things we see along the road beg that the question "Why?"or "What?" be asked, as in "WHY is that thing there?" or "WHAT was that person thinking when he did that?" These are the places that we refer to as head scratchers. Sometimes the reasons for their existence turn out to be quite logical or even mundane upon closer examination. But on first sight, these roadside oddities look pretty strange.

Many have gone underappreciated for years. Some have become so familiar to us that we hardly even notice them when we pass them. We think it's time now to slow the car down, pull off to the side of the road, and take a good long look at some of these roadside oddities.

Swampy, Man of Moss

Drive about twenty-five miles east of Beaumont, and you'll find yourself in the town of Orange in—you guessed it—Orange County. Separated from Louisiana by the Sabine River, this stretch of land is lush, marshy, and, in the summer months, nice and sticky. It's the kind of place where mosquito repellent qualifies as cologne.

Of course, the alligators love it. And so does Stan Floyd, who's hosted his Super Gator swamp tours here for fifteen years. He pretty much just supervises things now, overseeing the tours and his airboat-manufacturing business, but having dealt with alligators since he was fourteen, he can tell you just about anything you want to know about the critters.

Stan's assistant in charge of attracting the kids and looking generally fearsome is Swampy, a model of an as-of-yet-unclassified swamp creature who looms out front. Despite his red eyes and a Karl Malden–like nose made of "putty or something," Swampy tends to be more lovable than one would expect. His first incarnation surfaced around 1991. Since then, he's been rebuilt four or five times, says Stan, growing ever larger, resulting in the ten-foot beast he is today. Underneath his verdant overcoat is a metal skeleton that houses an electric motor. Switched on, Swampy performs a little quagmire jig.

A few yards behind Swampy, next to the former gas station that acts as tour headquarters, is where Stan keeps his pets. As a licensed alligator farmer, he keeps about twenty of them in a small pond for entertainment purposes. Despite the close quarters, they remain pretty tranquil.

Actually, the onlookers tend to be more hostile than the gators. "Our worst problem is keeping people from throwing objects over the fence trying to make them move," says Stan. "People are always throwing objects over our fence."

There used to be a group of eight-foot banana trees next to the pond, but somebody had ripped them out and thrown them at the alligators, trying to rouse them. Someone else did the same thing with the frame that supported the adjacent building's air conditioner. Of course, none of it ever does any good. The gators just ignore it. It's tough to prevent, though, since it happens when Stan's not around. Evidently, he could use a good security guard.

Sounds like Swampy needs to be reassigned.

Devil's Rope Museum

It's one exhibit where DO NOT TOUCH signs are entirely unnecessary. In fact, it could be the only museum in the world where the acquisitions serve as their own antitheft devices.

More types of barbed wire than you ever thought existed are on display in McLean, each painstakingly mounted and labeled.

According to the museum, more than two thousand variations of wire have been catalogued. And that's not including the punchpress wire, the planter wire, the decorative wire, and the expansive display of barbed-wire splices.

Many specimens of wire, the museum tells us, are rare, generating a desire in some people to collect the stuff. Books and magazines are published on the subject. Collectors' associations hold shows and trading events. Hobbyists even pit their collections against other "barbarians" in competition. As they say, it's a hobby you can really get "hooked" on. Single-strand, two-line, ribbon, Merrill Four Point Twirl, Barker Hanging Spur Rowel, Double Clip Butterfly—it's all here. And it's proof that if something can be accumulated in quantity, someone will open a gallery for it. Plus, there are the augers, post mauls, fencing gadgets, and automatic barbed-wire–stringing contraptions—everything you need to establish your own ranch or POW camp.

As a bonus, the museum also offers an exhibit on ranching paraphernalia, including cowhand implements, with names such as tooth float and nose grab. It's probably one of the most frightening museum displays, especially with its grouping of mystery devices labeled CASTRATION. In all fairness, though, this shrine to hooked barriers is well put together. Its curators did a first-rate job of converting what was once, interestingly enough, a factory for the only hooked barrier ranked more impregnable than barbed wire: the brassiere.

Goff's Charcoal Hamburgers

Until its recent move, the Goff's on Lovers Lane had been a Dallas landmark for more than fifty years, the first of what became an eight-restaurant chain. Boasting virtually the same decor, the same chairs, and the same menu since it first opened, Goff's remained a local favorite partly due to its old-style, burger-joint atmosphere.

More popular than the character of the restaurant, however, was that of proprietor Harvey Gough. Gough, whose parents opened the restaurant in 1950, was notorious for his acerbic attitude. Contrary to every accepted philosophy of customer service, he abused, berated, and insulted his patrons every chance he got. He would often let a diner know his or her order was ready by calling out, "Hey, doo-doo!" and would bark a curt "Dismissed!" when handing over the tray. If someone complained about the cleanliness of the utensils, Harvey would lick the customer's fork and hand it back, snapping, "There, now it's sterilized." Men with untrimmed locks were lucky to receive even that much courtesy; "longhairs" were often refused service entirely. One of Harvey's favorite tricks was to ask you if you wanted your carryout drink in a sack; if you said yes, he'd pour it into a paper bag for you. Of course, Harvey's unpredictable behavior and caustic remarks only made Goff's more of a draw.

Then there was the statue. Those who didn't know Goff's by the reputation of its owner knew it by the eight-foot Communist standing out front. In 1992, Harvey traveled to Ukraine, where he acquired a statue of former Soviet leader Vladimir Lenin as a souvenir. He purchased it from a crane factory for $500 and spent approximately $5000 to have it shipped to Dallas. Harvey placed the statue in front of his restaurant, overlooking a street rife with free enterprise. In true Gough fashion, he attached a plaque at Lenin's feet that read AMERICA WON.

Sadly, Harvey closed the original Goff's at the beginning of 2005, moving the establishment closer to Southern Methodist University. That meant Lenin had to go as well, but since there was no room at the new location, Harvey put him up for auction on eBay.

Lenin sold for more than $9000. Score another point for capitalism.

Halfway Stone of San Antone

This photo was taken near the city offices in downtown San Antonio. Apparently, someone figured out that this exact spot was the halfway point between St. Augustine, FL, and San Diego, CA. *—Karen Ballentine*

U.S. Border Patrol Museum

Tucked away in the western tip of Texas, on the northern edge of El Paso, a stark, windowless building houses a shrine to those who tend to America's periphery. It honors an elite group that, in a swell of concern over smallpox and dirty bombs, remains focused on the ongoing threat to homeland security that goes by the name of Undocumented Immigration.

It is the U.S. Border Patrol Museum, a somewhat imposing structure just a stone's throw from Mexico. Here one is invited to explore free of charge the world of the Men in Green and to learn what it takes to stem the tide of those huddled but illegal masses.

Just inside, visitors encounter R.A.D., the Robot Against Drugs. Once the border patrol's spokesdroid, educator of children on the dangers of drug abuse, he was forced to resign a number of years ago. Living out his remaining time at the museum, R.A.D. sulks next to

the main entrance, like a Wal-Mart greeter who didn't adequately plan for retirement.

Off to the left, one finds even more surplus machinery. Somehow the museum has managed to cram into one wing a Jeep, an ATV, a snowmobile, a helicopter, two cars, and an airplane. Plus, in the corner, an unsettlingly sexy mannequin shows off a mountain bike and a motorcycle. And just outside, set against an incongruous desert backdrop, there's a thirty-two-foot speedboat.

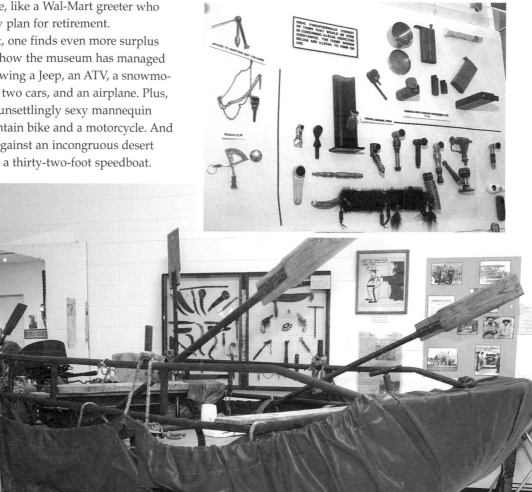

Left, an unsettlingly sexy mannequin shows off a mountain bike and a motorcycle, two modes of transportation employed by the Border Patrol in chasing down "illegals." Top, a display of illegal drug paraphernalia. Above, an example of an ingenious boat seized from a "coyote," or smuggler of illegals. Built from found materials, it once remained buoyant with the help of an air bladder; passengers kept it filled by continuously operating a bicycle pump all the way from Cuba.

Visitors to the museum are greeted by R.A.D., the Robot Against Drugs, who was once the Border Patrol's spokesdroid educating children on the dangers of drug abuse.

At the other end of the museum, several displays convey the history and function of the agency. Of particular note is the presentation on "signcutting"—the art of tracking. A small diorama demonstrates the sort of clues one would look for in the deserts along the Texas border, including tiny footprints next to scaled-down barbed-wire fences and a surprisingly abundant scattering of miniature abandoned flour tortillas. One imagines two perplexed patrol officers scratching their heads over such a scene: "Now, what do you think would leave behind all these tortillas?"

"Beats me, Phil. Better bring in an expert."

Perhaps the best exhibits, though, are the examples of ingenuity seized from various unsuccessful immigrants, or illegals, as they're referred to here. Cases hold a shotgun fashioned from metal pipe and electrical tape, and a .17-caliber pistol worn as a ring. There's also the boat seized from a coyote, or smuggler of illegals, welded from two truck hoods. Another vessel, built from found materials, once remained buoyant with the help of an air bladder, which passengers kept filled by continuously operating a bicycle pump all the way from Cuba.

The collection isn't extensive, but it's sure to expand. After all, further acquisitions are certainly to come. For as long as there are outsiders willing to assume all of our undesirably arduous and low-paying jobs, the U.S. Border Patrol will be there to stop them.

Alley Oop Fantasy Land

The oddly named town of Iraan, whose moniker derives from the names of its founders, Ira and Ann Yates, was the source of two noteworthy exports in the 1920s and 1930s. First, like that country with a similar-sounding name, Iraan had plenty of oil. The reason this was significant is because wells drilled here shattered the long-held belief that there was none of the black stuff to be found in Texas west of the Pecos. Second, this was the town in which a reasonably famous caveman was discovered. His name was Alley Oop.

It was while working as a newspaperman in Iraan that comic-strip artist V. T. Hamlin came up with the idea for a strip featuring a prehistoric protagonist, his dinosaur companion, Dinny, and his dishy girlfriend, Ooola (as in "ooo-la-la"). They spent much of their time in their native land of Moo, but on occasion, the characters were transported through history with the help of Doc Wonmug, a scientist from the future and the inventor of a time machine. The strip still continues in syndication, though it's not as prominent in pop culture as it once was. Years ago, you could say that Alley Oop was the Dilbert of his day. "The king of the jungle jive" even inspired a song that you've probably heard at some point or another on your local oldies station.

In 1965, Iraan sought to honor Hamlin's creation, or possibly capitalize on it, by opening Alley Oop Fantasy Land, a seven-acre park on the west side of town. It still exists today. Inside, you'll find a large steel rendition of Alley Oop smoking a four-and-a-half-foot stogie and sporting a giant top hat. More impressive is the sixty-foot-long concrete Dinny. Unfortunately, there's no giant Ooola.

At the back of the park is the Iraan Museum, which appears to feature more local prehistory than Alley

Oop-related material. Display cases labeled MAN IN THE TRANS-PECOS, EARLY HUNTER-GATHERERS, and WHAT IS ARCHAEOLOGY? line the walls. The thing about museums in small towns like this one, however, is that they're often difficult to find open. On one Saturday, a sign announced a closure "due to funeral."

It's hard to say what kind of commotion the place caused forty years ago, but today it's pretty quiet. Should you ever decide to visit, odds are you'll have the grounds to yourself. Plus, it's free. What appears to have been a ticket booth stands just inside the gates, but it's been boarded up.

Ellis County Courthouse

It's difficult to drive a state highway or farm-to-market road through Texas without eventually running into one of its county courthouses. With more than two hundred and fifty counties in the state, each required to have its own judicial structure, the infamous arm of the

Texas law is evident in the buildings' virtual ubiquity. In fact, more historic courthouses stand in Texas than in any other state. And considering the prominence given to the county courthouse in both a community's physical layout and in its history, it's no surprise that so many legends revolve around these imposing halls of justice.

Stories of lynchings, riots, and hauntings all share the courthouse as their backdrop. But in Ellis County, the legend involves the courthouse itself. Though there are variations of the narrative, the basic story tells of an itinerant stone carver who was hired to create the ornamental faces that adorn the courthouse façade. He's usually said to have been an Italian or German immigrant, despite having the Irish name of Harry Herley.

While staying at a boardinghouse in Waxahachie,

Herley supposedly fell in love with his landlady's granddaughter, Mabel Frame. Hoping that the young woman would return his affection, he spent hours creating beautiful likenesses of her in the capitals topping the courthouse's pillars.

Despite his efforts, Miss Frame never returned his love and soon married another man, leaving Herley feeling humiliated. Consequently, his work took a drastic turn. The images he chipped into the building's red sandstone became increasingly grotesque. Beauty turned to monstrosity. Admiration became mockery.

Herley is said to have developed contempt even for the town itself. Soon residents began noticing similarities between themselves and the sculptor's work, and the faces they saw were less than flattering. Venomous eyes stared back at them. Scowls and absurd, cockeyed mugs looked out over the streets of Waxahachie. Strangely, one carving resembled a particular part of the female anatomy.

Local historians will tell you the only part of the story that's true is that one of the men involved in the courthouse's construction was indeed a carver named Harry Herley, though his work was done in Dallas and it's unlikely that he had ever met Mabel Frame.

Regardless, any day of the week you can run into tourists and teachers all retelling the story to their children—and the children all pointing at that piece of anatomy, supposedly Mabel Frame's hoo-ha, or passion flower, or whatever they call it where you come from.

Roads Less Traveled

Certain roads are just not quite normal. These strange byways possess a special mystique that sets them apart from ordinary stretches of concrete and asphalt. Throughout Texas, we find hills that defy gravity and railroad crossings where the usual laws of physics don't seem to apply. So strange are the happenings on these lonely avenues that stories of ghosts wandering their environs are told without a hint of disbelief.

It could be that such roads act as pathways to our innermost fears. If that is, in fact, the case, then a trip down one of these legendary routes may be for some a journey of profound self-discovery. Of course, there are also those who enjoy traveling such roads purely for the thrill of scaring the wits out of themselves and their friends. Night riders on jaunts like these are so jacked up to witness something out of the ordinary, the overanticipation alone might cause their eyes to play tricks on them.

Whether these roads are actually epicenters of supernatural activities, merely the fevered delusions of rowdy, nocturnal joyriders, or a little of both is open for debate. Whatever the case, one fact is indisputable: There are roads less traveled throughout Texas that possess some kind of indefinable, yet undeniable, power.

Ghostly Hills and Gravity Roads

One of the most common "road" myths across the state of Texas is the story of gravity roads or hills. These are places where the laws of gravity just don't seem to apply. The stories of the various mystery spots around the state are remarkably similar, yet have unique plot twists. Most of the legends involve at least one violent death and a spirit of some kind that pulls or pushes vehicles uphill.

The preferred scientific method of testing these anomalous roads is to pull your car up to the spot in question, throw it into neutral, and remove your foot from the brake. Then, ever so slowly, the stories go, your car will begin to travel, as if forced by unseen hands, uphill. It usually works, and the sensation can be very unsettling.

Those seeking more concrete evidence of the spectral nature of the phenomenon often sprinkle flour or baby powder on their car's bumper. After the antigravity experiment, they check their bumper for signs of ghostly handprints in the powder. And many very frightened individuals swear they've found them!

Skeptical types claim that these apparent antigravitational pulls are merely the result of optical illusions that make the viewer believe they are looking uphill when, in fact, they are really facing down. To these people we say the following: We know our ups from our downs as well as the high roads from the low.

Ghost Tracks of San Antonio

At the intersection of Shane and Villamin roads in San Antonio is a gravity hill that comes complete with a tragedy and a ghostly legend. Way back when, the story goes, a bus that was filled with unfortunate kids got stuck on the railroad tracks that cross the intersection. The bus was struck by a speeding train, and everyone aboard was killed. The surrounding streets are said to be named in memory of the fallen children. The legend also says that if a driver is foolish enough to stop his car on the tracks at this same intersection, the car will roll off and away from the tracks, pushed by the ghostly hands of the dead children. People have reported feeling the rocking of the car as if pushed by many hands as well as hearing childish whispers and phantom footsteps outside their car.

The first thing a weird investigator will note is that yes, indeed, the streets around this intersection do have eerie childlike names—Cindy Sue, Laura Lee, Bobbie Allen, Richey Otis, even Shane. And it is a spooky area, heavily wooded and deathly quiet. The place where the accident supposedly happened is a desolate corner, and it isn't hard to imagine its being haunted.

However, when the *Weird Texas* team tested out the legend for ourselves, our car stayed firmly planted on the tracks, fortunately at a time when no train was passing. Not a real smart thing to do, and we don't suggest that anyone else try this!

Also, there is no official record of any accident, much less one involving a train and a school bus full of kids, at this intersection. The nearby streets, we were told, were named after the developers' children, who are still alive and well. Nevertheless, there are those who insist that they've had paranormal experiences at this intersection, and the ghostly stories persist.

The Children of the Tracks

The tale of those railroad tracks in San Antonio is a tragic one, although those who suffered the tragedy seem to have returned to literally lend a hand. Many years ago, a bus full of schoolchildren, who were on their way home from a class outing, had stalled on the tracks. It was late, and the kids had fallen asleep, so their teacher, a nun, was trying to restart the bus without waking them. Suddenly, she heard a train coming. Its light was off, so she hadn't noticed it. She knew she didn't have time to wake the children to evacuate them, so she made one last ditch effort toward starting the bus. She failed.

The bus was ripped in half by the speeding train, but the driver's area was thrown from the tracks, with only the nun inside. She was unhurt and witnessed the horror that followed. The train tore asunder the remaining section of the bus with the children entrusted to her care still inside. All of the kids died.

Weeks later, still wrought with immense grief, the nun decided to take her own life. She parked her car on the same tracks where the accident took place. As a train approached in the distance, the nun began hearing the voices of children. The voices grew louder and louder, and then she felt her car begin to move. Just before the train struck, her car was pushed from the tracks and out of harm's way by some unseen force. She leapt out in amazement only to see children's handprints covering her vehicle. Her kids had returned and saved her.

Since that day, the mysterious moving of cars has taken place. People come from far and wide to drive onto the tracks and place their cars in neutral in the dead of the night. After a short period of time, the car will be miraculously pushed off the tracks without any explanation.

My friends and I have made more late-night trips out to these tracks than I can even count, always with similar result: Our car gets pushed off the tracks. The children who died on these tracks return time and time again to make sure that no one suffers the same grisly fate they did. Still, it's probably not the best idea to trust that these ghost kids will push your car from the tracks, especially if you happen to be staring down an oncoming locomotive!—*Travis T.*

Nun Starts an Orphanage

I have heard that after the nun was saved from death by the children who had died, she went on to start an orphanage and took care of lost children. When she died, those at the funeral said they heard the voices of children playing and the voice of one lone adult laughing. To this day, it is said that if you park your car in neutral on the track in the middle of the night and stay very quiet, you will hear voices and your car will be pushed off the track.—*John R. Cobarruvias*

Rocking and Rolling over the Tracks

I have had the pleasure of visiting the train tracks in San Antonio. My husband was driving our car with me riding shotgun and his sister in the backseat. We covered the car with baby powder and parked on the tracks. My husband shut the car off and put on the emergency brake and pushed as hard as he could on the brakes. After a few seconds, the car started rocking as if someone was pushing us from behind. My sister-in-law burst into tears and said, "Look!" I turned and saw big and little handprints in the baby powder on the window next to her. The rocking continued all the while my husband had his feet on the brakes. Then the car rolled uphill as if we were driving, and then down away from the tracks to safety. It was an experience I will never forget.—*Audra Sweet*

Tracks Are No Laughing Matter

My sophomore year, I found myself in a car with four other guys testing out this railroad track legend for ourselves. My boy Hugo, the driver, got out and powdered down the bumper. He got back in the car, put it in neutral, and to our shock, we found ourselves actually rolling uphill! We were freaking out, yelling and laughing, when my boy Baldini yelled, "Shut up, shut up! Do you hear that?"

We all went silent instantly. Very, very faintly, we all swore we heard the sound of a little girl crying. We tore out of there and didn't calm down until we were halfway home. That was just about the time that we stopped to pick up some food and noticed that there were patterns in the baby powder. It had mostly blown off in the wind, but what remained appeared to have the patterns of fingerprints in it.

The rest of that trip was spent in silence. After my visit, I somehow felt as if I had sensed the presence and understood the suffering of the poor kids who died there.

–Mark "Wingman" Winger

A Scientific Mind Tests the Tracks

I suspect this is another one of those spots affected perhaps by the electro-magnetic forces of the Earth. One night, a guy drove us there to prove this antigravity thing really would happen. The van was turned off and placed in neutral while sitting at the bottom of the little hill. No one touched anything. We then rolled uphill and over the tracks. We did this more than once. *–Suzanne*

Austin's Own Gravity Hill

There is, we're told, a gravity hill located off Well's Branch Parkway in Austin. Locals say that if you go up to "Jacob's Hill," stop on a bridge, put your car in neutral, and turn everything off, your car will roll across the bridge. The locomotion is supposedly supplied by the ghosts of two children who were killed by their father nearby. The tiny, but kindly, specters now haunt the area and will push your car out of harm's way.

The directions we had were something like "It's a bridge on a road off of Well's Branch Parkway." This is the kind of place that, even though many people seem to have heard of, nobody knows exactly where it is.

The *Weird Texas* team drove around for hours, exploring every single road off Well's Branch, and even most of the roads off those roads. We did not find anything that looked like a bridge, unfortunately. There is a lot of new construction along Well's Branch, and this may have affected the location of the bridges. But although we never found what we were looking for, we've heard from plenty of people who did.

Gravity Bridge at Jacob's Crossing

Just north of Austin is a town called Jacob's Crossing. There's a bridge out in the woods over a ravine that used to be pretty well traveled before the Interstates started to be built.

Supposedly, a bus driver drove his bus full of kids off that bridge, and no one survived. The bridge is flat for the first little way but then starts to slope upward at an angle. Today, if you go out there, put your car in neutral at the base of the incline, put baby powder all over the back of your car, get back in, and wait, the car will be pushed up to the top of the incline by something invisible. Right as the car reaches the top of the incline, almost to the other side, the force stops and the car will roll back across the bridge, down the incline. If you get out and look at the back of your car, there will be several tiny handprints that belong to the children and two large prints, which are supposed to belong to the bus driver.—*DeargCeol*

Or Is It Jack's Bridge in Hutto?

One night, my best friend, Holly, and I drove out to Hutto, where there's this bridge in the middle of nowhere on a country road. It's known as Jack's Bridge. We parked on the bridge and started taking pictures with her digital camera. She got spooked because she said she saw a little boy, and she did not want to be there. I drove out of there a little scared myself. We pulled in to the nearest gas station to view the pictures when she freaked out that there was this little boy in one of them. I was shocked! One day or night, I plan on going back and doing it again . . . not with Holly. She will not go back!—*PinkandBrunette*

The Screaming Bridge

They say it happened one dark night as a carload of excited teenagers was returning from a high school football game, driving down an old country road just outside Arlington's River Legacy Park. The kids were excited and distracted as they approached the narrow little bridge that ran across the Trinity River. They didn't see the car coming at them from the other direction until it was too late. There was a terrible head-on collision, with both vehicles exploding violently and plummeting off the bridge and into the waters below. There were no survivors.

Ever since that night, the span has been called the Screaming Bridge, no doubt named after the terrified cries of the doomed teenagers. The road to it has long been closed off, and the only way to reach it now is on foot through the park. Local lore states that if you can find Screaming Bridge and look down into the water from it, you will see eerie glowing tombstones, one for each of the dead kids. They also say that if you dare to sit in the middle of Screaming Bridge on the anniversary of the night of the deadly accident, a thick fog will rise up from the river, and the phantom headlights of the speeding cars will appear at either end of the bridge, as the tragic events of that fateful night replay themselves again and again to their violent conclusion.

Like some other haunted spots, this one is elusive. Everyone seems to know about the legend, but nobody knows exactly how to get there. It's almost as if Screaming Bridge doesn't want to be found! However, a park ranger did confirm its existence and also that the road that led to it had long ago been closed down.

Playing Taps on Patterson Road

In Houston, there is a legendary byway named Patterson Road, which unfurls peacefully through a lush and tranquil swatch of marshy and forested land. But some say the tranquillity hides a darker past, for this area may have been the site of a violent and bloody Civil War battle.

While the whole road has an underlying air of the unknown, there is a particular concentration of spectral angst centered around the old bridge that passes over Langham Creek. Many drivers crossing the span have reported hearing numerous tappings on the outside of their cars, especially along the doors and the backs. It's as if unseen hands are knocking at, even swaying, the cars.

Some say this is the work of the turbulent spirits of the soldiers who so violently lost their grip on mortality here long ago. But are they warning drivers off, or are they trying to escape the place of their bloody deaths? In other words, are they trying to climb IN and come home with you? No one claims to know for sure, but if you find yourself stopped on this haunted bridge, take heed—the spirits are restless.

Overpass of the Dead

There's an infamous, gloomy overpass in Humble. It was built to cross over a set of train tracks that leads into a deep, dark wood. There are rumors of a very old graveyard in the area, which was dug up and moved into the woods to pave the way for the new construction. But some say that all did not go as planned. Locals will tell you that the spirits were not as appreciative of this modern progress as the living.

The overpass and its surroundings have gained a reputation for being an extremely evil area. Some of the businesses along the tracks and woods have reportedly experienced strange disturbances, such as demonic voices emanating from inside their buildings after the doors have been closed and locked. The woods adjacent to the tracks have been a source of fear as well, as passersby have reported seeing spectral figures and red lights floating through the dark forest. The woods themselves are considered by some to be a gateway into hell. In the words of one local resident, they are "pure evil."

Today, the path to the track and woods is blocked by a high, barbed-wire–topped chain-link fence. Obviously, someone doesn't want anyone on those tracks. Underneath the overpass, the atmosphere is shadowy and cold, the reverberations of the traffic passing above sounding like demon whispers in the rafters. This is a creepy place with a powerfully unsettling atmosphere. One can't help but wonder, What really lies beyond the restricted area in the darkness of those thick woods? Maybe we're better off not knowing.

Demon's Road

There is a spooky, isolated back road in Huntsville that winds past lonely meadows and dark, wooded groves. Its real name is Bowden Road, but some locals call it by another, more sinister moniker: Demon's Road.

People are wary of traveling this road after dark, for stories persist of haunted things along its way, things such as the "faceless creature" that's been seen lurking in the woods. Claims of mysterious handprints appearing on the outsides of cars as they travel along the road are not uncommon. Strange apparitions and ghostly lights float across the open meadows and fields around the road. Some people have claimed to have seen, and in some cases, even to have been chased down the road by, an unearthly-looking hooded figure. Without a doubt, this is one road with a diabolical reputation.

We drove down its dusty length in the last minutes just before dusk. The shadows grew longer around every curve, and even in the fading daylight, the road had an air of menace. It's very isolated and very long, and we imagine it would be quite a wild, scary ride in the dead of night, when the unknown are said to roam and stake their claim on Demon's Road.

Lindsey Hollow Road—Waco

I feel I had a real paranormal—or at least unexplained—experience on Lindsey Hollow Road, near Cameron Park in Waco. Legend says that the ghosts of two brothers haunt this lonely, shaded road. The two were horse thieves, who laid in wait along the desolate road looking for victims to rob. Supposedly, in the 1880s, a group of vigilantes took matters into their own hands on Lindsey Hollow, and the brothers' bodies were found hanging from a tree about a hundred feet off the road. Some locals have claimed that the brothers linger there still, tied to the location by their violent end.

There are many reports of paranormal experiences along this road. People say they have felt paralyzed, heard disembodied screams, and seen spectral apparitions. Some have even claimed to see the shadowy images of the brothers' hanging bodies in the old tree.

I was wandering around one day, at the intersection of Lindsey Hollow and Procter Springs, wondering which tree was supposed to be the hanging tree. The area was very still and silent, and I was pretty engrossed, when suddenly I heard what sounded like a very loud footfall in the brush right behind me, followed by a faint jingling sound. I didn't pay very much attention at first, not until I heard it again.

It was just behind me, as if mimicking my own footsteps each time I moved—CRUNCH-jingle . . . CRUNCH-jingle—keeping close behind me as I edged back toward the road. I stopped, stood very still, and listened hard—nothing. I took another step, and again—CRUNCH-jingle—a bit behind me and to my left. The weird little metallic noise reminded me of something I couldn't quite place. It continued to happen again and again wherever I moved. It was really tripping me out.

And then, it suddenly occurred to me what the sounds reminded me of: the jingling of a spur on a

cowboy boot! I will admit to getting a chill or two up my spine as I realized this. It was then that I decided to head back to my car. As I moved closer to the road, I distinctly heard the noises following me again, steadily, until I stepped off the curb into the paved road, at which point they just stopped. I have to wonder, Did I encounter one of the doomed spectral siblings on Lindsey Hollow Road?
—Shady

Spooky Old Hollowman's Road

When people talk about Old Hollowman's Road, a deserted road in Mesquite with only an abandoned house on it, it's in that "Don't speak its name" kind of way. Besides supposedly being a place where the bodies of murder victims were disposed of, the entire road has been closed off, and there are whispers of a number of unsolved disappearances.

The legend of Hollowman's Road is a spooky one. Thrill-seeking teenagers would some-times dare each other to walk the length of the road, past the old house, alone at night. Rumors say that some of the teens disappeared, never to be seen again. In the 1980s, a Dallas man is supposed to have murdered a woman and her young son and dumped their bodies near the old house on the road, adding to its sinister reputation. Even in the safety of daylight, many who visit the place feel overwhelmed by a sense of dread and the feeling of being watched.

Did that stop the *Weird Texas* team from checking it out? Of course not. For once, our destination was clearly marked on a map. Hollowman's Road was shown running between two larger routes marked Lawson and Bruton. So far, so good. But despite driving up and down the lengths of both, we found no marker for Hollowman's. We were undeterred and started again, going more slowly and trying to pinpoint the area on the map where the road is marked.

As we drove along, we suddenly noticed something bizarre: a headless skeleton hanging from a fence post. We pulled over to check it out and realized that this was the exact spot where the map showed Hollowman's Road. The post the skeleton was hanging on was part of a wire fence, and beyond it we could see the remains of a paved road, weedy and grown over. Off in the distance was a rickety old abandoned house.

Then we noticed the metal pole where a street sign could have once been. There was no sign there now, though. We got out of the car and immediately felt a freaky "Someone is watching us" feeling. We took a closer look at the skeleton; it was one of those classic rubber ones, sans skull, and it was attached to the post with bits of wire. The fence closed off access to the house and the road. As we were pondering a way to get over it, a sheriff's car cruised by slowly.

Okay, maybe trying to get over the fence to the house wasn't the best idea. And to be honest, we didn't feel too comfortable there, anyway. There was certainly an intense feeling of malice all around. We got a few pictures and started to head off. As we pulled out, we had a creepy feeling that eyes were following us.

Since we didn't see an actual road sign saying HOLLOWMAN'S ROAD, we can't say for sure that this was it. But there was no other road anywhere in the area, and this one came complete with abandoned house (and spooky skeleton).

What do you think?

Trans-Mountain Road—El Paso

I distinctly remember the first time I heard about the "Ghost Monk" of Trans-Mountain Road (State Highway 375). I was in fourth grade, it was Halloween, and my really cool teacher had come to school that day dressed up as the Grim Reaper and toting a satchel filled with spooky materials to read us in honor of the day. She even turned out most of the lights and read to us in the eerie, dark classroom. She told us many creepy tales that day, but the story about the Monk was the one that made the most of an impression on me.

She started out by reading an old newspaper piece about a man who had had a car accident while driving down Trans-Mountain Road late one night. The man survived the wreck and claimed it was caused when he swerved to avoid a strange figure, which had suddenly stepped into the path of his headlights, a figure that looked remarkably like an ambling old monk leading a donkey by a rope. Of course, official word was that the man had been overtired and had hallucinated or fallen asleep at the wheel and had imagined seeing the monk. But the odd thing was, he hadn't been the first to witness the spectral monk wandering the lonely bends of Trans-Mountain Road late at night, and he wouldn't be the last.

Over many years, the legend of a Ghost Monk haunting the twisting and isolated mountainous road has been well-known in this area. Countless people have claimed to see him, and it's not unusual for some of Trans-Mountain's late-night car accidents to be attributed to the phantom's appearance. Descriptions tell of a haggard and grizzled old man dressed in a rough monk's robe sashed with a worn rope. Sometimes he is seen leading a donkey, sometimes not. He is rumored to haunt the road in the dead of night, either standing or walking at its edge, or sometimes walking directly across the road itself. When I was a teenager, we spent many a spooky night traveling the inky darkness up and down Trans-Mountain, half hoping and half dreading a glimpse of him. We never did encounter him but heard of many others who said they did.–*Shady*

Monk and His Donkey Walk Trans-Mountain Road

One of my childhood friends was in a minor accident on Trans-Mountain Road while driving with her mother years ago. She still swears that it all happened because they saw the famous ghost that walks along this road, a man dressed in a monk's outfit accompanied by a donkey.–*Wendy Ramos*

The Lonely Ghost

Old Greenhouse Road in Houston is not only a lovely country road, it also harbors a melancholy legend all its own. Local lore says that an elderly woman was killed in a tragic car accident on Old Greenhouse, right at the treacherous curve that leads onto a bridge spanning Bear Creek.

Indeed, the curve leading onto this bridge is extreme, and with the road surrounded on all sides by a thick, dark woods, it's not really possible to see the upcoming bridge until you are literally right on it. It's the kind of road formation that could be called a "dead man's curve," except that it was supposedly a woman who lost her life here.

And legend claims that you just might see the elderly ghost lady herself if you follow the ritual of Old Greenhouse Road: You must journey the road in the dark of night, then slow down and turn off your headlights just before you drive very slowly around the curve and onto the bridge.

Witnesses have said that if you do this, a swirling mist will form over the bridge and slowly whirl together until it assumes the form of a spectral figure. Her face looks unutterably sad, and there is something about her that speaks of a profound loneliness. If you are brave enough to stick around, this solitary road ghost will begin to approach your car. Is she trying to make friends, or is she sending a warning about the treacherous bridge? Nobody knows, and the few people who claim to have actually seen this apparition didn't stick around long enough to find out. Who can blame them?

The Ghost Cows of Farm Road 511

Drivers in the southeast tip of the state, almost at the Mexican border, whisper about a well-known ghost-road legend. The specter shows up in the town of Brownsville, along a fairly well-traveled route called Farm Road 511. It seems to be a perfectly normal road by the light of day, but locals warn of traveling it late at night, lest you encounter the road's ghostly inhabitants. As you drive down certain dark and desolate stretches of 511, your headlights may suddenly wash over a large cow standing smack in the middle of the road, not six feet ahead of your bumper.

That's right—a ghostly cow! You may swerve or pull off the road to avoid it, risking an accident, only to look back out at the road and see that nothing whatsoever is there.

Some people have gotten out of their cars and searched up and down the road, only to find no sign of a cow or anything else, living or dead. So many ghost-cow sightings and resulting car accidents have occurred on this road that the local newspaper and other media have reported on the story. It might sound humorous until you realize that accidents have been caused, creating the potential for someone to get hurt or even killed in these inexplicable encounters.

So if you find yourself traveling down Brownsville's Farm Road 511 in the dead of night, beware of the ghostly bovines that are said to lurk just around the next dark curve in the road, waiting to claim their next victim.

The Mysteries of Ascencion Boulevard

In the flat, dusty Texas desert sits the tiny town of Horizon. It's a small place, just outside the El Paso city limits, but a world removed from the civilization of the big city. In fact, in Horizon there's nothing around as far as the eye can see but tumbleweeds and desert horizon. A long, winding road runs through the town, past the middle and high schools, and continuing out into the barren desert. Even though the street sign says Ascencion Street, all the legends about the road call it Ascension Boulevard. And the byway's reputation is chilling.

Even the word *ascencion*, Spanish for "ascension," is spooky when you consider the legend. You see, they say that if you drive down this road at night and turn out your headlights as you approach Mountain View High School, the ghostly figure of a man will appear, walking along the roadside. Nobody seems to know the identity of this phantom, but somehow he's always mentioned, along with the other well-known legend of this byway: that there are many bodies buried alongside it.

Believe it or not, stories like this may not be too far-fetched. The desert roads on the outskirts of the city have been used as body dumping grounds in the past. Nobody ever mentions a specific gravesite location or known victim or how the spectral man on the roadside might be connected to them (victim . . . killer . . . accident casualty?). But Ascencion Boulevard is rarely mentioned without a story about the bodies.

Horizon is an eerie place, with tumbleweeds skittering down its sidewalks. And there is something else odd about it: Down the road a little, set back off Ascencion Boulevard, is something that looks like a tombstone standing among the dunes and cacti. We almost didn't even notice it, but the odd shine of some reflectors that decorate it caught our eye. There is no graveyard here, yet the stone is complete with name, birth and death dates, a cross, and flowers. Someone clearly cares for this place. On a recent visit, the flowers were fresh and candles stood inside a little cubicle.

Is it someone's grave? The site of a car accident? Or the spot where one of the many dumped bodies of the desert was found? There is no clue, nothing to explain this lone marker.

So we are left with yet another mystery of the desert to ponder. What is the stone all about? Who, or what, was Oscar, the name engraved on its base? What, if anything, does he have to do with dead bodies and a ghostly nightwalker on Ascencion Boulevard? We don't know, and maybe we aren't meant to. The desert keeps its secrets.

Is it someone's grave? The site of a car accident? Or the spot where one of the many dumped bodies of the desert was found?

Duel with the Marfa Lights

Roy, a friend of my dad's in the '70s, was once driving from San Antonio to West Texas along US Highway 90 when he had a unique introduction to a mystery that local believers and skeptical researchers have never adequately explained: the Marfa Lights.

These lights appear outside the city of Marfa as glowing orbs, floating a few feet above the ground, and zoom quickly and erratically across the desert. Sometimes they've been attributed to atmospheric reflections of distant car lights. This might make sense, except that they've been seen for well over a hundred years. And mysterious though they may be, they also appear to play games.

Roy said he had been driving his small pickup truck for about eight hours and had outdriven the coverage of most radio stations long ago. It had been quite awhile since he'd seen another car on the road, and he took notice when a pair of lights appeared in his rearview mirror. He glanced down at his speedometer to make sure he wasn't speeding and relaxed when he saw he was doing less than five mph over the limit. That wouldn't pique the interest of even the most jaded county sheriff.

My dad said that Roy had been driving with the lights a comfortable distance behind him for several minutes when they sped up and approached his truck rapidly. For a few seconds, he honestly thought he was about to be rear-ended. Before an impact occurred, however, the lights stopped a few feet short of hitting his truck. At sixty mph, in the middle of an otherwise deserted highway, it probably wasn't too much to ask for the courtesy of a little breathing room. So Roy tapped the brakes.

The driver of the vehicle behind him stayed close, too close. Annoyed, Roy jammed hard on his brakes for a fraction of a second. To his amazement, the vehicle behind him stayed the exact distance from his rear bumper as it had been.

Roy decided to try a different approach. He floored the gas pedal, making his small truck shudder and lurch ahead. The speed crept up to eighty mph. The lights behind him reacted in perfect unison, staying several feet behind his truck as it approached speeds Roy had never pushed it to before.

Enough was enough. Roy eased off the gas and let the truck coast down to a sane speed. Then he stood on the brakes. His tires screeched and smoked, and the truck pitched and slid slightly to the side. The whole time the lights stayed in exactly the same spot until the truck came to a stop. Roy then saw something completely unexpected: The lights shot out, off the road to the right, and fired across the desert like missiles. He craned his neck around to try and visually follow them, impressed by the driver's taking off on what was sure to be very rough road. He was about to drive on when a thought occurred to him. He frowned, put his truck in reverse, and slowly backed up maybe a couple of hundred feet. He checked the barbed-wire fence line on either side of the road for a gate or other break of some kind where his pursuer might have slipped through. But there was none.

Roy said he was pretty spooked, all right. Off in the distance, he could see the lights move swiftly across the horizon. —*Tim Stevens*

> **Roy had been driving with the lights a comfortable distance behind him for several minutes when they sped up and approached his truck rapidly. For a few seconds, he honestly thought he was about to be rear-ended.**

hosts aren't real, right? But if they aren't, then why are stories of them so pervasive in our culture? And why do so many people swear to have had encounters with them?

There are many theories as to why ghosts may exist. Sometimes, it's said that ghosts are souls who do not know that they have passed on. Others believe that ghosts know their bodies are dead, but their souls are restless for some reason, and so they refuse to move on.

Many people may publicly profess disbelief in the supernatural and the afterlife, but how many of those same folks would secretly like to be proved wrong? For to believe in ghosts is to accept the idea that there is more to this world than we mortals comprehend.

Haunted Places and Ghostly Tales

Of course, ghosts are notoriously camera-shy and materialize only when the spirit moves them, so it is rather difficult to document them in any concrete way. But our ghost files are brimming with firsthand accounts of otherworldly visitations. Some readers say they have caught only fleeting glimpses of spectral visions, while others have witnessed fully formed entities. More often, though, people tell us that rather than having seen a spook, they felt the presence of something or someone not of our plane.

In this chapter, we recount the experiences of ordinary people who have had encounters they cannot explain. Since they can't come up with an explanation, we will not even venture to try. It is up to you, dear reader, to decide if the phantasms described in the following pages are simply the product of someone's overactive imagination or if there is much more to them than that.

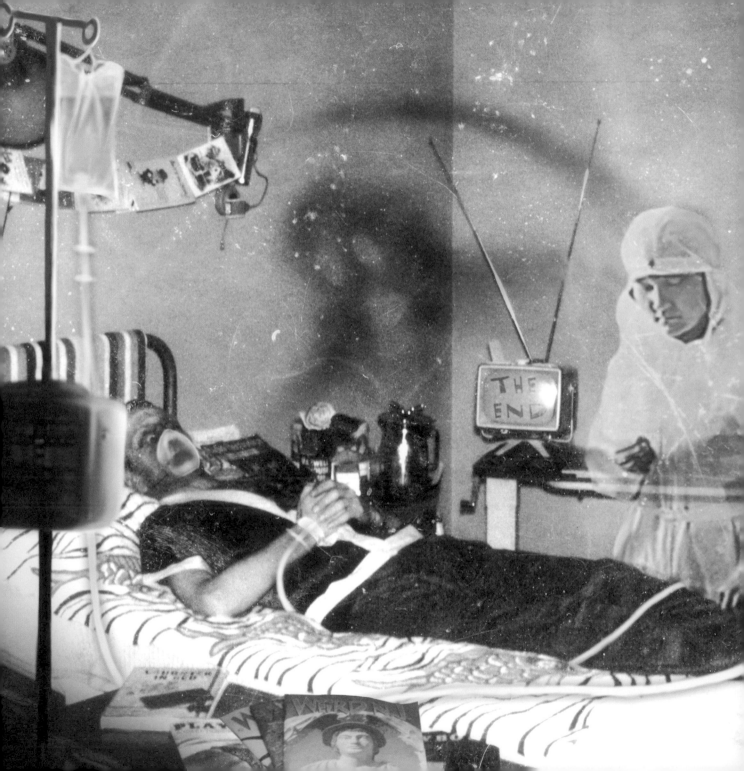

Bexar County Hospital's Angel of Death

Growing up in San Antonio, I have heard and seen some pretty weird stuff. But there are a few not-so-known incidents that happened to local businesses that do not want the strange events known, one of which is the formerly known Bexar County Hospital. My sister worked on the oncology ward as a medical clerk. She told us stories of a lady in white making her way down the hall performing her own Dr. Kevorkian rituals.

At the time, there was a rash of deaths taking place on the ward, and they were going in order from room to room down the hall. Now, while it seems it would be common to have deaths in this type of ward, the fact that it was progressing in order according to room number was what was bringing it to the staff's attention. Several patients, before meeting their demise, would ask who the nurse in the old-time uniform was that was coming in their room in the wee hours of the morning.

Many patients had video and diagnostic monitors on them with displays at the central nurses' station. Nurses could quickly review the patients' stats there so as to not disturb the patients during the night. But abnormal things started to happen. Patients would be seen talking with or holding their hands out to someone not seen on the monitor. Privacy curtains would suddenly close around the bed, obstructing the camera's view. One nurse had to repeatedly replace a tracheotomy tube that kept popping out of a patient's neck. The nurses watched the monitor to see if the patient was doing this himself and were startled to see it come out seemingly of its own accord. When they started watching the monitors more closely, the staff caught glimpses of a white figure moving around patients' beds.

The strange deaths stopped when one patient died and the next room in the progression was vacant. A patient's room across the hall was experiencing problems with the electrical wiring, and it was suggested that they move her into the vacant room, but staff members did everything they could to relocate her to another area. That is when management asked what was going on. The staff was told to keep quiet about their suspicions and that people would get fired if it leaked out. Several staff members, including my sister, soon turned in their resignations.—*Anonymous*

Camp Lulu

Summer camp. We all went there as kids or wished for it. Idyllic days playing in the sun, and songs and stories told around a fire at night. But are all the tales of ghosts and ghouls told around the campfire just that— tall tales? Stories of the macabre used by counselors to keep the little campers in check? Perhaps—perhaps not.

In Brownsville, there used to be a place called Camp Lulu. And it had its own terrible tale. Legend has it that a counselor simply lost it one day, and that he attacked and killed several of the girls in his charge. They say that because of this grisly act, the camp was closed down immediately.

But there's more to Camp Lulu's story. Locals say that to this day, if you venture there after sundown, you can hear the tortured cries of the victimized young campers. Perhaps their final moments of life were so traumatic that they are unable to let go. Perhaps they want the last ghostly tale of the camp to be their own. No one knows for sure.

According to the locals, however, the current owner of the property will chase you off the land if he sees you there. It is said that he's trying to protect the tortured souls of the unfortunate young girls who met their demise on his property all those years ago. So if you stumble upon Camp Lulu, beware of not only the undead souls who linger there but also the living who stand as sentinels for those who haven't quite passed over.

Bloody Center Theatre

Here in Corpus Christi, there is a place called Center Theatre. Back in the '40s, late one night, a woman who worked in the theater was cleaning up. Her jealous husband showed up to confront her because she had been cheating. He stabbed her many times and left her to bleed to death. Still to this day, the bloodstain remains where she died. They tried to clean it many times, and they say that it came up completely, but it always comes back. The theater itself has a very eerie feeling, and there is said to have been sightings of the woman all around it. You really have to see the theater—it is old, creepy, and very WEIRD.—*Tiffiny Fuller*

Ghosts of the Ashton Villa

When my mom, my sister, and I were in Galveston for a vacation back in 1997, I wanted to visit the Ashton Villa, not for its historical value, but for the ghosts I had read about. We arrived late in the afternoon and took one of the last tours of the day. Only two other people, a woman and her teenage daughter, joined us and our guide.

Now, let me explain a few things about the house. It was built in the 1800s and withstood a terrible hurricane that nearly destroyed the island. It sits almost in the middle of the town, actually in a bad part of town today. So the house is kept locked, and only one set of keys exists, for the tours. Only one group of people is allowed in the house at a time, and the doors are locked behind them when they enter.

The house was freezing when we walked in the door. "That's just the ghosts," our guide said teasingly. I had told her I was interested in the paranormal. It took some prodding on my part, but after a while, she told me little things, like stuff they would find out of place or how the clock that was broken would change time. The rooms of the house are set up to look like they did when the family lived there.

We were looking at the upstairs sewing room when we heard a crash. It sounded like a door had slammed. Everyone froze, but I spun around to see what the noise was. The frosted glass in the old veranda doors was vibrating, and through the glass, I spotted a man in a suit with short brown hair. Then he was gone. Our guide, meanwhile, looked white as a sheet and in a small voice said, "I heard that too."

We continued on, looking at the other rooms. Now the guide was very open to talking about anything paranormal in the house, considering our little run-in. We got to talking about the children that the couple had. They had two girls, Emily and Bettie, and a boy, Charles.

Charles committed suicide when he was twenty-one. He was wearing a suit when they found him. She showed us a family picture, and I flipped out—Charles was the guy I had seen behind the frosted glass.

We finished up the tour in the ballroom, and the guide showed me a very interesting picture. It showed a maid in the room. She said they used it as a guide to re-create the room's decor for the time period. But above the maid in the old photograph was the disembodied head of a man. There was no way it was a trick. It was just there, floating in the air above the woman. The guide said the attic was full of at least three dozen pictures with the same disembodied head in them.

I believe I caught a glimpse of Charles. No one else was in the house at the time, and where I saw him it would be impossible for any actual human to stand. I never really believed in ghosts until that day. But it goes to show you—you never know unless you go through it yourself.–*Angi K.*

The Lady of White Rock Lake

The story of the Lady of the Lake (or sometimes the Lady in White) is one of the most well-known ghost stories in the Dallas area. An encounter with this spirit usually goes this way: A man is driving on one of the roads that run around White Rock Lake late at night, when up ahead at the side of the road he sees a strange sight: a lone young woman who is dripping wet and wearing a 1920s-era evening gown. The man pulls over and asks the woman if she needs some help, and she asks him for a ride to a house on Gaston Avenue. The man obliges, driving through the night; the young woman remains silent beside him. When they finally reach their destination, the man turns to ask the woman exactly where he should pull over, and to his shock, she is gone—just silently disappeared, leaving nothing but a wet stain on the car's seat.

Legend says that the ghostly lady was once the daughter of a wealthy family. One night, on the way home from a party or a ball, there was a terrible accident, and the car she was riding in wound up in the lake. Her companions survived, but she drowned. Some say she is still trying to make her way home.

White Rock Lake is an absolutely beautiful spot, though it can be creepy after dark. Thick woods surround the dark waters of the lake, and a lonely road winds around its shores. There are giant, pure white birds, cranes or egrets, perched or swooping everywhere, making mournful cries. It's easy to see how one of these, with their tall white bodies and eerie calls, could be mistaken for a ghostly Lady of the Lake on a dark night. If you go, watch out for them. And watch out, too, for any late-night damsel in distress. She'll just leave a soggy puddle in your car.

Fort Bliss Is Anything but Blissful

In the mid-'90s, I landed a civilian job at Fort Bliss, a military base in Texas. The job was nothing too difficult—the only bad part was that I often worked a graveyard shift and would have to stay overnight. That's how I learned about the scariest place I will ever see in my entire life: Building #4.

Almost as soon as I started working at Fort Bliss, I began hearing tall tales about how haunted Building #4, or B4, was. In its early days, I was told, it served as a hospital, and at one point, it was even used as a morgue when the base's regular morgue was filled to capacity. In the early part of the twentieth century, before vaccines and medical advancements, many men died lonely deaths from diseases like influenza and whatnot. Because of the amount of suffering and death that took place here, rumors persisted that many troubled spirits still clung to B4 as their home, even from beyond the grave. Ghosts were seen, noises were heard, inexplicable events occurred regularly. I was told that some of the toughest guys at the base avoided stepping foot inside the unused building.

On those lonely nights of the graveyard shift, I often found myself driving out to B4, just to check things out for myself. I have to say, it definitely gave off a bad vibe. It was two stories high, with a stairway on the outside leading up to the second floor. During one of my first trips there, I thought I saw movement inside one of the upper floors' windows, as if someone was staring outside, then moved away. I wrote it off as a trick of the brain. A part of me wishes that would have scared me off forever and ended my fascination with B4.

Instead, I found myself a bit obsessed with B4. My favorite story was about the ghost of the Doctor. He was supposed to wander around in a medical uniform from the '20s, with high boots and, best of all, a surgical mask. The other ghost most people talked about was a dark-haired woman who would be seen outside the building, sometimes staring up at it.

I became so obsessed that I decided it would be a good idea to go inside the building myself. The guy who worked the shift before me agreed to stay late one night to accompany me. We brought a video camera, a powerful flashlight, and all the courage we could muster.

We went in through the back, and immediately, the adrenaline took over. It was quiet and much colder than the air outside. We made our way all through the first floor and began to feel more comfortable. I made my way upstairs. My co-worker was filming downstairs and said he would follow me up in a minute. I went from room to room, thinking about the men who had withered away here. It must have been a miserable place to spend your final days.

Down the hall, I saw the light mounted on the video camera peeking out from one of the rooms into the hallway. I made my way down to the room to meet up with my friend, only to find that the room was completely empty.

"Where'd you go?" I yelled out to him, not understanding how he could have left the room without my seeing him.

"Nowhere, I'm still down here," he answered back from downstairs.

I suddenly felt my entire body tingle as I realized that the light I had seen wasn't him at all. It was something from someplace else. I let out a scream that came from deep, deep within my stomach and launched myself back down the hall and downstairs. I was out of there before my friend could even ask me what was wrong, and he was right behind me.

I never went back inside B4. I had learned an important lesson: Being intrigued by the paranormal was okay—but after that night, I learned to always keep my distance from it.—*Jake B.*

Poets' Library and the Waving Statue of Pippa

Baylor University's Armstrong Browning Library of Waco is an incredible research library–museum devoted to the lives and works of the Victorian poets Robert and Elizabeth Barrett Browning. Some of the Brownings' original works are kept in this library, as well as many personal artifacts such as jewelry, locks of hair, furniture, photos and letters, and much more.

The Brownings shared a great love story. Elizabeth, fragile and a semi-invalid, was rescued from the clutches of her overbearing father by her younger suitor, Robert. (He had fallen in love with her after reading a volume of poetry she'd published. Things like that seemed to happen in Victorian times.) They married, and Robert whisked his bride away to Italy, where her health

miraculously improved. In true fairy tale fashion, the two lived happily ever after, really. In fact, Elizabeth wrote her famous "Sonnet 43," the one that begins *How do I love thee? / Let me count the ways* for her husband.

The Browning collection is in Waco thanks to the dauntless work of Dr. A. J. Armstrong, a former head of the English department at Baylor. Armstrong was passionately interested in the Brownings and managed to track down many of their possessions after they died. He assembled what is now the largest single collection of Browning artifacts in the world, and this library was constructed specifically to house them.

There is a legend that Elizabeth Browning haunts the building. Her spirit is said to be drawn there by the pull of the things that once belonged to her and her beloved husband and by her passion for her lifelong work. People claim to have seen her walking in the library at night, usually in a long, white formal gown. Most of the sightings have taken place on the third floor, which is the top floor of the building. Some people say that they've seen her figure peering out from the upper windows at night. And as in a classic ghost sighting, the light of a candle has been seen passing from room to room in the windows of the upper floor late at night, when no mortal soul is supposed to be in the place.

Another legend associated with the library centers around the statue out front. Many people assume that the statue is of Elizabeth, but it's actually of the character Pippa, from Robert Browning's work "Pippa Passes." She's standing in front of the building with her arms down close to her sides. However, on certain nights, the shadow she casts onto the library wall shows her arms waving high above her head. Or so the story goes.

When the *Weird Texas* research team checked it out, we found that the library building is a very impressive

After looking around downstairs, we decided to take a look at the supposedly haunted third floor. As we rounded a corner, we were momentarily stunned by a humongous and vivid painting of a bloody severed head tucked away in a stairwell. Kind of disconcerting, but we recovered and moved on.

Up on the third floor, we found only an empty hallway with several closed, locked doors. As we were just standing there, wondering what to do next, one of the doors suddenly opened, and a woman came out. No, it wasn't Elizabeth's ghost, but a lady who worked in the library. She greeted us and offered to show us the Elizabeth Barrett Browning salon, which we didn't even know existed.

The woman took us down the hall and unlocked the door to an amazing room. It held many of Elizabeth's things: her writing desk, jewelry, furniture, paintings. The only word for it is exquisite. This room was made just to hold the things Elizabeth Barrett Browning loved. Is it any wonder she would return to it again and again?

We asked our guide if she had ever seen the ghost, but she hadn't. She did say, though, that she gets very creeped out when she is alone on the third floor in the evening, and she sometimes gets the feeling that someone is watching her.

place, regally proportioned, with stained-glass windows everywhere. The inside is breathtaking. The ceilings are high, with elaborate moldings, and the sun streams through the stained glass. The furnishings are antique, and the floors are burnished wood. It's certainly the sort of place where a Victorian ghost might feel right at home.

As we left the library, we couldn't tell if Pippa's statue was looking at us in a rather knowing way when we passed by, but we did feel as if somebody's eyes were upon us.

The Ghost Nun

Since 1923, this historic and beautiful religious academy has served the ever-growing communities of El Paso, Texas, and Juarez, Mexico. It is one of the city's oldest structures, and its history is apparent with a glance at its classic architecture, its immaculate grounds, and especially, its looming old tower, which dominates the view. But there is one bit of dark history, or more accurately, folklore associated with this noble institution, and it centers around the stately tower.

Even though there is no historical evidence to support the spooky story, the haunting of Loretto's Tower is one of El Paso's favorite ghost tales and was being whispered during dark nights way back when my grandmother attended boarding school there. The lore states that on certain nights, the specter of a ghostly nun can be seen pacing slowly back and forth up in the highest reaches of the tower, her shadowy figure, in its old-fashioned habit, just visible through the arched openings. The reasons for this restless apparition seem to differ depending on the teller, but they all involve an illicit pregnancy on the nun's part. In some versions, she was locked away in the tower to cover her shameful betrayal of her holy vows; in other versions, the unfortunate nun took her own life in the tower to spare herself and the academy embarrassment.

While there may be no historical record of any such event associated with Loretto, it's the very unprovability of such tales that sometimes teases us with its mysterious possibilities. Whatever the case, there are still those who are convinced that they have seen the ghostly nun of the tower roaming among the shadows in the night.—*Shady*

Ghosts Come Out to Play at Galveston Wal-Mart

The city of Galveston sits on a barrier island along the Texas coastline southeast of Houston, roughly a hundred miles west of Louisiana. In 1900, it was the site of the deadliest disaster in the history of the United States, when a hurricane caused the loss of between six and eight thousand people. Major fires and epidemics in succeeding years took further lives and left Galveston's citizens reeling. It's no wonder that throughout the twentieth century, the number of ghost sightings continued to increase.

Where a Wal-Mart now stands, legend holds that an orphanage once stood. During the hurricane of 1900, a number of children were tied together in a line so that none would wander from the group as the storm pounded the building. Sadly, the storm surge swept them all away when it tore the building to pieces. Now, more than a hundred years later, the toy aisle of the Wal-Mart is a busy place late at night. Balls and other toys are knocked off shelves for the employees to pick up. And moving the toy section makes no difference. The children always seem to find it.—*Tim Stevens*

The Sobbing Girl of Matz Street

There is a street in Harlingen called Matz Street, and should you find yourself alone there after midnight, you might see what appears to be a young girl shuffling down the street as she quietly sobs. After the initial surprise of seeing a girl in such a condition at such a late hour, many would-be Samaritans have tried to stop and help her, only to receive no answer from the weeping apparition. Some have said that if she is approached, she may turn to look at you with a tear-streaked face, but she will not respond to your offer of assistance. In fact, she will slowly vanish from sight right before your eyes. No one knows who she is or why she cries, but many claim to have seen the sad and ghostly wraith girl of Matz Street.

Haunted Brownsville Well

In South Texas, in a small farmhouse twenty miles north of Brownsville, is a well. In that well are large, red ladder rungs. This well is not round, and it has a storage shed on the back. Climb down. When you get to the bottom, you should be on a small concrete platform. There is a crack in the stones that you can shine a light through.

Inside, you will see a cave. It is said to be haunted. They say there's a small girl with a large eyeless dog. The scary thing is that a nineteen-year-old guy that went missing was found a week later in the well with a small doll in his hands. The doll had no eyes.

—R. Kames

Bolivar Lighthouse

It seems that everyone in Galveston knows something or other about the infamous black lighthouse on the tip of the Bolivar Peninsula. From 1872 to 1933, this historic lighthouse shined its beacon into the night, guiding ships into the Port of Galveston from the Gulf of Mexico.

Well-known for its history, this old landmark also has its share of ghost stories and local legends, some of which have persisted from as far back as the 1950s, and even earlier. Many of the stories date from times when the lighthouse was unoccupied and local teenagers would dare each other to enter the supposedly haunted structure. The ghostly tales revolve around a young man who is said to have committed a particularly heinous crime: He murdered his own parents in the lighthouse, though the story is silent as to why. His angry, doomed spirit has remained there ever since. Some claim to have seen his ghostly presence lingering in the lighthouse windows.

The entire property is now private and closed to the public. Its occupants, whose family has owned the lighthouse for decades, have no knowledge of any deaths in or around the tower. Nonetheless, Bolivar's ghostly reputation is still deeply rooted in the area's folklore. It's all part of the lighthouse's undeniable intrigue and charm.

The fact that over time, the majestic lighthouse has weathered to a jet-black color only adds to its mystique. Though logic and science tell us that years of saltwater air and oxidation have given the towering landmark its dark shade, superstition is strong, and there are those who see spectral significance in the darkening of the edifice.

Bumping and Grinding in a San Antonio Hotel

I was in San Antonio for a high school journalism convention, and we stayed at the Gunter Hotel, a historical site now owned by Sheraton. There was a murder committed there in 1965 in room 636 involving a man in his thirties butchering a young blond woman (supposedly a prostitute) and dismembering her with a meat grinder. The maid discovered the mass of blood in the room when trying to clean and screamed when she saw the man run from the room with a blood-soaked bundle. The man was found in a neighboring hotel, St. Anthony, where he shot himself as the police entered the room. There are rumors of the ghost of the young woman, seen by the hotel staff in room 636.

My staff and I went to the sixth floor and noticed the floor plan, how the rooms skip numbers and how the wall is blank where the floor layout should have a room at the end. There is even a change in the top paneling, and you see the difference in the age of the molding. When you knock, it's creepily hollow.

Supposedly, people have done séances on that floor, but the two times I've stayed there, nothing extraordinary happened, except for strange noises, which were probably due to paranoia. –*Ruth, formerly of Waldwick, NJ*

Hey, Daddy!

The doctor my mom was working with got a chance to move into this really nice, new building right next to the office where they were working. For a while, the old office lay vacant, until a sleep and neurology doctor moved in and began to remodel the place. My mom was at the front desk when she received a phone call from the old office. The woman on the other end of the line asked if anything strange had happened when they used to work there. My mom said no and asked her to go into detail. The woman ended up going over to my mom's office, and she told her this: The doors open and slam shut. Pictures and other stuff that's hung on the walls just flies through the air at them. They also hear a voice that sounds like a little girl's, saying, "Hey, Daddy!"

My mom said that maybe it started up due to the remodeling. The woman agreed with her and also told her that no one will go in to clean or fix up the place. Her boss had a ten-year-old daughter who would not come in the office. She told her dad that the last time she was in there, a little girl was standing in the bathroom staring at her. She said that the little girl scared her. Her boss swears that he has never told his daughter about any of this because he felt she was too young. –*Kammy*

Who Lurks in the Firehouse?

The Lockhart Volunteer Fire Department station house, built in 1906, had several occupants before becoming just the firehouse. The Army National Guard once stored munitions firing pins there; Social Services occupied the second floor; a bank and temporary jail facility were also located in this two-story building. Some believe that several of the former occupants are still hanging around, even after death.

We were given a gracious tour of the building by Aaron Slaughter, a five-and-a-half-year veteran of the Fire Department. He gave us information on the background of the facility along with his experiences with a former resident.

In the spring of 1947, a thirty-eight-year-old fireman named Louis Wolff, who was off-duty at the time, heard the sirens of a fire truck that was responding to a call. Being only a few blocks away, he ran toward the truck and attempted to jump onboard while it was moving, and he lost his grip and was crushed under the wheels. Wolff was the only Lockhart fireman killed in the line of duty, and a plaque adorns the wall of the foyer in his honor.

Aaron has told us about instances where he would be sitting in the dayroom upstairs and would hear someone coming up the stairs. The footsteps would stop at the dayroom door, only no one was there. Aaron has also been in the dayroom watching TV when out of the corner of his eye, he would catch someone walking by the door. After going to the kitchen-office area to see who was there, he found the room was completely empty.

Fireman Darren Brock recounted an event: When he was sleeping on one of the beds in the dayroom during the wee hours of the morning, he heard footsteps coming up the stairs. They stopped at the dayroom door, and while no one was there, he felt like he was being watched.

Twelve-year veteran fireman Captain Bruce Smith has had too many encounters to recount. Most of them are the footsteps coming up the stairs, but he has another very interesting story. The station had a Dalmatian during that time, and while Captain Smith was sleeping in what is now the storage area, the dog bolted up in the middle of the night and started barking wildly. The dog ran to a door off the kitchen area still barking and then just as quickly started to backpedal away from it. The dog stopped barking and ran off into another room. Captain Smith did not seem like a person who would make up stories.

All three firemen are proud of their community and of their building's history. They don't even mind their visitor, who they feel may be former fireman Louis Wolff. He probably visits the station to see how things are going and who is on duty at night. In fact, they say that if you rub his plaque in the foyer, Louis will pay a visit within the next few days. We look forward to following up with Aaron since there was a lot of plaque rubbing done on the day of our visit.–*Marlene Stevens*

A Confederate Ghost

The Thompson Island Bridge

in San Marcos is said to be haunted by the ghost of a long-dead Confederate soldier. He died there at his post while guarding it during the American Civil War. It is believed that he still appears there, dressed in his gray-and-yellow uniform, cap, and cape and armed with a Kentucky muzzle-load rifle. Although sightings are infrequent, the dead soldier's ghost seems to be more active before and during wartime.

His ghost has been reported walking near the bridge since the 1920s. In 1939, two men fixing a flat tire on the bridge were startled by the figure of a tall man wearing a rebel cap. Because the man was carrying a rifle, one of the two businessmen went for a gun in the car, but the apparition disappeared before he could confront it. Legend says the ghost is a man who lived in a cabin near the bridge before the Civil War. When he and his brother went off to fight for the South, they promised each other that they would return home, no matter what happened.

The bridge is located over the San Marcos River on the road between San Marcos and Nixon.
–Tim Stevens

Ring of Ghosts

Howdy, *Weird Texas*.

There's a county in Texas called Brazoria, where over a hundred eerie things go down. If you take County Road past the Primitive Satanist Church (wait, it gets worse) and turn right just before Dead Man's Curve (which got its name due to the fact that so many people drove into the river on the hairpin turn), you will be on a small country road with no name. Along one side of the road is a full-on swamp with alligators, snakes, and about a foot of fog covering the ground. To your right are old oak trees with Spanish moss hanging down to the ground, just like in the opening credits of Scooby Doo.

At the end of the road, you have to get out and walk about another half mile. Remember, you can't see your feet due to the fog, and there are wild noises coming from the virgin Texas forest. You'll know when you get there because it's an abandoned seventeenth-century church. I am talking gargoyles and the whole bit. It was built by Spanish missionaries who were later killed and eaten by the local Indian tribe. There is a cemetery in the back with ancient tombstones, all with burn marks on them from where the Indians tried to burn it to the ground.

Now for the scary part: There are two sets of ghosts who hang around this structure. One is the Ring of Children. During frontier days, as the story goes, a group of children was playing ring-around-the-rosy in the woods. A sect of black magic practitioners came upon them and slayed them all. You can still see their ghosts if you and your friends stand in the middle of the graveyard and play ring-around-the-rosy. I've seen the fire in the distance and heard what sounded like small voices singing, but my nerves broke and I ran.

The other ghost of the area is known as the Banshee. A local deputy actually saw the Banshee and unloaded his revolver into her. She is rarely seen but more often is heard screaming in the woods when you are at the abandoned church. I have also heard this, but in another part of the woods. It sounds like a lady constantly being strangled to death and wailing at the top of her lungs. My dad, who was with me, said it was a panther stalking us. Either way, we thought it was a good idea to leave immediately.–Ran Scot

Cemetery
Safari

How people choose to be remembered after death is often a revealing look at the way they spent their time here on earth, or would have liked to. Some people who got little attention in life have become almost famous after their passing, living on in the memorials they left behind.

There are fascinating cemeteries all over the state of Texas. A walk through any one of them can be like a living history lesson, taught by those who preceded us and who know where we are all headed in the end. Some cemeteries have given rise to legends of hauntings and curses, while others are of interest simply for the offbeat tombstones to be discovered in them.

Each of these tombstones tells a story, and every graveyard that we may whistle past offers reminders of life's triumphs and tragedies to anyone who takes the time to read the words inscribed there. The departed speak to us from beyond the grave, and their words are written in stone. Sometimes they are words of warning or advice. Some tell tales of earthly woe, while others are actually lighthearted and inspiring.

Of course, there are hundreds of famous or noteworthy people buried throughout the state who distinguished themselves in one way or another in life. But these people have had their time in the sun. In this chapter, we place the spotlight on those dearly departed folks who waited until after death for their turn to really shine.

National Museum of Funeral History

The caretakers at Houston's National Museum of Funeral History would prefer that visitors think of their exhibit not as morbid entertainment but as an educational experience, though that's a little hard to do when they stock their gift shop with things like coffin soap and Death Salsa.

Still, that doesn't mean you won't learn something there. For example, did you know that the term *casket* is an American euphemism that equates a coffin to a keepsake box? Or that before the development of chemical embalming, the dead were preserved for viewing in windowed "corpse coolers" filled with ice? You might also be interested to know that nineteenth-century mourners commonly wore jewelry fashioned from the hair of their deceased family members. And that's just scratching the coffin lid. The reserve of macabre knowledge conveyed through the museum's exhibits could fill a Mortuarius edition of Trivial Pursuit.

One such exhibit, though devoid of gruesome details, covers the development of cadaver preservation. Featured is a life-size diorama honoring the work of Dr. Thomas Holmes, the "father of American embalming." Holmes, depicted in his morgue tent hand-pumping the fluids from a fellow mannequin, advertised his "petrifying" services during the Civil War by circulating flyers to battle-bound Union soldiers.

Continuing the theme, a replica of an early-1900s embalming room stands in contrast to Dr. Holmes's open-air facility. The display illustrates later advancements in bodily preservation

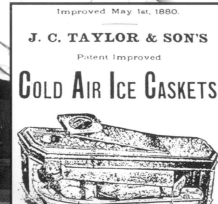

Improved May 1st, 1880.

J. C. TAYLOR & SON'S

Patent Improved

COLD AIR ICE CASKETS

Dr. Thomas Holmes, the father of American embalming, is depicted in his morgue tent hand-pumping the fluids from a fellow mannequin as part of his "petrifying" services.

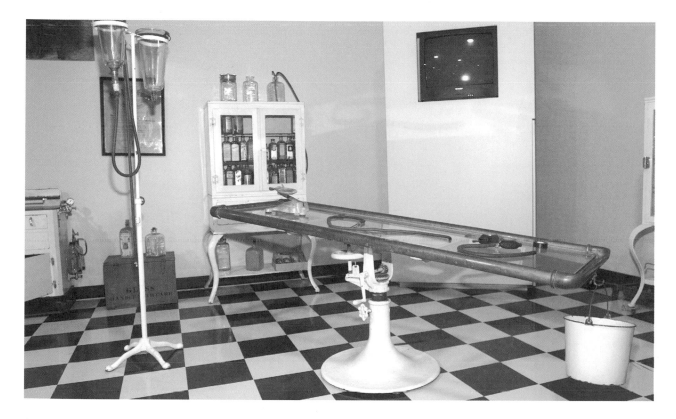

that, to sum up, basically involved exchanging the gravity-powered draining bucket for an electric pump.

Most of the museum, however, focuses on the more ceremonial aspects of death, with an impressive collection of postmortem paraphernalia. A convoy of hearses, both horse-drawn and motorized, borders a maze of coffins configured in every size and shape imaginable.

The most unusual example among the hearse collection is the museum's 1916 Packard Funeral Bus, the Swiss Army knife of funeral vehicles. It carried the deceased, his pallbearers, the flower arrangements, and nearly two dozen mourners, consolidating the usual procession of vehicles into one ultimate party bus. Unfortunately, the unbalanced design sometimes caused the whole thing to tip backward on the job, tossing its occupants about and overturning the casket, which understandably forced it out of service.

A replica of an early-1900s embalming room. This display illustrates body preservation that employed an electric pump rather than the earlier gravity-powered draining bucket.

Amid the caskets are numerous gems, such as the molded-glass number and the coffin built for three. Also included is the world's largest collection of Ghanaian "fantasy coffins," which are hand-carved to resemble, among other things, a lobster, a shallot, and an outboard motor.

All in all, the museum does a wonderful job of representing the history and diversity of interment practices without actually addressing the unpleasantness of death itself. Actually, the place makes the whole affair seem so agreeable that it almost defies its own motto, which insists, "Any day above ground is a good one."

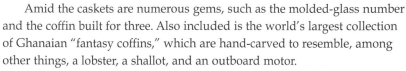

Far left, a re-created Victorian-era funeral parlor complete with everything necessary for a fancy wake—except a corpse, of course. Top, nineteenth-century mourners commonly wore jewelry fashioned from the hair of their deceased family members. Bottom, an ornately decorated horse-drawn carriage circa 1900 designed to carry children's coffins.

Madge Ward's Granite Grand

You probably wouldn't expect a graveyard to be the must-see attraction of your vacation, but if you're visiting family in Tyler, odds are that's exactly where they'll take you. Seems there isn't much else to do in the area, because Rose Hill Cemetery gets more than its fair share of traffic, most of which consists of people eager to see the way-out gravestone of Madge Ward.

Ward was an entertainer in life, and though she's been dead since 1995, she still attracts an audience.

Locals drive by to point her out to their friends, out-of-towners pile out of rented minivans to get a closer look, and even a tour bus or two has been known to roll by, pausing momentarily so its passengers could snap a quick photo through the windows.

Unless you have a serious short circuit between the left and right sides of your brain, you should be able to figure out just what the deceased did for a living. Yes, Madge Ward tickled the ivories.

For most of her long life, she performed her one-woman show at resorts and hotels and on cruise ships around the world. She entertained troops during World War II and taught music to schoolkids.

Near the end of her life, Ward commissioned a Tyler memorial builder to design a gravestone that would convey her passion to the world after she was gone. The result is an eight-foot-tall, twenty-five-ton grand piano inside which Ms. Ward rests eternally. The largest single-person monument on the grounds, the granite piano took more than a year to design and build. The price tag has been kept a secret, but custom monuments like Ward's typically cost tens of thousands of dollars. According to the piano's designer, she had been saving for it for thirty-five years.

Unfortunately, Ward never got to see her grand piano in person since the monument wasn't set in place until just after her death.

But it's just as well, since she didn't have to hear the subsequent whining from some of the locals. After the piano was erected, it struck a sour note with a number of Tyler residents, who called officials to complain. Apparently, not everyone appreciated Ward's individuality.

It's a good thing she didn't play the tuba.

Jesus in Cowboy Boots

There are approximately forty thousand graves in Evergreen Cemetery, yet one headstone gets all the attention. Word of mouth brings people from near and far to the town of Paris to find the grave they've heard so much about. They don't know who's buried there. They just come to see the Jesus in cowboy boots.

Willet Babcock, the man underground, owned a furniture factory in Paris and another in nearby Clarksville. A pioneer in plant automation, Babcock was instrumental in turning Paris into the cabinetmaking center of Texas in the 1870s. He was also reportedly a board member for Evergreen Cemetery, where he retired for good in 1881. His wife, Belinda, is interred next to him.

Of course, nobody's aware of any of this because . . . well, it all falls by the wayside once you stick Christ in a pair of snakeskins.

The truth is, no one's sure that's actually Jesus up there on the Babcocks' pedestal. Some think he looks a little too feminine. Besides, closer inspection shows that the individual isn't carrying a cross, just leaning on one.

According to Jim Blassingame, the superintendent of Evergreen, a lot of people think the figure is just an angel. It also looks as if he, or she, could be mourning over a grave. A local historian theorizes that it's really a Shakespearean character, as Babcock was supposedly an admirer of the bard. So what's the story?

There are a few who think the Babcocks were atheists. Evidently, theirs is the only marker with a statue that isn't facing east, the traditional placement. Plus, since anything upside down is a sure sign of godlessness, the atheism theorists point out the inverted torches carved into the pedestal's base. The snakeskin boots are apparently the kickers, so to speak—just a final act of blasphemy, like putting the Virgin Mary in a Stetson.

Superintendent Jim has his own hypothesis: "I think the man had a sense of humor about the whole thing, and that's why he set it up that way, so it would give everybody something to work on. Had the man died today, you would probably see the same statue up there with Nikes. He was just a pretty cool guy."

Hey, Lee Harvey Oswald, Where's Nick Beef?

He's probably the most infamous and controversial nobody in history. Having spent most of his life under the radar, Lee Harvey Oswald suddenly experienced worldwide scrutiny like few before him, a dissection of his life and persona that continues even today. He was only twenty-four when vigilante justice ended his life, a shocking moment captured on live television. It occurred just two days after the assassination of President John F. Kennedy, a crime for which Oswald was accused and then later convicted by the Warren Commission.

The same day Kennedy was laid to rest in Arlington, Virginia, Oswald was buried in Fort Worth. The ministers who were supposed to perform the service were no-shows, so an alternate had to step in. Reporters covering the event were compelled to serve as pallbearers. The entire affair reportedly cost just over $700, paid for by Oswald's brother.

His original headstone, a bit more decorative than the one there now, bore Oswald's full name and the dates of his birth and death. It was later replaced, supposedly after its theft, by a more modest stone bearing just his surname, the only word anyone needs to identify the man buried below. "Oswald" conjures just two images: a cartoon rabbit and the man convicted of killing the President.

Conspiracy theories and zealous speculation, unlike Oswald, refuse to die. In 1981, they even followed him to the grave. When a British writer sought to prove that the man buried in Fort Worth was an imposter, Oswald was exhumed. Independent pathologists concluded that the body was that of Lee Harvey Oswald, though naturally the episode prompted only more skepticism. The director of Oswald's funeral, who some say wasn't even present at the disinterment autopsy, claimed that the exhumed body showed no evidence of a craniotomy, which Oswald had undergone before burial. His conclusion: Someone had dug up the body and switched the heads.

Today, Oswald's gravesite is less a center of controversy than a tourist attraction. Management at Shannon

Rose Hill Memorial Park receives numerous queries every week from trivia seekers hoping to locate the grave just to get a look. The office staff won't tell anyone where it's located, but that doesn't stop people from asking. Self-affirmed "researchers" or those claiming that their children need extra credit for a school project try to finagle the information. It never comes.

Years ago, a headstone was installed next to Oswald's, marking the final resting place of the oddly named, and nonexistent, Nick Beef. The plot was supposedly purchased by a local comic or disc jockey who had the marker installed, then, depending on which version of the story you believe, either told his audience to ask about the location of Nick Beef if they wanted to find

Oswald or sold said information through a newspaper ad. Either way, it didn't work. The staff quickly caught on to Mr. Beef's ulterior motive, so even though they know where his headstone is, they won't tell you.

Even so, many find Oswald's grave on their own. Some take a picture. Others leave the occasional flower, maybe an American flag, or sometimes, strangely enough, coins. Vandalism tapered off years ago as emotional reactions to the assassination subsided, leaving the grave to become little more than a curiosity. But the burial park staff say Oswald is still their most famous resident. Yet, they say, "He's very quiet."

The Mourning Woman

Sure, cemeteries aren't the most uplifting of places, but finding a grave where someone has gone to a lot of trouble to be remembered and then learning that no one has a clue as to what the story is can be a little depressing. Such is the case with the grave of John Davis in Memphis. Then again, maybe it was the Carlsons who commissioned the vague marker. Or it could be Mr. and Mrs. Boykin. Nobody's really sure.

These five apparently related people, all of whom share a plot in the center of Old Fairview Cemetery, are watched over by a sixth figure whose identity is unknown. The figure appears in the shape of a woman whose body, as one local described it, is "all curled up in grief."

Those who run the funeral homes and monument shops in the Memphis area are generally aware of the unusual statue, but no one can offer any details about its origin. Longtime residents insist there's no story behind it, or at least none they know about.

It's surprising that, with such a strange form lying in a small-town cemetery, not a single rumor circulates regarding its origin. The best anyone can offer is that the statue may have arrived from Italy sometime around the 1930s. If so, she probably mourns for John Davis, who died in 1924. Judging from their positions, however, the two do not appear to be associated.

So who is she and for whom does she grieve? For now, that question will just have to remain open.

Grave of the Last Living Aunt Jemima

A number of America's most endearing commercial icons live on today, decades after being introduced to the American public. Unfortunately, their real histories have often been lost to the passage of time and focus group retuning. Take, for example, the new, hip, animated Colonel Sanders. Who ever thought that the man who built one of the world's most successful franchises on a $105 Social Security check would someday shake off death to bust phat rhymes about his menu?

Then there are those who fade into a barely noticeable logo, reduced to a face peering through a porthole in the corner of a box. Such was the fate of a once-celebrated flapjack personality.

When mill owner R. T. Davis purchased the rights to a ready-made pancake mix in 1890, he retained its original label, continuing to sell it under the name Aunt Jemima. He then developed the character as a beloved maid who was renowned for her cooking and her secret recipe.

In 1893, he hired a woman to appear in person as Aunt Jemima at the World's Columbian Exposition. Extolling the virtues of the easy-to-use mix, the newly cast Aunt Jemima performed for the public and shared with them her famous pancakes. With this, Davis had created the first living trademark and had established a marketing strategy that continued successfully for decades.

In total, seven women played Aunt Jemima. The last to take on the role was a Texan named Rosie Lee Moore, who was born just outside the town of Hearne. She was working in the advertising department of the Quaker Oats Company, which had acquired the Aunt Jemima brand, when she was offered the role in 1950.

For seventeen years Moore played the pancake queen, touring the country, giving demonstrations, and telling stories of her culinary adventures, including a tale about how she had revived a shipwrecked crew by cooking her invigorating griddle cakes for them.

ROSIE LEE MOORE
WIFE OF TRAVIS HALL
JUNE 22. 1899
FEB. 12. 1967
ROSIE WAS "AUNT JEMIMA" FOR
QUAKER OATS CO. FOR 25 YEARS.

Moore continued the appearances until her death, in 1967, at which point Quaker Oats retired Aunt Jemima as a living character, ending a popular campaign after more than six decades.

Moore was buried near her birthplace, though sadly, she lay without a marker for over twenty years. In 1988, Hearne sought to remedy the situation by erecting a headstone, which notes Moore's career as Aunt Jemima, though oddly bumping it up to a quarter century. Her grave was declared a historical site, no doubt in an attempt to boost local tourism by promoting her story.

Unfortunately for Hearne, there was a stigma attached to Aunt Jemima because of the negative social stereotype with which she was associated. The character was originally depicted as a southern "mammy": a dark-skinned, heavyset plantation cook dressed in an apron and checkered kerchief. (The name itself was lifted from a popular song performed by a vaudevillian in black-face.) Even though the icon's image had been progressively updated, finally losing all the characteristics of the original logo, opposition to it still existed.

Town promoters had planned ways to further publicize Moore's success, but they faced increasing controversy and got only as far as a small window display at the chamber of commerce. Today, even that is gone. The cemetery where Moore rests is mostly neglected, and about the only evidence you'll find of Aunt Jemima is a few nonspecific dolls in the bottom corner of a case in the chamber's office. Hearne officials appear to have given up advertising their once famous resident, now spending their efforts on publicizing their former German POW camp instead.

The Old Wink Cemetery

With less than a thousand residents, Wink is the kind of town where everybody knows everybody else and anyone can tell you, at any time, exactly where to locate someone else. There are, however, a few exceptions. Northwest of town, just outside city limits, reside a number of locals whose names and whereabouts no one has been able to pinpoint. This is odd, since they haven't

moved in nearly eighty years.

These lost souls inhabit what has come to be known as Old Wink Cemetery, located somewhere near the intersection of F.M. 1232 and C.R. 201. There's no sign, no gate, and not a single headstone. Many of Wink's residents aren't aware the gravesite even exists.

It was in the late 1920s when Wink came to life, the

result of a lucrative oil boom. Business was good all around, and people moved to the area in droves. Not wanting to be left out of the economic upturn, a local mortician decided he could make a killing selling burial plots. Pulling in $10 a plot, he was seeing a good profit, considering that the land he was peddling belonged to the local university, which had no knowledge of his operation.

The problem was, the mortician couldn't have picked a worse spot to plant his clientele. His spurious little cemetery lay beside a gully, which was soon dammed up to catch the water being drained from nearby oilfields. The site flooded, submerging the graves and covering the area with mud.

When relatives of the deceased learned of the situation, they filed suit against the mortician, who promptly skipped town. He subsequently died in a karmic car accident before the case made it to trial.

Records concerning Wink's ghost cemetery are sketchy, but it's believed that, in the end, a total of twenty-six people were buried there. Some references indicate that only seven or eight of the graves still exist, possibly after family members disinterred their relatives and moved them to other locations. A levee was built long ago to protect the area, but shifting sands, overgrowth, and brush fires have obscured all traces of the remaining graves. Only one had displayed a permanent marker—a simple concrete slab—but as of yet, no one has been able to find it.

In 1964, a local historical society organized an effort to preserve the memory of the site. Research was gathered, and a historical marker was placed near the cemetery's most likely location. The marker, meant to honor the dead and ensure that their existence would never again be forgotten, was later stolen. You could say it was gone in a wink.

Creepy Crypts

Cemeteries are supposed to be final resting places. There are some, though, where the spirits are not resting peacefully. Texas cemeteries have more than their share of unearthly tales associated with restless spirits and ghostly hauntings. Here, *Weird Texas* correspondent Shady takes us on a tour of some of the state's creepier crypts and telltale tombs.

The Glowing Grave of Karen Silkwood

When we first heard about the Glowing Grave of Danville Cemetery, we had no idea what the background was, beyond a vague story about "a woman who died in the '80s after being exposed to radiation" and that her grave supposedly glowed green on some dark nights.

So when we did some research, we were surprised to find that the woman was none other than Karen Silkwood. (You may have seen the movie *Silkwood*, which was based on her life.) She indeed suffered exposure to dangerous levels of radiation when she worked for the Kerr-McGee Nuclear Corporation, and she became a vocal crusader against the plant's shoddy safety practices. In 1974, while she was on her way to meet an Atomic Energy Commission official and a reporter to discuss her findings, she was killed in a car accident, causing much speculation about foul play.

Karen Silkwood is interred in Danville Cemetery, and locals swear that on some moonless nights, you can see a bright green, pulsing glow emanating from her grave. Ghostly traces of the high levels of radiation her body was exposed to, perhaps? A nighttime trick of the light? Or the chilling incarnation of Karen Silkwood's restless spirit?–*Kilgore*

The Children's Cemetery

Tucker Cemetery in Austin is a pretty well-known place. The story we got again and again from locals was that it is a haunted old cemetery, and if you were brave enough to drive toward it in the dead of night with all your lights off, strange things would happen. Door locks, for example, even manual ones, would pop up and down, as if spectral children were playing with you as you neared their resting place.

No one seemed to know the name of the place, however. Everyone just referred to it as the children's cemetery on Stoneridge Road, which made it kind of hard to locate. Luckily, when we found the road on the Austin map, we could see a small cemetery marked alongside it as well. Since it was the only cemetery on that road, we were fairly certain that would be it.

The area is heavily wooded, and the roads are very twisty, so it took a bit of maneuvering to figure things out. Finally, we found the place, and was it spooky! It sat back off the road, nestled in the woods, with a small, sandy parking area directly in front of it. A bright (almost cheerily so) blue wooden sign outside the fence announced TUCKER CEMETERY—ESTABLISHED JAN 1880.

Even though it was afternoon, the areas just beyond the parking lot were heavily draped in the shadows of thick foliage. The only sound was the crunching of leaves under our feet and the intermittent clicking of my camera.

Once you step inside, it's immediately clear why people call it a children's cemetery: The entire place is filled with very tiny graves. The air was hot, humid, and steeped in sadness. Bright flowers and even brighter collections of teddy bears, baby shoes, nursery books, and other childhood items covered many of the plots, even some of the oldest ones. Many of the same family names appear on the tombstones, going back for decades. We found a pink marble stone engraved with smiling cartoon lambs at the grave of a pair of twins and could only wonder how they died. There was no information beyond their names and a simple date, 1957.

We even saw the gravestones of people who are still alive. Take the one for ED & LORRAINE, THE BEST EVER CEDAR CHOPPERS. It seems that Lorraine is still alive, even though her name and photo are on the tombstone alongside her husband's. The deer that sits on Ed's grave creeped us out a little—it looked oddly angry. But the grave itself was rather sweet and touching, with its retelling of Ed and Lorraine's story engraved there.

Nothing weird happened to our car while we were there, but then again, we didn't go in the middle of the night.

El Paso's Evergreen Cemetery

You might say that Evergreen Cemetery in El Paso is near and dear to my heart, as odd as that is to say about a cemetery. It's one of two cemeteries my friends and I were fascinated by when we were growing up (Concordia, across the freeway from Evergreen, is the other). By day, we would wander through them, me usually with a cheap disposable camera in hand, marveling over the countless varieties of intricate stonework and statuary. By night we'd HAUNT them, flashlights in hand, clinging close together and slinking through the tombstones, half dreading and half hoping to get a glimpse of the ghosts that are said to haunt Evergreen at night. We did hear many a creepy, unidentifiable sound echoing across the graves, but we never actually saw any ghosts.

Evergreen Cemetery is a very old and strangely beautiful place. Some of El Paso's most exquisite statuary is located within its grounds, which are studded with rich evergreen trees woven among the headstones. Between this location and another on the east side of town, Evergreen's forty-seven acres have seen an estimated forty-seven thousand burials, including an array of interesting and famous folks including a *Titanic* survivor, several El Paso mayors, a Mexican president, and several well-known Utah St. madams.

Unfortunately, for some reason, this cemetery's stone inhabitants seem to suffer a higher-than-average loss of heads, wings, and limbs—perhaps due to their intricacy, their age, or some combination of both. Whatever the cause, it does make for some unsettling imagery as you wander through the grounds.

For many years, people have claimed to hear childish laughter coming from inside the cemetery walls late at night. Some say that the noises are the ghosts of the children buried within, rising to laugh and play together among the tombstones under the moonlight. Others say it's the statuary itself, the chipped stony angels and children climbing off their tombstone perches for a few hours of nighttime fun amid the evergreens.

Either way, it makes for a very creepy mental picture, something not easily dismissed if you happen to be wandering around inside Evergreen's walls after dark, surrounded by the eerily watchful statuary on all sides. Brrrrr!

Lying Down on Smiley's Grave—Dallas

Even the name Smiley's Grave sounds creepy and unforgettable. And this place is both.

It is said to be the grave of an entire family who all died on the same day. Some claim it is because the father killed the family, then himself. They also say that if you lie down on his grave at midnight (some say at midnight on Halloween), it will be hard to sit back up, as if invisible arms are pulling you down from beneath the grave. It's Smiley, trying to add another member to his ghostly family.

Smiley's final resting place is easy to find. It's good-sized and seems to be divided into two sections: Mills Cemetery on one side, Garland Cemetery on the other. We were there on a very hot, humid day, and oh man, was there a bad smell—a very, very bad smell! A horrible odor of rot and decay and, well, things dead.

From a distance, Smiley's grave seems unremarkable. Its tombstone is regularly sized and shaped. It's not till you get up close that you notice that there is not one but five names on it, and sure enough, all of them died on the same day. The names of mother, father, and three daughters are engraved with their birth dates, and underneath is the line ALL DIED MAY 9, 1927.

One can't help but wonder how the poor family died. Was it a murder-suicide, as the legend says, or perhaps a fire or some other disaster? Someone told us that the family died of a shared illness, but it would be odd for all of them to die on the exact same day.

Of course, we had to lie down on the grave, even though it wasn't midnight (or Halloween). We got comfy and waited a minute . . . but there was no phantom embrace.

Smiley's grave is in a beautiful old cemetery, worth a visit for those inclined. But that creepy death stench. Whew!

The Black Jesus

Oakwood Cemetery in Huntsville is famous for being the final resting place of legendary Texan General Sam Houston. It is also well-known for a less famous, much darker legend—that of the so-called Black Jesus.

Located at the very edge of the lush, green cemetery sits a recessed wildwood landscaped by the Powell family in the 1920s, after the tragic passing of their five-year-old son. It is a well-tended, circular clearing with benches on either side and family graves at its center, edged by gorgeous palms and shaded by the thick forest pressing against its back. This quiet nave is dominated by a hulking, black, deeply-muscled, bearded statue that seems to watch you from every angle. This is the sculpture that the locals call the Black Jesus.

Originally, the Jesus, who stands with his hands turned palms up at his sides, was a shining bronze. It wasn't long, though, before it was weathered to an inky black. According to local lore, the dark color could not be cleaned away, as if the statue itself was cloaked in the blackness of mourning. Adding to the mythology of the place, the graves inside this hushed area are laid out with their feet facing west, while the rest of the graveyard's occupants have been laid out in the usual feet-facing-east orientation.

According to the legend of the Black Jesus, if you dare visit the statue at night, you might see his hands change to a palms-down position instead of their daytime, palms-up position.

We didn't get to test this eerie theory, as we visited during the day. But we did notice something weird about the statue: The hands did seem to change position when looked at from different angles. It also has those eyes that follow you wherever you go. The clearing had a quiet, watchful vibe, even during the day, so we can only imagine how spooky the Black Jesus might be in the deep of night.

The Kissing Statues

Forest Lawn Memorial Cemetery in the lovely small town of Beaumont has a legend of its own, but it's slightly different from other cemetery legends. Rather than being spooky, this one is more on the romantic side.

In the midst of this lushly green, landscaped graveyard stands a well-known memorial that locals refer to as the Kissing Statues. It is an intricate, life-size, and exquis-

pull your car around the drive behind the couple in the darkness of night and shine your bright lights on them, the statues will turn and begin to kiss. Witnesses have reported seeing the girl's face turning sideways toward her lover as his white marbled arms reach around to caress her back and the two share a long, loving, if spectral kiss. Eerie, yes, but the twist makes this an intriguing and unforgettable graveyard visit.

itely rendered likeness of an eternally loving couple. The statue itself is a marvel to view—every tiny detail, every fold of fabric and bulge of vein under the skin is delicately and perfectly carved. If it were not for their slightly weathered state, you might expect this pair to take a breath or turn their eyes upon you at any second, even in the bright sunshine.

However, nighttime is when this memorial turns from sentimental statuary to local legend. It is said that if you

Halloween Ghost Lights at the Round Mound

In 1978, when I was in college at Abilene Christian University, the local paper ran a story about a cemetery near Fort Phantom Lake called the Round Mound. The story said that if one were to visit the cemetery at midnight on October 29, 30, and 31 (Halloween), they were guaranteed to see apparitions of some of the people buried there on Halloween night.

Not one to turn down the chance to see a ghost, I went with a couple of friends to the cemetery when instructed. The first night, only a few others were there. The headstones described many of the people buried there as Civil War–era veterans who had protected settlers against warring Indians.

On the thirtieth, there were quite a few more cars. People milled about reading the headstones' inscriptions by flashlight.

The following night, Halloween, we got there at about eleven thirty. The place was packed. Cars were parked in every available space in and near the graveyard. Literally hundreds of flashlight beams illuminated the area. Whatever eerie feeling one might have had by being in the cemetery at night just didn't happen.

Midnight came and went. The excited chatter began to die down, and many people began to leave. My friends and I wandered around the graveyard, resigned to the fact that we were wasting our time. Mary, one of our friends, pointed out a truck that was driving around in a dense growth of trees just behind the cemetery. It was a minute or so before I said that there was no road back there. Nor was there a truck—just lights. Then we saw that other lights were hovering on the edge of the graveyard. They weren't casting beams as from headlights or flashlights. Mary approached one of the lights. She looked at it closely for a few seconds, then turned and ran back to us.

"Let's go," was all she said. She was, for lack of a better word, unsettled. As we were leaving, we noticed that only a few people were pointing at the lights. They were the ones who had been there since the first night.

—*Tim Stevens*

Concordia Cemetery

Concordia Cemetery in El Paso is one very fascinating necropolis. This gigantic old cemetery goes way back in time, and its ghost stories are many.

Concordia first started out as a ranch, but it claimed its first burial (a lady of the ranch, who had been gored by a pet buck) in the mid-1800s. The city of El Paso purchased part of the land for the burial of paupers in 1882; by the 1890s, other sections had been purchased by different groups and were segmented into areas for Chinese, Jewish, black, Jesuit, Catholic, Masonic, military, city, county, and other ethnic and social groups. As of today, the fifty-four acres of this vast graveyard are the final resting place of around sixty-five thousand souls.

There are many noteworthy occupants at Concordia, from Jesuit priests to Kansas St. madams to Mexican presidents. But its most well-known resident by far is notorious gunslinger John Wesley Hardin. Hardin was famous for supposedly killing more people than Jesse James AND Billy the Kid combined. He was killed in the Acme Saloon, in downtown El Paso, in 1895. Despite efforts to have his remains moved to other locations, court injunctions have seen to it that the gunslinger remains undisturbed in Concordia. And there are those who claim to have seen his pistol-packin' ghost wandering the acres of the old boneyard.

But Hardin's ghost might not be the only one wandering around

Concordia. Local lore says that on some dark nights, the thundering hooves of phantom cavalry horses can be heard ringing through the tombstones. Remnants of the time long ago when Fort Bliss was on these grounds? Another well-known bit of spookiness is the children's laughter emanating from Concordia. It seems impossible, yet neighbors surrounding this spooky place have been hearing such things for years.

Concordia's sinister reputation goes beyond its ghostly tenants. For a long time, this old cemetery lay in a state of disrepair. Because it is owned by both public and private institutions, no one organization is responsible for its upkeep, security, or preservation. In years past, this resulted in chaos. The cemetery became a haven for various criminals, homeless folk, Satanists, drug addicts, and more. The broken-open tombs (which have now been repaired) held numerous possibilities for unknown hazards. Anyone, or anything, could be lurking inside.

Concordia

YOU ARE IN THE FAMOUS CONCORDIA CEMENTERY (CITY AND COUNTRY PLEASE HELP)
IMPORTANT FACTS * THE BUTTERFIELD OVERLAND STAGE PASSED HERE! * FORT BLISS WAS HERE! * HEROES, BUFFALO SOLDIERS, CHINESE RAILROAD BUILDERS MEXICAN PRESIDENTS (OROSCO & HUERTA) KIT CARSON'S HALF BROTHER * BILLY THE KID'S CAMPANION * LADY FLO * PARSON TAYS, *FATHER PINTO * MSGR. BUCHANON , *JAMES BIGG'S (THE AIRFIELD) * DIAMOND DICK (ERNEST ST. LEON) * JOHN WESLEY HARDIN * THE MORGAN CONTRACTORS *SOLDIERS FROM MOST OF OUR WARS, * CYRUS JAMES..... THE INCREDIBLE LIST GOES ON.....

In one infamous event, a grisly murder occurred within the walls of Concordia. Police eventually decided it was a drug -and/or gang-related killing motivated by revenge. A carload of men drove the victim into the cemetery one night, beat him with rocks and bricks (and, supposedly, pieces of tombstone), then ran him over repeatedly. After they were finished with their deadly work, the men drove off and left their victim's battered body there with the rest of the dead, to be discovered the next day.

Luckily, in recent years, some concerned citizens of El Paso have formed the Concordia Heritage Association, and their volunteers have done a tremendous job of cleaning, repairing, and preserving the cemetery, making it a safe place for El Pasoans to visit.

Abandoned in Texas

id you ever get the feeling you were being watched? It's a very unsettling sensation, one that's all the more unnerving if you happen to be alone in a place where no living person is supposed to be. Some of our scariest, and most thrilling, times have been spent exploring abandoned locations around the state. Stepping into a strange world that others once inhabited, and then deserted, is a very weird trip. Who were the people who once lived here? Why did they leave, and where did they go? These are the questions that race through your mind when you're inside these forsaken monuments of rotting wood, broken glass, and peeling paint.

Then there are the stories that surround these places. Anything left abandoned long enough will almost always become the subject of local mythology. But have these stories sprung forth from overactive imaginations, or do some weird things really go on behind these forlorn façades? Think about that as you enter another darkened doorway to explore the mysterious abandoned places of Texas.

The Abandoned Frat House

There are those rare moments in life that can completely change your outlook on the way the world works. In finding the Pike House of San Marcos, we discovered one of those moments. We will never, ever forget that place.

First of all, let us tell you what we'd heard. In San Marcos, there was a huge, abandoned building near a place with the creepy name of Purgatory Creek. People said it was originally an insane asylum that had sat empty for some time, haunted and deserted, until the Pi Kappa Alpha (Pike) fraternity turned it into a frat house back in the '60s. At some point during one of the fraternity's hazing periods, legend has it, a pledge or pledges were killed carrying out some ritual. The story goes that the brothers had the pledges write down the events of that night in their pledge books, then burn them and finally nail them to a wall.

The house is supposed to have been abandoned since then, even more haunted than before. But anyone brave enough to venture inside the very dark, very spooky old place might still find the burned pledge books nailed to the wall, bloody handprints and splatters there too, crime scene tape, and Polaroid photos.

Now, stories like this are fairly common, and when we first heard this one, we were skeptical. We'd heard too many exaggerations about such places and thought that the legends of Pike House might just be another crock. But we had some good directions to the house, so we decided to check it out.

Once in San Marcos, we found the place easily. When we rounded a curve in the road and first saw it, our jaws dropped, and our eyes flew wide open. We couldn't believe it! The place was incredible, even from a distance—huge, decrepit, creepy. It sat back from the road, looming above a huge green expanse of lawn, right in the middle of a very nice suburban neighborhood. We found a place to park just around the corner by a really neat little park called Wonder World, which incidentally had an antigravity house, a fault line cave, and an observation tower.

Anyone brave enough to venture inside the very dark, very spooky old place might still find the burned pledge books nailed to the wall, bloody handprints and splatters there too, crime scene tape, and Polaroid photos.

There were NO TRESPASSING signs posted all around the old frat house, but in the time that we were there, we saw many neighborhood people cut across the lawn during their afternoon strolls and even ride their bicycles around the grounds. Nobody seemed to be bothered by our checking the place out; in fact, we got several friendly smiles and waves from neighbors who were out tending their lawns or playing with their kids. As we circled around the house, we noticed that one of the boards had been torn off a window and lay propped against the wall beside it. The window stood wide open like an invitation. There was just no way on earth we could resist, so in we went.

This place was DARK—very, very dark and very creepy. We went through a doorway on the left and found ourselves in a big dim room with a collapsing ceiling. The first thing we noticed was the fraternity crest on one wall, then faded Pi Kappa Alpha symbols on another. It was a frat house! We were pretty excited to find that part of the legend to be true. We spent a while wandering carefully through the place. It wasn't easy,

because it was super-dark in there, but as we went from room to room, our excitement grew. Lo and behold, we saw many faded smears and handprints (which could be considered bloody-looking, we supposed) on the walls! There were also coils of yellow CAUTION tape strewn around several different rooms. We were more and more thrilled with every step. Slowly, all the pieces of the legend were coming together in front of our eyes! We began to realize how jaded and cynical we had become about finding genuinely creepy places. Discovering this one reminded us why we love doing this! But the best was yet to come.

In a kitchenette, we found the words I'm Sorry scrawled below a skull, and in an adjoining room, the wall was decorated with splatters and smeared handprints accompanied by the message Help Me. Then, in a hallway, we discovered a Ouija board hand-drawn on a built-in shelf. This place just kept getting better and better. We saw more caution tape and smeared

handprints on the stairwell and considered going upstairs to explore the upper levels, but we thought better of the idea because of the state of the ceilings in most of the rooms, which were seriously collapsing.

So we exited the house and went back out into the stifling heat. We were still pretty exhilarated from our jaunt inside when we ducked under the porch to check it out. We turned around a corner and were stopped dead by what we saw: There, under the porch, was what looked

like part of the basement, and great googlymoogly— there were the BURNED PLEDGE BOOKS nailed to a wooden beam! Our hearts started pounding. We couldn't believe that they actually existed! They were black and stained and had obviously been there a very long time. We stood staring in awe for a few more minutes before emerging back out into the sunlight.

We never located the rumored Polaroids, but finding the crazy old place, the CAUTION tape, the handprints and blood smears, and the pledge books themselves—well, it was more than we'd ever expected. We even found out that the place had been used as a hospital in the past (not a mental hospital, but a hospital nonetheless). It reminded us how many genuine mysteries still exist to be uncovered out there. This has to be one of the best places we have ever explored, hands (bloody ones) down.

School's Out Forever in Gail

There used to be a town in Texas called Gail, the few remaining structures of which lie just outside Big Spring. Though the town is no more, the old Gail School remains, an abandoned shambles.

The school's list of tragedies is rumored to be what led to the town's demise. The sad chain of events seems to have begun when a girl was found hanged in the bathroom. Some said she failed a class and got so depressed that she committed suicide. Others suspected a murder. No one knew for sure. The controversy caused tremendous tension for the staff. Having no answers, the school principal is said to have taken his own life by shooting himself right in his office, which strikes us as suspicious.

The school was immediately shut down. Locals say the town's demise followed the school's very soon thereafter, leaving only the empty institution and the few remaining farmhouses that still stand today.

Legend says that anyone who enters the school risks dangers of many sorts. If you can negotiate the debris in the darkness, you may make it to the principal's office. Some folks say the old administrator is still lingering there. That cold breath you feel on your neck in the dark and dreary room may be the principal himself.

And what of the mysterious hanging student? She is said to be waiting in the old bathroom, still hanging around in the dark. If you look into the blackness, beware: They say she'll be staring right back at you.

The "Temple" of Valentine

Every year around Valentine's Day, the post office in the small city of Valentine receives a huge volume of mail to be processed using their postmark. Other than this fact, there isn't much to distinguish this small West Texas town from the countless others with no more than a few hundred in population. But Valentine did have one other oddity that made an impression on me at a young age: an abandoned house.

My grandparents were teachers who lived in Valentine for a few years. Between the ages of five and eleven, my brother and I spent a week or two with them for several summers. With little else but 1960s television to keep us busy, we spent a lot of time exploring the outdoors, barns, and vacant buildings.

One day, we made an unusually macabre discovery. The small house our grandparents lived in was on a dusty lot, located on a dusty street corner, with the hot air always full of . . . well, dust. Directly across the street was a vacant painted-cinderblock one-story house with a flat, gravel roof sitting in a weed-infested lot. It was an odd creation, but there was a bizarre element that stuck out even more: The home's previous owner had added some walls around the house that served to obstruct the direct view of the front. And in these walls, sculpted mortar had been shaped to resemble demons' faces and the naked upper torsos of overly endowed women.

Upon walking outside on our first day there, our attention was fixed instantly on that house. And almost as instantly, our grandparents told us the place was off-limits. We were crushed, but undeterred. Days went by with the hot sun cooking parched land at temperatures of well over 110 degrees. Even the buzzards sought shade. My brother and I spent those afternoons reading and occasionally glancing out the window at what we'd come to call "the temple." We had to take a look.

I don't remember how it happened exactly, but we soon found ourselves standing among the tall weeds, staring up at the demon heads and naked ladies. At that age, it was really difficult not to just stop and stare at the sculptures, poorly crafted or not. But we knew we were standing in plain sight and didn't want our grandparents to call us back so soon. We hurried along the wall to the side that faced the house and found many more of those adornments. There were freakish characters with rams' heads, and snakes and pigs. It seemed like a tribute to all the dark things one could imagine. And the creator of these things imagined a lot.

The front door, however, was plain. And it was ajar. We stepped inside, into the darkened interior, and let our eyes adjust. The house appeared to be just one large room. Unidentifiable junk littered the floor, but there were two things we picked out that needed further investigation: a refrigerator and a large concrete slab.

The refrigerator stood alone along the wall closest to the slab (which, for lack of a better description, looked like some kind of altar). We were surprised to find the light inside the fridge worked, meaning that the house still had power. But for whatever reason, we didn't make the logical leap to turn on any lights. The refrigerator was disgusting. There were no jars with floating eyeballs or large bags of lobbed-off heads, but it wasn't difficult to imagine they'd been in there at one time.

Then we walked up to the altar. It was simply a flat concrete table, four feet by eight feet, like the ones found at parks. Except this one had a dark, grisly stain on it that was spread over more than half the surface. We shuddered, thinking what that might mean.

It was some time later—perhaps years—that we confessed to our grandparents what we'd seen. They told us that a reclusive man had lived in the mysterious house and had abducted several children and sacrificed them.

He was caught and was committed for life to some mental institution. I don't know if any of that was true, but the state of the house didn't make that notion unbelievable.—*Tim Stevens*

Buried Sins of La Lomita Mission

As defined by a popular dictionary, a mission is a ministry commissioned by a religious organization to propagate its faith or carry on humanitarian work. It's a noble purpose normally held in the highest regard by the faithful. One such building in Mission has a more sinister tale that belies these good intentions, however. Legends hold that at the height of La Lomita Mission's popularity, unbeknownst to anyone in the surrounding town, the priests were having sex with the resident nuns. Since all of this took place before reliable birth control, unwelcome children soon began to be born to the not-so-celibate nuns. These people of the cloth, fearing they would be excommunicated if the children were discovered, committed the most gruesome of acts: They buried the bodies of the infants in the backyard of the mission.

This hideous practice couldn't be concealed forever, though, and the story continues that the unholy folk were found out by some townspeople, who were so horrified that they stormed the mission. Two of the padres were killed, while a third fled, only to die during his attempt to escape. No one knows what became of the nuns.

The mission stood empty for some time. Rumors claim that the bones of the fallen priests were on display as a reminder of its horrific past. For a time, the mission was said to be an insane asylum of some kind, in which ghostly apparitions were often reported by staff and patients. Finally, the evil vibes in the place became too much to bear, and it was closed permanently.

The Parkland/Woodlawn Hospital

An abandoned old hospital is the perfect place for a haunting, and Parkland Hospital in Dallas is said to have a few ghosts. The original old clapboard hospital on the site was replaced by the current building in 1913. It became known as Parkland because it was built on beautiful, sprawling grounds called Oak Lawn. The place, which was expanded several times, became famous for its intricate brick architecture, Greek Revival entrance, and lush parklike setting.

In 1954, in response to a need for more space, a new Parkland Hospital was constructed near the old facility, which was then renamed Woodlawn. The new Parkland became the main hospital, and of course, it was the hospital John Kennedy was taken to after he was shot. For a time, Woodlawn was used to treat patients with chronic diseases and psychiatric problems, then it was closed as a health-care facility in 1974. Ownership was transferred to Dallas County, and the former hospital went through many incarnations. At different times, it housed a rape crisis center, the Dallas County Fire Marshal, an alcohol rehabilitation center, and a minimum-security prison.

So this place has a lot of history. It's not surprising that people claim it could be haunted. There have been reports of strange noises, voices, lights inside the hospital at night, and even apparitions. The most famous is the specter of a little girl who they say fell out of a tree and died on the grounds. Supposedly, she appears near a tree and says, "You're too late to help." Then she vanishes with a scream.

Haunted or not, the old hospital is an incredible complex, with gorgeous brickwork and distinctive style. Leafy trees dot a brilliant green lawn, all impeccably maintained. Someone's paying a bundle to keep up these grounds. And the place is huge. Simply walking around it takes about half an hour. Unfortunately, walking around it is about all you can do. The place is tightly boarded up, and there is no access. Whatever happens inside stays inside, at least for the moment.

We did recently read the following in a Dallas publication: "ASLA Dallas will work in partnership with the Dallas Chapter of the American Institute of Architects (AIA) to restore the abandoned Parkland Hospital and turn it into the first-of-its-kind health education facility for the citizens of Dallas." So maybe the old place is gonna get new life again sometime soon. We can only hope that the new facility will set aside a little space for the residents of the former institution who never checked out.

Beaten by a Ghost at Zelder's Mill

While traveling down Highway 183 in central Texas, you can see the densely packed growth along the highway suddenly open up. Then you see the outskirts of Luling, a dilapidated old mill along the San Marcos River. Known as Zelder's Mill, this thriving grist and sawmill helped establish the small community in 1874. Now it barely stands, unused since the 1960s.

The aura around this crumbling building is impressive. Even the river that flows past the mill seems to quietly sneak by as if to go unnoticed. There's a hush to the area even with the highway right overhead. Maybe this is the reason the specter haunting the area tries to keep noisy intruders away.

Local teenagers will tell you that the area under the bridge is a favorite spot for late-night get-togethers. But only thrill seekers come here. Some have experienced a barrage of rocks being thrown at them from various directions until they are forced to flee. A man hunting for wild turkey along the riverbank said a dark specter came out of the wooded area and took his gun from him. It then beat him with it before mangling and twisting it into worthless scrap. Could this be a former watchman of the mill still protecting the area?—*Marlene Stevens*

Sea-Arama Marineland Goes Belly Up

Long before San Antonians filled the splash zone at Shamu Stadium, Texans were crowding the benches at Galveston's immensely popular Sea-Arama Marineworld. An exciting aquatic adventureland, the water park made a big impact as one of the earliest marine attractions. It featured sea lions, performing dolphins, the occasional orca, and even a touch of alligator wrestling. It also had the added benefit of providing a glimpse of sea life without having to go to the beach.

Sadly, by the late 1980s, Sea-Arama had begun to suffer a serious loss in attendance. As other, more flashy parks arrived on the scene, Sea-Arama's owners had trouble keeping things afloat. Much to the delight of animal activists, who were quick to cite the two orcas and eleven dolphins that had perished at the park, this part of Texas history closed its doors in 1990. After the aquariums were drained and the animals dispersed to other locations, the property was put up for sale. But so far no suitable suitor has arrived.

The walls of the long-abandoned buildings are now cracked, and the tanks are overgrown with algae. The once-impressive modernist façade has turned into a decaying hazard, while other structures have succumbed to gravity completely. Peeling and crumbling, Sea-Arama has become Galveston's version of the Roman Colosseum—though, of course, without all those dead Christians.

What will eventually befall the relic has yet to be determined. There have been reports of a new water park opening there, but no one's offering specifics. For now, all we have to go on is what the graffiti tells us: that J.H. is running the place, and it will, until a purchase is made, continue to serve as STONER LAND.

Hospital Returns from the Dead

The old Jefferson Davis Hospital in Houston is one of the state's most legendary abandoned places. Immense, historic, and incredibly creepy, with a foundation literally built right on top of an old cemetery, this bastion of abandoned spookiness sat vacant for over twenty years behind its razor-sharp, wire-topped fence, a beacon to the bravest of urban explorers and ghost hunters.

But all of that is ending, and not the way most people assumed it would. After a 2003 incident in which a

group of teenage explorers were robbed at gunpoint by some criminals while inside the old hospital, the city fathers decided to tear down the place. But a coalition of volunteers has come together to save and renovate the historic old building and make it into artists' lofts. That's right; people are going to live there! And given the history of this place, one can only imagine what they'll encounter late at night while supposedly in the privacy of their bedrooms.

The Jeff Davis Hospital originally opened in 1924 and was the first city-owned hospital that accepted indigent patients. It was built on land donated to the city by Houston's founders. What the founders didn't know is that the land actually happened to be a cemetery from the 1800s, filled with the remains of Houstonians from all walks of life: former slaves, Civil War veterans, victims of the yellow fever and cholera epidemics, and city aldermen. Whether or not the bodies were disinterred and moved is a matter of debate; it seems that no one is sure. But until the 1980s, some of the graves on the grounds were still marked, and bones were still being unearthed during various constructions on adjacent lots. So it seems possible that the hospital still sits atop the final resting places of many Houstonians.

There are those who believe that the angry spirits of these disrupted dead made their presence known from Jeff Davis's start. The hospital always seemed to have a higher-than-usual occurrence of strange encounters, apparitions, and anomalies. Many

patients, visitors, and even hospital employees reportedly saw eerie figures in the hallways and heard the crying of disembodied voices. Even years after the hospital was no longer in use and sat neglected and empty, rumors of hauntings and strange happenings persisted. Some say that the many patients who died there only added to the ghostly population. Often, those who were brave enough to explore its dark and rotting halls claimed to have felt watchful eyes on them or to have heard or seen some of the various spectral figures said to haunt the hospital.

As of this writing, reconstruction of the building is in full swing, with hard-hat-wearing workers scurrying on all floors to renovate the premises as security guards keep a careful eye. All of the windows have been replaced; the grounds have been cleaned and fenced in. Seekers of the weird may be disappointed to lose the old Jeff Davis of urban-exploration legend, with its many jagged, broken windows and halls filled with darkness. But it's cool to know that rather than being demolished, this spooky old treasure will be preserved. And it will be interesting to see what happens when the energy of the living fills its rooms once again. One can only wonder how the spirits will react to that. We shall wait and see.

Looking for Lost America on the Open Roads of Texas: 4,360 Miles in 126 Hours

By Troy Paiva

At least three times a year, I make an epic road trip. Two thousand miles in three days is not at all unusual. When I was a teenager, my friends and I would take off in our beat-up junk cars, storming across the Southwest deserts, just exploring for the fun of it. Driving in shifts round the clock, we'd cover thousands of miles in a couple of high-speed days, the vast expanses of desert compressed into scale models. I gladly volunteered for the late-night driving shifts and watched with fascination as countless abandoned buildings and towns unreeled in the windshield. To my friends, it was just an off-the-wall thing to do, but for me, the lure of the desert night began to take on mythical proportions. Once I had picked up night photography, in the late 1980s, these surreal safaris blossomed into new meaning and purpose. I started to document the decaying American roadside with longtime exposures lit by the full moon. Soon I began adding colored lighting during exposure, sculpting the shadows like a stage set. Now I travel alone, tossing a sleeping bag and tripods into the back of my crusty Subaru.

This run begins as I head southbound from my suburban San Francisco Bay Area home on a warm Saturday morning, then due east at Bakersfield. My destination: the open road of Texas. Alone, I am chasing the ghosts of the American West, wandering the highways as long as I can, covering as many miles as I can. Before I know it, I've driven 975 miles in fourteen hours. The day is a blur of concrete, sage, and green Interstate signs with only one short meal stop and a series of quick gas breaks. It's been a long day, but it's a familiar and satisfying pace. End of day one.

The next day, Texas Interstate 40's shoulder is littered with bloated, dead dogs and twisted carcasses of recapped tires. Bypassed Route 66 towns lie sleepy and arthritic alongside the freeway, with its endless convoys of semis throbbing past. The legendary old highway is reduced to a butchered afterthought, running from nowhere to nowhere else, its blind crests and tight curves impossible for today's high-speed tractor trailers.

Petro, Pilot, Flying J, Loves—these are the truck stops of the Southwest. Actually no longer called truck stops, they are now "travel centers." They are your friends. At night, they glow like gritty space stations inviting you in from the black void. They are a refuge for drivers, a place to cool your jets, get a cup of hundred-mile mud, and maybe buy a CB radio. I gas up anonymously, sticking my credit card in the slot, pushing a couple of buttons. Thanks to postmodern technology, I never have to communicate with a soul. The road gets a little bit lonelier.

I shuffle stiffly into the garish building to have a stretch and pick up a snack. The truckers' lounge TV is on the Weather Channel. Dazed long-haul drivers with the "thousand-mile stare" sprawl in overstuffed waiting-room chairs. On the wall, a big map of the U.S. with lit pins shows each location of this chain's travel centers. I look at the map and marvel at how

many I've been to, but also at how many more I haven't.

There's no WELCOME TO TEXAS sign on Interstate 40, just one that reads DON'T MESS WITH TEXAS. $10 to $1000 FINE FOR LITTERING. What do you have to throw out to get tagged for only ten bucks? At Vega, I turn north looking for photo ops, making a lazy loop through Dalhart, Stratford, Dumas, and back to Amarillo, as the glowing red sun sinks into the monsoon clouds. This area is billiard table–smooth farmland with hundreds of abandoned silos and grain elevators banging and creaking in the endless plains wind, but there's nothing I feel like shooting. I head west, back toward New Mexico and melting adobe homes in Cuervo and a rotting gas station–motel complex in Newkirk that caught my eye six hours earlier. I spend the night a few miles down a dirt road off I-40. The winds blast through the red rock canyons as I toss and turn, crammed into the back of the Subaru. End of day two.

Still Searching for the Abandoned Underbelly

I wake up with the feeling that I've been spinning my wheels and driving in circles. The trip odometer reads 1722. I vow to refocus my efforts and find the abandoned underbelly of Texas.

A hot wind blows north from Mexico, carrying with it a storm of tumbleweeds, paper cups, and plastic bags. The Panhandle continues to be a photographic washout. As I roll into Lubbock, the sun is nearly set and the sky begins to cloud up. As the last slivers of sun bury themselves in the purple cloudbank, I get lucky: The overcast sky suddenly splits, bathing the landscape with a bright monochromatic blue moon glow. There, on the shoulder, stands an abandoned farm, dark and mysterious, like a

real-life horror-movie set. The baked desolation of this lonely place on the Texas–New Mexico border cuts right to my soul. The atmosphere is timeless and still. The nearest dot on the map says Griffith, Texas, but I know there's nothing there. Not a soul around for miles.

The farmhouse is long abandoned but still locked up tight. I confine myself to the yard, filled with broken toys, junk cars, farm equipment, and even a few boats. The vibe is intoxicating, and I get into a groove, shooting for several hours.

Around midnight, the three-day drive and tonight's shooting catch up with me, but the area is just too flat and exposed to the ceaseless gusting winds to camp. I hustle north for Clovis, New Mexico, and a motel room. End of day three.

The next morning, I skip the free "continental breakfast" of stale convenience-store doughnuts and coffee and head south once more, back toward Texas.

Zigzagging through the endless oil fields, I eventually find my way to Odessa and Midland, Siamese-twin cities ringed with bypass expressways. Their sprawl goes on, mile after mile. It's 105 degrees and cloudy, and I begin to understand the expression "Texas hot." Thousands of oil derricks sprout from the ground, stretching to the horizon in every direction. Exploring the road towns along Interstate 20, I find classic abandoned scenes to shoot.

The night's photography, in Penwell and Monahans, goes well. Abandoned buildings and machines saturate with my flash and the moonlight. I get lost in the flow of my work, forgetting how far away from home I am.

On the outskirts of Penwell, I pull over and sleep for a few hours in the car. End of day four.

Since it is still over seventy degrees well after midnight, I sleep with the rear hatch wide open, my bare feet sticking out into the dry air. I parked close to train tracks on the edge of town, thinking they were abandoned. A few incredibly loud freight trains with containers stacked on flatcars thunder by in the middle of the night, making my car shudder. At 3 a.m., a van slowly rolls by and makes a U-turn right behind me, shining his lights right into the Subie's open rear door, scaring the hell out of me. But it's just some road-weary clown looking for a place to park for the night. He ends up a mile down the road. I make sure to roll by him before sunrise, whacking him with a hundred-decibel heavy-metal wake-up call.

I did a lot of shooting on day four of my Texas road trip. That, combined with the late start I got, made for a short driving day, only 489 miles. As the fifth day dawns, I arc onto I-20 under maximum acceleration, heading west. Texas freeways have fun on-ramps, a quick left-right like a road-racing chicane. You can cut the second apex late and get a strong launch onto the highway, releasing your inner Unser. It's time to start thinking about working my way back home.

I grab a quick lunch at a pancake place in El Paso—five different kinds of syrup on the table, and none of them is maple. I've obviously slipped into another dimension. Loaded up on a greasy brick of road food, I unglue myself from the vinyl booth, ready for the long run.

The stretch of Highway 10 between El Paso and Tucson has a tourist shop at nearly every exit. I decide to stop at one and shake out the kinks. The store is filled with insanely tacky tourist stuff, and I get the stink-eye from the "management trainee" Tammy Faye-Baker look-alike. I must resemble a wild animal by now: a four-day beard, dusty and stained shorts and T-shirt, in ninety-nine-cent flip-flops, hair sticking out in every direction. Frankly, though, I'm feeling pretty good, getting my second wind.

I sleep that night at my favorite secret camping spot near some abandoned trailers between Barstow and Mojave. The engine ticks as it cools, and the car rocks in the wind. End of day five.

TA Lifetime in 126 Hours

I am up at six o'clock again to watch the sun rise like an atomic fireball, red in the churning dust. An easy four hundred miles and four Krispy-Kreme doughnuts later, I pull into my driveway. The trip totals 4,360 miles in five days and six hours for an average speed of thirty-four miles per hour. This includes sleeping, shooting, and all other stops. No question, some kind of perverse personal record.

The American roadside of my youth dies a little more every year. Every trip brings new melancholy as familiar abandoned landmarks burn down, are melted for scrap, get bulldozed and subdivided, or just vanish into the desert sand. The rate accelerates every year. The little that remains by the sides of the old Miracle Miles withers in the blistering sun. But the soul-cleansing love of the road keeps me coming back, just as the roadside decline assures that I'll continue to bring my camera.

INDEX Page numbers in **bold** refer to photos and illustrations.

Dedications

Thanks to Mom and Dad for the support, both moral and financial, through all the failed attempts at fame over the years. Thanks also to all the people who allowed me into their homes, their yards, and their places of business to share their obsessions with me and for patiently posing for photos while I pressed the wrong buttons too many times. Plus, a generous helping of gratitude goes to the crew at Channel 11 for letting me slack off enough to get some of these stories finished, to the inmates at the Asylum for all the encouragement and help with an assortment of topics, to the fans of my Web sites for putting up with a lack of updates for so long, and to the fine folks at M&M/Mars for taking the peanut and covering it in a chocolate candy shell. Also to Denise for being there and to Penguin for keeping an eye on things. And, of course, much appreciation to the Marks for the opportunity to write this book in the first place and for overlooking the occasional expense marked simply "Recreation." Finally, thanks to Craig and Christian for the best times. I miss you guys.—*Wesley*

This work is dedicated to my beloved Mom, Cheryl Welsh (miss you so much, rest in peace). I would also like to send out thanks and LOVE to my husband, Markus, my best friend, Lobo, the terrific Marks of *Weird U.S.*, all of my dear friends/Scoobies near, far, and virtual (way too many to list here, oy), my wild 'n' crazy family, and the great state/people of Texas. Oh, and also to my sock monkey. Thanks for always supporting my dreams of exploring the weird, you guys. *Ad astra per aspera!*—*Shady*

To all my friends and relations, who have encouraged me over the years to research and write about the mysteries of Texas.—*Rob*

Contributing Authors

Tim Stevens is a native Texan who has collected numerous strange stories through the years and is always happy to share them with others. Having spent most of his life in San Antonio, he now lives near Austin with his wife, Marlene (who also provided stories for this book), two kids, and an assortment of pets. Tim sincerely wishes to thank the two Marks for the opportunity to contribute material to this *Weird* collection.

Photographer **Troy Paiva** captures the disappearing man-made world with his evocative and exotic night-photography technique. Troy uses old and obsolete, low-tech equipment to create brilliantly lit tableaux of the abandoned debris of a modern, disposable culture—taking pictures of junk *with* junk.

Author Credits by Chapter

Local Legends
Heather Shade and Tim Stevens

Ancient Mysteries
Rob Riggs with Wesley Treat

Fabled People and Places
Heather Shade, Wesley Treat, and Rob Riggs

Unexplained Phenomena
Rob Riggs

Bizarre Beasts
Rob Riggs

Local Heroes and Villains
Wesley Treat

Personalized Properties
Wesley Treat

Roadside Oddities
Wesley Treat

Roads Less Traveled
Heather Shade

Haunted Places and Ghostly Tales
Heather Shade

Cemetery Safari
Wesley Treat and Heather Shade

Abandoned in Texas
Heather Shade and Troy Paiva

Publisher: Barbara J. Morgan
Design Directors: Leonard Vigliarolo and Richard Berenson
Associate Managing Editor: Emily Seese
Editor: Marjorie Palmer
Production: Della R. Mancuso
Mancuso Associates, Inc., North Salem, NY

PICTURE CREDITS

SHOW US YOUR WEiRD!

Do you know of a weird site found somewhere in the United States, or can you tell us about a strange experience you've had? If so, we'd like to hear about it! We believe that every town has at least one great tale to tell, and we're listening. It could be a cursed road, haunted abandoned site, odd local character, or bizarre historic event. In most cases these tales are told only in the towns in which they originated. But why keep them to yourself when you could share them with all of America? So come on and fill us in on all the weirdness that's lurking in your backyard!

You can e-mail us at: Editor@WeirdUS.com,
or write to us at:
Weird U.S., P.O. Box 1346, Bloomfield, NJ 07003.

www.weirdus.com